FUTURE TRENDS IN
EAST ASIAN INTERNATIONAL RELATIONS

Of Related Interest

Future Trends in East Asian International Relations

Editor

QUANSHENG ZHAO
American University

Routledge
Taylor & Francis Group

LONDON AND NEW YORK

First Published in 2002 by
FRANK CASS PUBLISHERS

This edition published 2013 by Routledge
4 Park Square, Milton Park, Abingdon, Oxon OX14 4RN
605 Third Avenue, New York, NY 10017

*Routledge is an imprint of the Taylor & Francis Group, an informa
business*

British Library Cataloguing in Publication Data

Future Trends in East Asian international relations
1. East Asia – Foreign relations – Forecasting
I. Zhao, Quansheng
327'. 095'09051'01

Library of Congress Cataloging-in-Publication Data

Future trends in east Asian international relations / Quansheng Zhao.
   p. cm.
Includes bibliographical references and index.
ISBN 0-7146-5259-8 (hbk)
1. East Asia – Relations – Foreign countries. I. Zhao, Quansheng.

DS518.1.F87 2002
327'.095–dc21   2002001628

This group of studies first appeared in a Special Issue on
'Future Trends in East Asian International Relations'
of *The Journal of Strategic Studies* (ISSN 0140 2390) 24/4 (December 2001)

ISBN 978-0-7146-5259-7 (hbk)
ISBN 978-0-7146-8237-2 (pbk)

Contents

IV. ECONOMIC AND ENVIRONMENTAL DYNAMICS

V. CONCLUSION: FUTURE TRENDS IN EAST ASIAN
   INTERNATIONAL RELATIONS

Dedication and Acknowledgments

I dedicate this edited collection to Kenneth N. Waltz and the late Amos Perlmutter. Both played crucial roles in the creation of this publication, albeit in different ways.

Kenneth Waltz is the dean of international relations theory and guru of the school of realism, having provided insightful approaches in the international relations field for generations of students. His monumental *Man, the State, and War* (1959) and *Theory of International Relations* (1979) remain classic reading for students entering into the field. I was fortunate to be his student as well as teaching assistant for his international relations theory courses many years ago at the University of California at Berkeley. Much of my own theoretical thinking on international relations has been inspired by his groundbreaking conceptual framework.

Similarly, other authors of this publication, I believe, have had been influenced by him, whether by means of direct relationship or intellectual inspiration from his writings. Robert Scalapino, for example, has been Waltz's long-time colleague and friend, whereas Danny Unger was his student. Although these authors may not overtly employ or subscribe to Waltz's framework in their writing, one can see the imprint of his intellectual guidance on the contributions in this work. It is my great delight to have this opportunity to express my deepest appreciation for Kenneth Waltz's significant theoretical contributions and intellectual leadership in the field of international relations. At the same time, it is understandable and even desirable that scholars of international relations continue to debate and dispute Waltz's theory. Therefore, it is also my pleasure to see that diverse – sometimes even opposing – frameworks and viewpoints have been used by various authors in this collection.

The second person to whom I wish to dedicate this collection of studies is Amos Perlmutter, who was a renowned expert on strategic studies and the Middle East as well as my good colleague and friend at American University. Amos passed away on 12 June 2001 at the age of 69. For some time, I only knew him as a fellow swimmer at the university's pool. I soon realized that we were not only both alumni of Berkeley and former students of Robert Scalapino, but we also shared a keen interest in Asian studies. In short order, we began working on projects of mutual interest, and I came to appreciate his wise counsel and enthusiasm for those ventures.

After learning of my research interests in politics and international relations in East Asia, Amos invited me, in his capacity as co-editor, to join

The Journal of Strategic Studies as a member of its editorial board. We also agreed that I would be a special editor for this publication focusing on East Asian international relations. I presented the completed manuscript to him in early May 2001, right before my departure for a month-long research trip in Japan. He immediately responded with encouragement and approval, and we made an appointment to get together upon my return.

I was deeply saddened that we will no longer be able to get together due to his untimely passing, and I am already missing his presence in the swimming pool, not to mention the deep loss to the field of international relations. This publication, therefore, is most appropriate to dedicate to his memory and the time during which I was privileged to know him. I also hope to carry on to complete our joint projects in the spirit and direction in which he intended.

Finally, I would like to take this opportunity to express my sincere gratitude to each contributor in this work. All of the authors worked diligently in high spirits during several rounds of discussions and revisions. Their cooperative and professional attitude is highly appreciated. My assistant, Elizabeth Dahl, deserves special thanks, as she not only assisted with my own writing in terms of research and proofreading, she also helped to maintain contact with the authors and provided many suggestions during the copy-editing process as well as compiling the book index. Finally, I would also like to thank John Gooch, editor of *The Journal of Strategic Studies*, and Randal Gray, journals editor for Frank Cass, for providing helpful editorial guidance.

QUANSHENG ZHAO
Washington, DC

Amos Perlmutter, 1931–2001

Amos was born in Bialystock, Poland, on 14 September 1931. His parents moved to what was then Palestine shortly after his birth, and he was raised in Tel Aviv. He was a member of what Israelis called the '12th-grade generation' – those who were in the 12th grade when the State of Israel was created in May 1948, and who were conscripted into the young Israel Defense Forces (IDF) before they graduated from high school to fight in the 1948–49 War of Independence.

Amos came to the United States shortly after the war to pursue his education, and received his BA, MA, and PhD from the University of California at Berkeley. He returned to Israel in the late 1950s and, among other academic and policy-related positions, worked for a while for the Israeli Atomic Energy Commission. He also served as a member of Israel's delegation to the United Nations and as a political advisor to the chief of staff and high command of the IDF.

Amos returned to the United States in the mid-1960s, and in 1968 became a US citizen. From 1972 he was on the faculty of the School of Government at the American University in Washington, DC Amos is survived by his wife, Sharon Watts Perlmutter, of Washington, DC; and his mother, Berta Perlmutter, and sister, Elazara Hason, both of Israel.

Amos's scholarly writings addressed issues of comparative politics, civil-military relations, politics of modernization, authoritarianism, and international politics. His areas of expertise included the Middle East, the Persian Gulf, and North Africa. Among Amos's lasting contributions to both scholarship and policy was his courageous challenge to the orthodoxies which, in the 1960s and 1970s, dominated the study of civil-military relations and of the developing world. These orthodoxies, to which leading academics and policymakers subscribed, emphasized the modernizing role of the military in Third World societies. The military, it was argued, was the most rational, organized, and powerful institution in these societies, and by seizing power from corrupt and ineffective monarchies (as it did, for example, in Egypt in 1952 and in Iraq in 1958), the military would bring to the political, social, and economic life of a society the same degree of rationality, meritocratic procedures, effective organization, and efficiency with which it conducted its own affairs. In short, the military would be the agent of modernization – in otherwise traditional, corrupt, and dysfunctional societies.

Amos vigorously and persuasively challenged this view, which he considered naïve and ill-informed. His argument had three layers.

First, the role the military plays in society very much depends on the culture, norms, structures, and traditions of the specific society in question. He showed that whether or not the military takes political power in a country depends on the proclivity of that country to have a military active in the society's political life; thus, there are societies in which the military never intervenes in politics, and societies in which such interventions are frequent.

Second, in those societies in which the military frequently intervenes in politics, the motives for such interventions vary; at times the military intervenes in order to preserve the status quo, and at other times it intervenes in the name of revolution or reform.

Third, the military itself, regardless of the slogans its leaders use for public consumption, has corporate interests which are not identifiable with the interests of any specific class, or with any specific agenda – modernizing or not. This situation, in which the palace guard takes over the palace (that is, the state), was defined by Samuel Huntington as 'praetorianism'.

Amos developed his own critique of development theory and the notion of the military as an agent of modernization into a theory of praetorian societies – societies in which military intervention in politics is the norm, not the exception. In such societies, military intervention does not represent 'progress' and the military is not an agent of modernity. Amos's analysis my not appear so startling today, but when he developed it, he was defying the prevailing convention and raising questions about the work of the most influential scholars in the field. His arguments did little to endear him to the powers that be. (On Amos's scholarly contribution, see Gabriel Ben-Dor, 'The Restless Mind In Its Element: The Study of Civil-Military Relations and the Analysis of Politics in Israel', in *A Restless Mind: Essays in Honor of Amos Perlmutter*, ed. Benjamin Frankel [London and Portland, OR: Frank Cass, 1996]).

Beyond his scholarly pursuit, Amos was an energetic participant in the public debate on current issues as an analyst, commentator, and writer. He was a prolific writer indeed, contributing articles for the op-ed pages of leading newspapers; essays; book reviews; and letters to the editor. One did not always agree with Amos, but one could always rely on him to be provocative (the Palestinian-leaning Palestine Media Watch picked Amos as 'The most inflamatory columnist' of 2000 for his columns on the Middle East). Amos's last column, penned from his hospital bed and entitled 'Arafat's Failed Utopia', appeared in the *Jerusalem Post* on 8 June 2001, four days before he died.

Amos was also a scholarly entrepreneur. He cofounded two journals – *The Journal of Strategic Studies* (of which he was coeditor when he died), and *Security Studies*, of which he served as coeditor for six years. He was instrumental in the creation of several other academic journals.

Amos wrote 15 books. Among them *Making the World Safe for Democracy: A Century of Wilsonianism and Its Totalitarian Challengers* (1997); *FDR & Stalin: A Not So Grand Alliance, 1943–1945* (1993); *The Life and Times of Menachem Begin* (1987); *Israel, the Partitioned State: A Political History since 1900* (1985); *Two Minutes over Baghdad* (1982; with Michael Handel and Uri Bar-Joseph); *Modern Authoritarianism: A Comparative Institutional Analysis* (1981); *Political Roles and Military Rulers* (1981); *Politics and the Military in Israel 1967–1977* (1978); *The Military and Politics in Modern Times: On Professionals, Praetorians, and Revolutionary Soldiers* (1977); *Egypt, the Praetorian State* (1974); and *Military and Politics in Israel: Nation-Building and Role Expansion* (1969).

Amos was what we would call a 'character' – *sui generis*, a category of one. Those who knew Amos recognized in him a certain insatiable quality – a hunger that would not be quenched. He was a man of big appetite. No one ever accused him of timidity, or meekness, or reticence. On the contrary – there was a passion in him, a contagious vitality. Everything he did, he did with gusto. He may not have always been disciplined, but he was always energetic and enthusiastic.

His passion for books, which he collected by the thousand, was legendary. Six years ago Nicholas A. Basbanes wrote a book entitled *A Gentle Madness: Bibliophiles, Bibliomanes, and the Eternal Passion for Books*. He could have had Amos in mind, because Amos had an eternal passion for books. He was deeply interested in, and knowledgeable about, a surprisingly wide range of topics. He loved travel, good food, and good conversation. Yes, he could be opinionated and argumentative. Those who were close to him, however, knew that he was always generous and warm and helpful. He was there when you needed him. He was a good friend to his friends.

BENJAMIN FRANKEL
Security Studies

Amos Perlmutter: A Personal Tribute

There have been many deserved tributes to Amos Perlmutter, the founding co-editor of *The Journal of Strategic Studies*, as a man, political scientist and as a much published author and media contributor and I would like to add to these his many contributions as a publisher *manqué*.

I first met Amos Perlmutter in the late 1960s when publishing his first book *Military and Politics in Israel: Nation-Building and Role Expansion* (1969) a title as relevant now as then. At that time the company had been publishing for just 12 years and was still finding its way in academic social science publishing. From that first meeting, accompanied by the usual bear-hugs, loud laughter and coughing fits that always characterised these meetings, there evolved Amos's keen and intuitive interest in publishing and ideas which would both interest and benefit his academic constituency.

Throughout the 1970s, 1980s and 1990s Amos encouraged and attracted a wide circle of his academic colleagues to publish with us and stimulated us too to publish in new areas that had not yet been fully understood or developed. He recommended new authors and always particularly bright young scholars for whom he invariably and uncannily correctly predicted an important academic future.

Many of our early forays into military publishing came from Amos's ideas and encouragement and his own suggestion of publishing a new international journal on *Strategic Studies* (1978) and later on *Security Studies* (1991). These quarterly journals both stemmed from the need that Amos foresaw for new scholarly periodicals dealing with the then ever-widening interest in strategic studies.

He devised the 'mission statement' for each journal, identified and invited the initial editorial advisory boards and commissioned and selected the first articles to be published in each. He worked easily with his co-editors over the past two decades always encouraging new young scholars and formulating new ideas.

Amos played a huge part in the development of many of the Frank Cass publishing areas, both in books and in journals. He possessed a gargantuan zest for life, was a great friend over nearly four decades and with his beloved wife Sharon found much happiness and contentment in the latter years of his life.

The Journal of Strategic Studies and *Security Studies* are a lasting testament to his intuitive ideas.

FRANK CASS
London, April 2002

PART I

POST-COLD WAR TRENDS IN THE ASIA-PACIFIC

1

Trends in East Asian International Relations

ROBERT A. SCALAPINO

Despite numerous problems, relations among and between Asia-Pacific nations are more positive at present than at any time in the past century. The current concern over terrorism, moreover, has generally strengthened and broadened relationships. Perhaps three factors have accounted for the positive atmosphere.

First, whatever the degree of success or crisis, the domestic economy, and in larger measure, issues at home that are products of the age of globalization, take priority in virtually all nations.

Second, since the end of the Cold War, no imminent threats are perceived in terms of state-to-state relations although from some quarters, concerns about future threats are voiced. Nevertheless, the basic trend is toward engagement, not confrontation.

Third, multilateral structures, informal as well as formal, are now available to supplement the still dominant bilateral relationships, enabling a variety of regularized dialogues on a full range of issues.

Optimism concerning the current scene must be tempered. There are certain factors that cast clouds over the horizon. Military modernization is proceeding in virtually all nations, with verifiable arms limitations and controls still minimal.[1] Moreover, nationalism is reasserting itself in many nation-states, with uncertainty as to whether it will assume a moderate or militant form. Indeed, at present, three semi-conflictual forces vie for recognition in every state: internationalism, nationalism, and communalism. Communalism refers to the quest of individuals for a more meaningful source of identification and psychological comfort in this revolutionary age. It can take the form of a strong identification with ethnicity, religion – especially fundamentalist religion or cults – or greater affinity for one's immediate region or locality. Any one of these commitments, if given priority, may pose a serious challenge to national unity. Thus, how a nation copes with these three forces constitutes one determinant of whether stability or instability, unity or disunity, can be achieved.

MULTILATERALISM – ADVANCES AND CHALLENGES

With these basic considerations in mind, let us first examine the multilateral structures currently operating in the Asia-Pacific region. As in other regions, all of the Asia-Pacific states (if one does not count Taiwan) are members of the United Nations, and the UN has played an important role in peacekeeping operations in certain instances, as well as providing a forum for the discussion of key issues from those relating to human security (environment, resources, demography and human rights) to those focused on specific controversies of a regional or bilateral nature. It has also provided a platform for national leaders to express their views on a variety of subjects before a global audience. There is a growing sentiment, however, that if the UN is to be truly effective as a peace-making and peacekeeping organization, significant reforms are necessary, although there is no consensus as to the precise reforms desirable. Clearly, the requirement of unanimity among the permanent members of the Security Council for any action represents a serious impediment in many situations. Further, there is presently no permanent UN peacekeeping force, with only ad hoc groupings available.

A similar situation exists at the regional level. The Association of Southeast Asian Nations (ASEAN) is the most senior regional body, having been initially established by five states of the region to cope with what was perceived as the threat of communist expansion. Today, it includes all ten states of the region, including the three so-called Indo-China states, two of which – Vietnam and Laos – remain communist. Despite their ideological-political differences, these latter states were most anxious to join ASEAN, especially Vietnam, so as to provide a collective covering, given their uncertainties about China. Yet the enlarged membership makes consensus more difficult. The timing of moves toward a freer, more open economic order is now more complex, given the status and policies of various states.[2]

Further, political issues are less easily resolved. Certain states, notably Thailand and the Philippines, have recently taken the position that it is legitimate to raise questions about a state's domestic policies, especially if those policies impact upon others.

Thus, even within ASEAN, the complex issue of 'humanitarian intervention' has been raised. In the broader environment, nations such as

China take the position that the preservation of national sovereignty is paramount, and there must be no intervention in a nation's internal affairs. Yet in this age of globalization, can a clear line be drawn between what is 'internal' and what is of broader consequence? For example, if Sumatran farmers burn off the land to provide space for crops, and the resulting pollution sweeps over Singapore and Malaysia, is that a domestic matter or a regional matter?

Both Asia and the world are far from a consensus on this complex problem. Further, with existing international and regional bodies unable to deal with such a challenge, humanitarian intervention is certain to be one of the enduring issues of the twenty-first century. The discussion and debate will center upon such questions as to whether and under what conditions it is justified and what are the desirable safeguards or required agreements.

Meanwhile, the ASEAN Regional Forum (ARF), spawned by ASEAN and with a nearly complete membership of the Asia-Pacific nations illustrates the current advantages and limitations of this type of organization. Like the UN, ARF enables national leaders to meet periodically, holding side meetings that on occasion produce significant results. Indeed, the ASEAN Post-Ministerial conferences have been institutionalized. It also enables a discussion of many regional problems in an inclusive forum. Yet in the final analysis, ARF remains a 'talk' not an 'action' body, and its very size and diversity impose inhibitions on the application of concrete measures.

Other multilateral organizations also exist such as APEC (Asia-Pacific Economic Cooperation), ASEAN Plus Three (Japan, China and the Republic of Korea (ROK)), and the recently created Asian-European Meetings (ASEM). In the economic realm, the Asian Development Bank plays an important role in addition to the global International Monetary Fund. As yet, no official Northeast Asia Dialogue exists, but a Track One and One-half Northeast Asia Cooperation Dialogue (NEACD) has operated since 1993, with the four major nations and the two Koreas as members (although the Democratic People's Republic of Korea (DPRK) has not attended since the first meeting). NEACD, meeting yearly, discusses a wide range of issues, and makes certain recommendations to governments. Perhaps at some point in the near to medium future, an official NEACD will be established, possibly with a limited agenda initially.

Meanwhile, multilateral bodies of a more informal type are playing an increasingly critical role in the region. Some are trilateral such as the US-Japan-ROK regularized meetings focusing on the Korean issue but touching related matters. The Four Party meetings on the same subject involving the United States, China and the two Koreas exemplify a quadrilateral body, although these meetings have been suspended for more than one year. A very different five-party combination is represented by the so-called Shanghai Five, involving China, Russia and the three Central Asian states of Kazakhstan, Kyrgyzstan, and Tajikistan. Recently, Uzbekistan was added and the group was renamed the Shanghai Cooperation Organization.

These developments illustrate the fact that a new or at least different form of internationalism is playing an increasingly important role in regional and global affairs. Nations having a common interest in a given problem or set of problems are joining in informal coalitions, with in-depth, regularized discussions aimed at reaching a consensus on the issues at stake. Thus, two basic strategies regarding Asia-Pacific security are now simultaneously in operation: a concert of powers and a balance of power. In some degree, virtually all states of the region are committed to this course, with the United States being a key actor at present on both fronts.

Despite the growing importance of multilateralism in diverse forms, however, bilateral relations, especially those between the leading nations of the Asia-Pacific region, still represent the most critical variable affecting both economic and political-security relations at the international level. Prior to discussing these, however, it is important to assess with broad strokes of the brush the current domestic situation in the leading states of the region, since this is a critical element in the creation and implementation of every nation's foreign policies.

THE DOMESTIC SCENE IN THE MAJOR POWERS

Geographically, the United States is not a part of East Asia. Yet in every respect – economic, political and strategic – it is a crucial player in the region. Moreover, the United States is at once the world's only superpower and its most revolutionary society, measured in terms of the pace and depth of change. Consequently, it combines a long period of unprecedented growth and prosperity with a growing anxiety among many of its citizens regarding certain very fundamental issues produced by the domestic revolution. 'Who am I? What are my values?' are common if often unspoken concerns. In practical terms, the issues of paramount importance are education for one's children; the trauma of urban life, including congestion, pollution and crime; the preservation of the family; and the future of such programs as social security and Medicare. Will the events of 11 September 2001 causes a long-term readjustment of priorities and commitments?

Not without reason, the United States is often accused of arrogance in its dealings with others, or seeking to convert the world to the American way of life. Yet there is an aspect of the American scene that is overlooked. For the American people, foreign policy is of secondary importance except in times of crisis. Indeed, an increasing number of Americans are now raising questions as to whether US involvement in the world is not too costly in both economic and human terms. Conserve funds for greater expenditures at home, and take fewer human risks by having others play the principal peace-making roles, it is asserted. Neo-isolationism is far from the majority sentiment in the United States today, but its adherents have loud voices and appear to be growing. Moreover, there is a certain connection between neo-isolationism and unilateralism, namely, acting alone when United States' vital interests are involved, and acting swiftly without undue complications. The only popular conflicts in recent years have been those that were US directed, concluded quickly and with minimal casualties. Collective efforts, some assert, are always lengthy and without clear resolution. Thus, the current struggle against terrorism poses profound challenges involving both official and public attitudes.

Nonetheless, the probabilities are that the United States will continue to work with others in seeking a peaceful, prosperous world, and that its basic foreign policies will continue to rest upon the two fundamental principles outlined earlier: a concert of powers and a balance of power. Yet such policies will not be without challenge, and the attitudes and policies of US allies as well as others will play an important role in shaping the American course.[3]

Turning to Japan, the domestic scene is less clear. Once labeled 'the Father of the Asian Miracle', Japan has been in economic remission for nearly a decade. Growth slackened in the early 1990s, and the economic scene remains generally dark as 2001 comes to a close. Japan stands as a prime illustration of the principle that no economic strategy, however successful, is permanently valid. In an earlier era, Japan's strategy was based upon the government serving as convoy leader, selecting key industries for special support; permitting limited transparency that served to protect privilege; collusive bureaucratic-business alignments; protectionism over the domestic economy; and an emphasis on export orientation. In this age of economic globalization, the weaknesses of such a system are exposed, among them, lagging competitiveness, corruption, and the reluctance of entrepreneurs to adjust to the new era.[4]

Yet Japan remains the world's second largest economy. Moreover, the prospects are that a new generation of entrepreneurs will now enter the scene, more prepared to seek leadership in the information technology (IT) revolution, and more internationalist in outlook.[5] Clearly, Japan must adjust quickly to the rapid aging of its population and the need to integrate its economic strengths with the human and material resources of its neighbors.

The essential reforms necessary have been made more difficult in the past decade by political trends.[6] The so-called 1955 system provided long-term political stability, with one party – the Liberal Democratic Party (LDP) – consistently in power, and all other parties representing permanent minorities. With the decline of the LDP in the early 1990s, political fragility ensued, with coalition governments and generally weak leaders. Changes were frequent, making fundamental policy changes nearly impossible. The current Prime Minister, Junichiro Koizumi, represents a change, being outside the LDP old guard, and acting with greater independence than his predecessors. He has promised major reforms, calling upon the Japanese people to endure pain while the essential changes are made. In his opening months, his popularity has remained high, remaining at 70 per cent even after some decline. But given Japan's uncertain economy and the power of such interest groups as the agriculturalists, can he carry out the promised reforms and will his popularity hold? In any case, it is not surprising that a significant number of Japanese citizens have recently exhibited pessimistic attitudes toward their future and that of their country.

From this environment, two somewhat contradictory trends are emerging. Despite the domestic problems, nationalism has been reasserting itself in Japan, its manifestations diverse: a request that Japan be accepted as a 'normal nation', with the right to employ a full range of policies in protecting and advancing its national interests; acceptance as a major power, with a permanent position on the UN Security Council; the reestablishment of the flag and national anthem in schools; official visits to the Yasukuni Shrine, the memorial to Japan's war dead; and with respect to its bilateral relationship with the United States, a shift from patron–client relations to partnership.

If these manifestations of nationalism represent one trend, another trend lies in Japan's efforts to center its foreign policies on economic interaction with its neighbors –with extensive aid programs to societies in economic trouble despite its own problems, expanding trade and investment with such nations as China and the Republic of Korea, and advancing economic interaction with virtually all of the ASEAN members. Japan has also been an active participant in various multilateral undertakings, and has taken the lead on occasion in proposing an Asia-centered economic consortium.[7] Japan's security stance remains centered upon the alliance with the United States, but guidelines have been revised and legislative action taken to expand its military commitments, including the right to dispatch security forces to combat areas abroad for auxiliary support short of combat. Combined with economic and political realms that reach out to the entire

Asia-Pacific region, Japan seeks to play a more significant role on the international stage, troubling some of its neighbors.

China presents a different picture in domestic terms.[8] The People's Republic of China (PRC) is a nation in transition, with domestic changes quite as profound as those of its initial revolutionary era. The economic transition is toward a market-oriented economy although in reality, the economy is hybrid, with one important sector still state-owned. Nonetheless, the more dynamic portion of the economy is that in the private sector. Politically, the transition is from a Marxist-Leninist-Maoist state to an authoritarian-pluralist society, with politics still authoritarian, albeit, much more flexible than in past times; a civil society emerging apart from the state; and a mixed economy with the private sector rising rapidly.

China, in essence, is en route to becoming a major power, but one with significant ongoing major problems. Its growth rate during the past several decades has been truly impressive, and hundreds of millions of Chinese have benefited. Moreover, the indications are that China's growth will continue at a rate superior to that of most, if not all, other Asian states. Yet Chinese leaders must cope with massive un- and under-employment, significant unrest in rural areas, a major East–West developmental gap, a fragile banking-financial structure, many failing state-owned enterprises (SOEs), and massive corruption. These problems will not be solved quickly or easily.

Meanwhile, on the political front, three broad trends are underway.

First, one-man dominance has ended and the nation is rapidly on its way to collective leadership, with technocrats replacing ideologues in virtually all of the significant positions.

Second, rapid economic development has made increasingly urgent the problem of allocating power among center, region, province and locality, with a strong need for a more institutionalized federal system.

Third, the power of ideology has faded despite the effort of party leaders to promote it, and in considerable measure, its place is being taken by nationalism – now the primary instrument employed to seek unity and loyalty from the citizenry.

The priorities of current Chinese leaders are strongly focused on continued economic development and resolving or at least mitigating economic problems. The prevailing slogan is 'make China rich and strong', and both parts of this slogan are given weight. Thus, military modernization advances in tandem with efforts for livelihood improvement. Under these conditions it is understandable as to why many neighbors ponder whether China's future will feature continuing commitment to the Five Principles of Peaceful Coexistence as constantly pledged, or the Middle Kingdom psychology as once prevailed. Will China live up to its promise to treat all nations as equals and resolve all disputes peacefully or will it seek to dominate the region as the central Asian power?[9]

The final major power in the region is the Russian Federation. While its capital, Moscow, is distant from East Asia geographically, its domain stretches across the Eurasian continent, with a lengthy boundary with China, and with the Russian Far East an integral part of Northeast Asia.

As is well known, Russia has been through recurrent trauma for more than a decade, and the ordeal is not over, although some promising signs are on the horizon. The old Stalinist economic order collapsed quickly, but the nation was not prepared to operate a new market-oriented economy effectively. Confusion, corruption, and a sense of helplessness ensued, with neither a coherent entrepreneurial class nor an economic structure equal to the emergent challenges. Slowly, these elements are developing, but genuine recovery under a new order does not seem likely in the near term.

Meanwhile, in the aftermath of widespread disillusionment with Yeltsin's leadership, the Russian people sought a strong man to lead them. Their interest in leadership far surpassed their interest in political institutions. In Vladimir Putin, many Russians believe that they have found an answer to their needs, but Putin's ultimate reputation will depend upon the success of his economic and political policies. He has pledged a commitment to market principles, is seeking foreign investment, and promises to root out corruption. On the political front, he has sought some recentralization of power, and treated certain enemies fiercely, but insists that his commitments to political pluralism are firm.

Any verdict on Putin's policies – and the direction of his nation, economically and politically – would be premature at this point although he remains a popular figure at present, symbolizing a new and forceful generation. It seems likely the pain of transition will continue for some time, but that ultimately, Russia will reemerge as a major power. It has the resources, the educated people, and the geopolitical position to support that course. The question of its economic and political system, however, remains open.

Like Japan, although with different tactics employed, Russia is seeking to reestablish its status as a major power. Putin is pursuing a Eurasian policy, placing emphasis upon Russia's relations with both the West and Asia. Despite past opposition to the expansion of NATO and to US missile defense programs, Moscow has shown an increasing interest in compromising on key security issues, and in cooperation with both the United States and West Europe. Indeed, the possibility of working closely with NATO has been broached. At the same time, in forming a 'strategic partnership' with China, seeking to reestablish close relations with India, and reaching out to various other Asian societies, Russia is seeking to strengthen its international role, reestablishing itself as a global power.

Against this background of domestic circumstances, how are the key bilateral relations to be judged at present, and what is their relevance to the broader strategic picture in East Asia? Let us commence with US-Japan relations.[10] These relations are proclaimed by both parties to be central to their respective foreign policies, and indeed, despite certain difficulties and a few challenging trends as outlined earlier, no bilateral relationship in Asia or elsewhere seem more firmly anchored. On the economic front, interaction is huge and still growing, providing both societies with indispensable advantages. To be sure, there are problems. The extensive trade imbalance in favor of Japan has only begun to decline. Soaring US prosperity made it a less contentious issue, but as the US economy falters, the trade imbalance may resume the importance it displayed in the 1980s. Further, competition may increasingly vie with complementarity in the IT field in the years ahead. Yet the problems that emerge will undoubtedly be subject to continuous negotiations in the World Trade Organization and at the bilateral level.

Security relations also present certain problems, notably, the heavy concentration of American forces and bases on Okinawa, and the resultant protests there, and the question of Japanese payments for the American presence. However, with the revised defense guidelines, formally enacted in 1999, both sides are relatively satisfied with the new division of responsibilities, admittedly vague (and purposely so) in some respects. The United States has long felt that Japan was not bearing its share of responsibility in security matters. Yet it did not want a nuclear or high-posture military Japan. The new agreements, while far from distributing responsibilities equally, point clearly in the direction of greater Japanese commitments and that trend has been powerfully underwritten by the recent Japanese commitment to send forces to the South Asian combat zone.

Most Asian nations look upon the US-Japan alliance as one conducive to supporting stability in the region, both because it signifies a long-term US commitment and because it reduces the chances of a militarist Japan. Even China, despite its increasing concerns following guideline revisions, shares in the latter view, albeit, more hesitantly than before.

As previously noted, Japan will continue to mount a more independent foreign policy in Asia, and will express itself more forcefully both with the

United States and others when leaders feel their national interests are involved. Moreover, the US-Japan relationship may never be as intimate in human terms as that between nations having strong cultural-linguistic bonds. Japan is a relatively homogeneous island society that finds genuine comradeship with foreigners difficult. Yet a younger generation of Japanese is reaching out – and there will be younger Americans ready to greet them. Above all, however, the broad interests of the two nations are more compatible than at any time in history.

The situation with respect to US-China relations is significantly different.[11] On the surface, indeed, relations between Washington and Beijing seem to be verging upon hostility periodically, with inflammatory incidents starting with the Tiananmen conflict, and more recently, the accidental US bombing of the PRC Belgrade embassy and the US reconnaissance airplane incident near Hainan, causing major protests and angry attitudes among the citizenry, invariably stimulated by the media of both sides.

Various Chinese, both at elite and citizen levels, regard the United States as prone to use its global power to promote its values and institutions internationally, interfering in the internal affairs of other nations and violating their sovereignty. Terms such as 'unipolarism', 'hegemony', and 'arrogance' are regularly applied to the policies of 'certain countries', with one country in mind.[12] The Third PRC National Defense White Paper issued in fall 2000, pointed directly to the United States in negative terms.

Yet while the 'American threat' is voiced openly by certain intellectuals along with some civil and military officials, it does not presently dominate Chinese policies toward the United States. Those policies are strongly shaped by China's economic priorities, as noted earlier, and in a broader sense, by the need to have a relationship with the United States that is conducive to maintaining peace and fostering economic growth in East Asia. Thus, PRC leaders encourage high-level visits, both by military and civilian leaders, to discuss and negotiate problems. Further, extensive American investment is sought and cultural contacts – some of them intended to improve China's image among Americans – are fostered. In addition, China has shown itself prepared to participate in a concert of powers including the United States when its national interests largely coincide with those of Washington such as with respect to Korea, and more recently, in condemning terrorism, although Beijing has clear reservations about the American military campaign over a possible protracted US presence in Central Asia.

While working with the United States on some issues, moreover, China seeks defenses against what it perceives as US pressure. In attempting to improve relations with all of its neighbors – and Beijing has made strenuous efforts in this respect in the past few years – the PRC is making an effort to create a buffer region around it. For this same reason, after years of wariness, the PRC has become a recent ardent exponent of multilateralism, as a means of countering unipolarism.

The 'strategic partnership' with the Russian Federation goes further than most of China's other bilateral relationships, with the goal that of capitalizing upon a common perception of threat – including mutual opposition to the TMD and NMD programs as well as overweening American global power.[13] As will be noted, the China-Russia relationship is far from a strategic alliance in its full sense, but it is a part of China's effort to build a balance of power 'with Chinese characteristics', to use an oft repeated Chinese phrase.

China's principal concern with respect to specific issues involving the United States is Taiwan, as is constantly made clear.[14] It refuses to acknowledge the existence of the Taiwan Relations Act, referring only to the necessity of abiding by the Three Communiqués, and insisting that the policy of furnishing arms to Taiwan is a blatant interference in China's internal affairs. Yet for the United States to abandon its commitments to Taiwan at this point would be politically impossible, given the sentiments of the American Congress and electorate. Thus, US policy will continue to walk down a tortuous path, proclaiming its adherence to a one-China doctrine on the one hand, and delivering defensive arms to Taiwan on the other, meanwhile urging both sides to refrain from provocative actions and to explore all possible routes to a peaceful resolution of the problem.

Unquestionably, Taiwan is the major security threat in East Asia today, and no resolution is in sight, given the deep distrust existing between the Chen Shui-bian government and Beijing. The greatest risks are not in the short term, but at a later stage, if the status-quo continues to prevail and new Chinese leaders face greater pressures to respond to the nationalist surge at home.

Turning to the American side of this bilateral relation, the picture is equally complex. In the recent past, a wide range of troublesome issues have emerged from those in the human rights field to alleged Chinese spying, missile emplacements on China's coast near Taiwan, and assorted economic issues. Yet every administration starting with Nixon and continuing through George W. Bush has sought a relationship with Beijing that is one of 'constructive engagement', based on the thesis that this is the most appropriate route to effecting change in China, both in term of domestic and international policies. Clinton's strenuous and successful efforts to get Congress to pass the Permanent Normal Trading Relations Act (PNTR) with China and Bush's shift from his campaign rhetoric to extensive dialogue with China's leaders are the most recent examples.

The US relationship with China at present is an excellent illustration of the twin foundations of US foreign policy, namely, the simultaneous application of concert of powers and balance of power strategies. Washington works with Beijing on such issues as Korea and counter-terrorism, and seeks to involve it in as many unofficial as well as official multilateral operations as possible. Yet as a hedge against the possibility that 'constructive engagement' will fail or in any case, based upon the thesis that it should be fortified by the availability of deterrence, the US maintains its strategic alliances with Japan and the ROK, and indeed, has recently strengthened them in Southeast Asia with such nations as the Philippines, Thailand, and Singapore.

For the present, despite negative verbiage on both sides and the creation of safeguards, the Sino-American bilateral relationship tilts toward efforts to resolve or contain disputes and counter the more extreme warnings. Unquestionably, Taiwan constitutes the most serious problem, and one that cannot be presently resolved. The greatest risks are not in the short term. At present, most PRC leaders believe that time is on their side. The Chen government is currently facing multiple economic and political problems. Opposition parties are being courted by Beijing with frequent dialogues taking place. Meanwhile, cross-strait economic and cultural interaction is surging forward. However, if the status quo continues, at some point in the future, new Chinese leaders may force greater pressure to respond to nationalist sentiments at home. Then a crisis could arise.[15]

Meanwhile, the China-Japan relationship is also complex if less likely to affect the entire regional picture.[16] On the economic front, major advances in interrelations continue, and the prospects for the creation of even more extensive connections are good. Presently, Japan is a major investor in China, and the two nations are leading trading partners also. At some point, moreover, Northeast Asia will witness the emergence of a Natural Economic Territory (NET) involving western Japan, the Russian Far East, the Korean peninsula and northeast China, the complementary assets of capital, technology, managerial skills, labor, and resources brought into optimal use. Such a development is in the interests of all of these states, and can do much to cushion their respective bilateral relations.

It is in the political-strategic arena that the relationship is delicate. The so-called legacy of history still casts a shadow over official and public sentiments despite certain efforts to downplay the issue. China continues to demand that Japan 'listen to the voice of history', and make even more fulsome apologies for its past behavior. Japan insists that it has apologized sufficiently, and that its current policies demonstrate its commitment to a peaceful and prosperous Asia.

Underlying these sentiments is a lack of closeness at the grassroots in the relationship. Chinese and Japanese, despite a lengthy history of cultural interaction and sharing, remain very different people, and deeply ingrained suspicion or hostility exists on both sides, especially among the Chinese. Thus, concern about the rise of 'Japanese militarism' is regularly voiced in the PRC, and a growing worry about a 'dominant China' is expressed in Japan. The rising nationalism in both societies together with Japan's moves to increase its strategic role in the region and China's continued military modernization add to the suspicions of the two sides.

Taiwan is also a somewhat troublesome issue although Japan's involvement is far less than that of the United States. Taiwan happens to be the one part of the former Japanese empire where sentiments toward Japan and the Japanese are strongly favorable among the people and cultural as well as economic intercourse is extensive. This stance is not calculated to please Beijing, and the revised security guidelines that leave the issue of the involvement of the Straits in Japan's security commitments unclear, do not make the issue less worrisome for China.

Once again, however, although the China-Japan relationship is delicate and replete with both short- and long-term issues of consequence, neither party constitutes an immediate threat to the other, and both have an overriding national interest in working together on a wide range of issues while advancing jointly on the economic front.

Some observers have suggested that a triangular relationship among the United States, Japan and China should be cultivated so that mutual suspicions and concerns may be reduced. Such an effort would be feasible at present only if the agenda were limited. However, with respect to Korea, such a relationship already exists, albeit, in imprecise form, and it might be expanded so as to relate to military dialogues, especially on issues of safety, piracy, and transparency.

Russia constitutes the fourth party among the major states, and as noted earlier, one that is seeking to improve its bilateral relations with others while reestablishing its major power status.[17] Russian relations with the United States, despite the objections held in common with China and set forth earlier, are on balance positive, and have further improved since the onset of the terrorist crisis. The United States continues to place its hope on a Russia that pursues market-oriented policies and maintains political openness while cooperating with the West as Putin has indicated. It does not worry greatly over the Sino-Russian relationship despite its orientation, believing that each nation has national interests that underwrite a relationship that is distinctly different from an alliance.

The most important aspect of the US-Russia relationship in the immediate future relates to strategic-political matters. Putin has shown a willingness to cooperate not only with respect to the anti-terrorist campaign but also on the issue of NATO and possibly with respect to the US missile defense program. No final agreements have been reached but the current atmosphere is positive. In some matters, the agreement to disagree harmoniously may be reached.

Russian relations with China, as indicated, have greatly improved in the recent past. However, there remains a huge cultural gap between the two societies, no ideological connections at present, modest economic interaction, and the problem of greatly diverse demographic factors. There are only eight million people in the Russian Far East, and it is not surprising that many of these view the 1.3 billion Chinese below them with some trepidation.

Once, during the Cold War Russia provided China and the United States with the primary reason for establishing a constructive relationship. Now, it might be argued that the United States plays a similar role for China and Russia. However, such a view is too simplistic given the present complexities of the Asia-Pacific region, and the basic needs of these two nations. A positive relationship is eminently desirable, and one that can support the type of agreements reached by the Shanghai Five; a comprehensive strategic alliance, however, is not desired by either party. Russia's recent overtures to India for a resumption of a close relationship are but one indication of that fact.

Meanwhile, relations between Russia and Japan remain relatively minimal despite ongoing efforts.[18] The pledge to reach a peace treaty by the end of 2000 has not been fulfilled due to the inability to find a satisfactory resolution of the Northern Territories (Southern Kurils) issue. And while neither party perceives the other as a threat at present, the legacy of the past remains alive, as in the case of Sino-Japanese relations. The Russian Federation, and particularly the Russian Far East, is geographically close, culturally distant. Yet if and when Russia's economic recovery ensues, the Russian-Japanese relationship can become vitally important – with pipelines and other infrastructure developments harnessing Russia's resources to Japan's urgent needs, and bringing Japanese technology into play in the Russian Federation.

REGIONAL ISSUES AND TRENDS

Let us now turn to issues confronting the small and medium states of East Asia. The most encouraging development is that which has taken place on the Korean peninsula.[19] Here, timing proved critically important. A new ROK President, Kim Dae-jung, opened the South Korean door through the 'Sunshine Policy' at a time when Kim Jong-il and his associates in the North had decided that economic changes were essential if the Democratic Republic of Korea or North Korea (DPRK) were to survive. Thus, tension reduction by way of economic interaction has taken place, with all of the major powers united in their approval of the new direction. Here, national interests largely coincide. None of the major powers want a collapsed DPRK, a nuclear DPRK or conflict. The alternative is an evolutionary course on the part of the North toward meaningful interaction with the external world, with the South being a key link in this process.

No one can predict with assurance the future course on the peninsula. There may well be temporary retreats and stalls as indeed is largely the case as 2001 comes to a close, with the greatest threat being that of a troubled South unable to sustain its current policies, accompanied by a tougher stance toward the DPRK on the part of the Bush administration. Nor can one rule out growing concerns in the North over the repercussions of a more open policy. Yet despite the uncertainties, the current scene on the Korean peninsula appears less threatening than anytime in the post World War II era, with the possibilities of some progress in North-South relations, especially on the economic and cultural fronts, not to be dismissed.

In Southeast Asia, the decline of ideological barriers, the growth of access to each other on the part of all states of the region, and the partial recovery of most states from the economic crisis offer hope.[20] Multilateralism is now significant in the region despite present ASEAN problems. However, certain Southeast Asian states currently face political instability, in some cases of major proportions.

This fact raises a profoundly important fact relating to security in East Asia and elsewhere. The greatest threat that lies ahead is not war between or among major powers, but rather the problems of ailing and failing states. Those problems, if protracted, inevitably affect the region and sometimes, the world at large. As noted earlier, they are likely to raise the issue of intervention, 'humanitarian' or otherwise, and no multilateral organizations – formal or informal – are yet capable of dealing with this problem adequately. At the moment, Indonesia is a troubling example insofar as Southeast Asia is concerned. Here, separatism is rife, economic issues are intensifying, and political leadership appears confused. ASEAN is thereby affected, but beyond this, so are all Asia-Pacific states.

Should outsiders stand by and do nothing? Measures such as economic assistance, already proffered, may not to be of sufficient help. External intervention, from whatever source, has dubious value and high costs and risks. The current scene in Indonesia epitomizes the dilemma likely to confront the international community in the new century.

However, notwithstanding the various problems that the Asia-Pacific region confronts today, the overall prospects are reasonably good for peace among nations and continuing economic development together with the further improvement of internationalism in its various forms.[21] There will be strife at the domestic level, and tensions in the relations between major powers, as has been indicated. However, major wars between large states are unwinnable, given the ongoing revolution in military affairs, and political leaders everywhere increasingly realize this fact.

Further, the IT revolution offers the opportunity for rapid participation in a new world order, the world of economic modernization. To be sure, that in itself creates problems. But these problems can only be intensified through conflict with others. Rationality has never pointed so clearly toward the path of negotiation and compromise, together with a pursuit of transparency and control in the military realm.

In each of these respects, a heavy responsibility rests with leadership. However, in very few nations do leaders hold absolute power at present. The rise of a civil society apart from the state has taken place throughout Asia-Pacific, along with a mixed economy.[22] Thus, non-governmental organizations (NGOs) and various other groups within the society are playing an increasingly significant role in policy-making and implementation, rational or otherwise. They, too, bear a major responsibility for the future.

Nationalism will vie with internationalism in influencing policy decisions, and this trend may represent the greatest challenge in certain societies. Can it be kept under control, with extreme forms avoided? Will leaders, or a sensationalist-oriented media, or groups intent upon pushing a strong-arm agenda foster a militant nationalism for their own purposes?

In sum, the future is certain to be complex and require constant attention, with warning signals taken seriously. Yet on balance, cautious optimism is warranted. Given the combination of the costs of modern war and the opportunities for rapid economic advances, there is a good chance that the new century can avoid the global disasters of the last one.

NOTES

1. Essays dealing with the impact of military modernization on US defense policy can be found in Ashton B. Carter and John P. White, *Keeping the Edge – Managing Defense for the Future* (Preventive Defense Project, Kennedy School of Government, Harvard, and Stanford University, Cambridge, MA and Stanford, CA 2000).

2. For an APEC Forum dealing with regional economic issues, held 30 March–1 April 2000 in Seoul, see Kyung Tae Lee (ed.), *Shared Prosperity and Harmony* (Seoul: Korea Institute for International Economic Policy 2000). On economic issues in Northeast Asia, see *Regional Economic Cooperation in Northeast Asia*, Proceedings of the 9th meeting of the NE Asia Economic Forum, 26–29 Oct. 1999, co-sponsored by the East-West Center and Tianjin Municipal Administration.

3. Essays dealing with America's Asia-Pacific alliances are contained in Robert D. Blackwill and Paul Dibb (eds.) *America's Asian Alliances* (Cambridge, MA: MIT Press 2000).

4. One good analysis of traditionally based problems is Brian Woodall, *Japan Under Construction – Corruption, Politics, and Public Works* (Berkeley, CA: Univ. of California Press 1996).

5. For a recent appraisal of economic trends and their social consequences, see a two-article series in *The Wall Street Journal*, 'Converging Forces – Distress, Deregulation and Diplomacy Breach Walls of Fortress Japan' (28 Dec. 2000) pp.1, 4, and 'Japan's Long Decline Makes One Thing Rise: Individualism' (29 Dec. 2000) pp.1, 4.

6. A comprehensive recent study of Japanese politics is Gerald L. Curtis, *The Logic of Japanese Politics – Leaders, Institutions, and the Limits of Change* (NY: Columbia UP 1999); see also Frank J. Schwartz, *Advice and Consent: The Politics of Consultation in Japan* (Cambridge: CUP 1998).

7. Yoichi Funabashi (ed.) *Japan's International Agenda* (New York UP 1994).

8. Among others, for a comprehensive picture, see John Bryan Starr, *Understanding China – A Guide to China's Economy, History, and Political Structure*, rev. and updated ed. (NY: Hill & Wang 2000); also Cheng Li, *Rediscovering China – Dynamics and Dilemmas of Reform* (Lanham, MD: Rowman & Littlefield 1997).

9. An excellent analysis of Chinese foreign policymaking using macro-micro linkage theory is Quansheng Zhao, *Interpreting Chinese Foreign Policy* (Oxford and NY: OUP 1996).

10. Among recent studies, see Michael J. Green and Patrick M. Cronin (eds.) *The U.S.-Japan Alliance – Past, Present, and Future* (NY: Council on Foreign Relations Press 1999), and The Edwin O. Reischauer Center for East Asian Studies, *The United States and Japan in 2000: Seeking Focus*, (Washington, DC: SAIS, Johns Hopkins UP 2000). For a somber view, see Yoichi Funabashi, *Alliance Adrift* (NY: Council on Foreign Relations 1999).

11. Contemporary studies of US-China relations of importance include Ezra F. Vogel (ed.) *Living with China – U.S.-China Relations in the Twenty-First Century* (NY: Norton 1997); Robert G. Sutter, *Chinese Policy Priorities and their Implications for the United States* (Lanham, MD: Rowman & Littlefield 2000); and Mark A. Stokes, *China's Strategic Modernization: Implications for the United States* (Carlisle, PA: Strategic Studies Institute 1999).

12. For an insightful Chinese view of US-PRC relations, see Chu Shulong, 'Bilateral and Regional Strategic and Security Relationship Between China and the US after the Cold War', *Contemporary International Relations* 10/5 (May 2000) pp.1–13.

13. See Wang Lijiu, 'New Starting-point, New Challenges – Sino-Russian Relations in the New Century', *Contemporary International Relations* 10/7 (July 2000) pp.9–20.

14. A typical Chinese perspective is given in Lu Qichang and Zhang Yanyu, '"Taiwan Security Enhancement Act" is a Dangerous Political Bill', *Contemporary International Relations* 10/4 (April 2000) pp.22–32. For recent essays on the Taiwan issue, see Paul H. Tai (ed.) *United States, China, and Taiwan* (Carbondale: Public Policy Institute, Southern Illinois Univ. 1999).

15. A variety of views on US policies toward Taiwan is presented in Jaw-Ling Joanne Chang and William W. Boyer, *United States-Taiwan Relations: Twenty Years After the Taiwan Relations Act*, Maryland Series in contemporary Asian Studies (Baltimore: School of Law, Univ. of Maryland 2000).

16. See the essays in Japan Center for International Exchange (ed.) *New Dimensions of China-Japan Relations* (Tokyo: JCIE 1999).

17. An impressive series of essays on Russian policies in East Asia are contained in Gilbert Rozman, Mikhail G. Nosov and Koji Watanabe (eds.) *Russia and East Asia – The 21st Century Security Environment*, Vol. 3 in series *Eurasia in the 21st Century: The Total Security Environment* (Armonk, NY: East-West Institute/M.E. Sharpe 1999).

18. A comprehensive treatment of Russian relations with Japan from the Brezhnev era through the Yeltsin years is Hiroshi Kimura, *Japanese-Russian Relations Under Brezhnev and Andropov* and *Japanese-Russian Relations Under Gorbachev and Yeltsin*, 2 vols (Armonk, NY: M.E. Sharpe 2000).

19. Recent studies of the Korean issue of note include Chung-in Moon and David I. Steinberg (eds.) *Kim Dae-jung Government and Sunshine Policy – Promises and Challenges* (Seoul: Yonsei UP 1999); Kongdan Oh and Ralph C. Hassig, *North Korea Through the Looking Glass* (Washington DC: Brookings Institution Press 2000); Scott Snyder, *Negotiating on the Edge – North Korean Negotiating Behavior* (Washington DC: US Institute of Peace Press 1999); Don Oberdorfer, *The Two Koreas – A Contemporary History* (Reading, MA: Addison-Wesley 1997); and Korea Institute For National Unification, *The Unification Environment and Relations Between South and North Korea: 1999–2000* (Seoul: Korea Institute for National Unification 2000).

20. An earlier series of essays, broadly gauged, are to be found in Richard J. Ellings and Sheldon W. Simon (eds.) *Southeast Asian Security in the New Millennium* (Armonk, NY: M.E. Sharpe 1996). For an excellent analysis of the economic crisis earlier encompassing East Asia, see Ungsuh Kenneth Park, *Balancing between Panic and Mania – The East Asian Economic Crises and Challenges to the International Financing* (Seoul: Samsung Economic Research Institute 2000).

21. For diverse perspectives, see Hung-mao Tien and Tun-jen Cheng (eds.) *The Security Environment in the Asia-Pacific* (Armonk, NY: M.E. Sharpe 2000); and Shanghai Institute for International Studies, *The Post Cold War World* (Shanghai: SIIS Publication 2000).

22. Perceptive studies of the emergence of a civil society in many Asian states are contained in Lowell Dittmer, Haruhiro Fukui and Peter N.S. Lee (eds.) *Informal Politics in East Asia* (Cambridge: CUP 2000). See also Larry Diamond and Marc F. Plattner (eds.) *Democracy in East Asia* (Baltimore, MD: Johns Hopkins UP 1998).

2

The United States and East Asia in the Unipolar Era

MICHAEL J. GREEN

In the decade since the end of the Cold War, the United States has struggled to define a security strategy for an era without peer challengers. Unipolarity has led some Americans to call for policies designed simply to sustain national preeminence. Others see an opportunity to advance American ideals. Many have simply lapsed into complacency and apathy about world events.

America's Asian interlocutors are also confused by the contradictions of this new era. Economic growth has created interdependence but at the same time heightened the sense of rivalry and insecurity among the major powers in the region. The United States has unparalleled global dominance but increasingly turns to regional friends and allies to play a larger role. The threat of total nuclear war with the Soviet Union is now gone, but new threats from weapons of mass destruction have emerged in North Korea, South Asia and even in the Tokyo subway system.

The fact that unmatched global US power does not easily translate into regional influence further confuses American security relations with East Asia. Asian states see the impact of America's economic and cultural 'soft power', yet the spread of McDonald's and America Online does not provide instruments of power that the United States can wield in pursuit of specific national interests. Malaysia's Prime Minister Mahathir attacks the pernicious influence of American-style capitalism, but even with the dollar as the predominant global currency, the United States remains the world's largest debtor. Asian states complain of American neglect of regional forums such as the Asia Pacific Economic Cooperation forum (APEC) and the ASEAN Regional Forum (ARF), but are even more annoyed with American initiatives to strengthen and institutionalize those forums. The US pursuit of global regimes for non-proliferation, labor and environmental standards further antagonizes Asian states that would just as soon not put regional stability at risk for the sake of universal codes of conduct. And, of course, Washington's human rights agenda drives many Asian leaders to distraction.

However, while Asian observers may see a confusing jumble of priorities in US foreign policy in the region – and while Americans themselves have often been uncertain about their purpose there – it would be a mistake to think that American security policy in the region has lost its bearings. There is still a clear and consistent hierarchy to US interests in East Asia that has its roots in the forming of the republic over 200 years ago. And while idealism and global regime building are central elements in American foreign policy in East Asia today, realism and power still trumps idealism. That is why the United States will have staying power in East Asia well into the next century.

To demonstrate this point, the essay is broken into two sections. Section I examines the enduring US interests in East Asia in more detail, with a particular focus on (a) historical roots, (b) what has changed with the end of the Cold War, and (c) competing definitions of security in the US debate. The subsections in section II examine how these interests affect US relations in East Asia, both in terms of broad regional themes and specific bilateral relations (though the treatment of the latter is brief, since these are treated in more detail in other studies in this collection).

US FOREIGN POLICY IN EAST ASIA

Enduring Interests

A mix of idealism and realism has always driven US foreign policy in East Asia. From the birth of the republic, presidents have returned consistently to the same three-note chord that describes US interests in the Pacific: physical security, economic prosperity, and the promotion of values. James Madison noted in the Federalist Papers that security against foreign danger was the primary justification for shifting power from the states to the central government (physical security). Thomas Jefferson promoted peace and commerce with all nations (economic security). James Monroe advocated the expansion of American democracy throughout the Western Hemisphere to protect the physical and economic interests of the young republic (promotion of values). The Clinton administration struck the same chord two centuries later. The White House National Security Strategy, the Joint

Chiefs' National Military Strategy, the Pentagon's Security Strategy for East Asia and the Pacific (1995) follow-up report in 1998 – as well as testimony and speeches by senior US officials and military commanders, all begin with a statement that the US interests after the Cold War are:

(1) To promote a stable and secure world, where political and economic freedom, human rights and democratic institutions flourish;

(2) To advance a healthy and growing US economy to ensure opportunity for individual prosperity and a resource base for national endeavors at home and abroad;

(3) To preserve the survival of the United States as a free and independent nation, with its fundamental values intact and its institutions and people secure.[1]

Now, to be sure, the consistent articulation of broad US interests from the founding fathers to George W. Bush masked decades of struggle between supporters of expansion engagement, and dramatic ebbs and flows in the nature of the direct physical threat to the United States. Moreover, while the chord has been the same for over 200 years, at times one of the three notes have drowned out the other two. Nevertheless, the interplay of security, economic and democratic interests in American foreign policy has unfolded with a logic that suggests that the end of the Cold War did not – and will not – lead to a new prioritization of these interests. Before examining the specifics of post-Cold War US security policy in Asia, it is worth examining three reasons why there is such consistency.

First, the geographic definition of security has steadily expanded in the United States beyond Madison's immediate focus on continental protection against foreign dangers. Two broad competing visions for US security policy in the twentieth century, collective security and balance of power, both emerged from an identification of US material interests with those of other states. When the United States was isolationist, it was so because the nation's physical security could not be put at risk by other powers (or so it seemed). The expansion of overseas investment and trade and the emergence of nuclear weapons ended such continental and isolationist options forever. Material threats and interests are now global and there is no other actor that can preserve stability and guard those interests for the United States in the way Britain did during the era of American 'jackal diplomacy' in the nineteenth century.

Second, the three notes in the US foreign policy chord are neither distinctly material nor ideational, and ideals are not inconsistent with power.

Conservative realists in the Morgenthau tradition have complained that the pursuit of American interests in Asia is constantly obstructed by idealism,[2] but the rhetoric of democratic expansion – and the reality of economic and political power – have always been difficult to disaggregate. The expansion of democracy equates with a reduction of potential physical threats to the United States, whether from communism, terrorism or nuclear weapons. President Truman echoed and expanded the hemispheric strategy of James Monroe when he stated in 1948 that 'the loss of independence by any nation adds directly to the insecurity of the United States and all free nations'.[3] More of *us* means less of *them*. At the same time, even the most idealistic Wilsonian calls to 'make the world safe for democracy', were at their core an expression of the national values necessary to win a broad national consensus for the use of force in pursuit of material, balance of power ends during World War I. The economic dimension is similarly intertwined with both traditional definitions of power and idealism. The emergence of trading blocs would threat US trade and investment and also increase the prospects for unstable multipolar rivalry and conflict. The economic globalism of the Bretton Woods system was self-consciously designed to parallel the security globalism of the UN system. Meanwhile, the expansion of democratic ideals that underpin the Bretton Woods system has helped to assure that the United States continues to play a central role in most new global and regional economic organizations that have emerged.

Third, while physical security, economic prosperity, and democratic ideals have all been intertwined in American definitions of security, it is fairly clear that in the twentieth century the use of force has increasingly depended on the material presence of a physical threat to US interests. Specifically, US security policy, including decisions on the use of force, has focused on preventing the emergence of a rival Eurasian hegemon with the capability to wage war on the continental United States. The United States was finally drawn out of isolation because of the looming threat of Nazi and Japanese control of the Eurasian landmass. The Japanese attack on Pearl Harbor on 7 December 1941 was only the immediate *casus belli*. Similarly, North Korea's attack on the South in June 1950 led to a robust US military response – primarily because of concerns over the impact of a South Korean defeat on the credibility of the US defense commitment to Western Europe and Japan, not because Korea itself was imbued with geostrategic or economic significance to the United States at the time. The war in Vietnam was also viewed through the lens of Munich and the failure of appeasement to check aggression, and the desire to prevent falling dominoes from spreading to Japan.

Moreover, where the pursuit of democratic ideals or economic interests did threaten to undermine fundamental security objectives, the material security calculation eventually prevailed. The New Deal idealism of the early occupation of Japan was reversed as the United States moved to build its former enemy into a bastion against communism in 1947.

Recognition of a 'democratic' Republic of China was dropped so that relations could be built with the PRC, primarily to strengthen the United States geostrategic position and prevent the emergence of a hostile Eurasian hegemonic power.

And President Carter's initial emphasis on human rights was largely abandoned after the Soviet invasion of Afghanistan threatened to expand Moscow's reach to the Persian Gulf.

How Much Changed after the Cold War?

The difficulty of organizing the three-note chord of US foreign policy interests after the Cold War was best captured in the very ambiguity of the Bush administration's 'New World Order' compared with the elegant simplicity of 'containment'. The 1991 Gulf War demonstrated that Americans were still willing to use force to defeat and contain hegemonic threats to American interests at the regional level.

However, President Bush's inability to translate his Gulf victory into electoral success at home revealed that Americans were unconvinced that physical security translated into economic security in this new era. Bush attempted to barter his foreign policy prowess for economic results by spotlighting trade disputes in his 1992 summit with Prime Minister Miyazawa in Tokyo, but the effort only made the President appear ineffectual. Candidate Clinton pushed a more consistent line on 'economic security' and won the election.

The Clinton administration came into power thinking itself liberated from the balance of power constraints faced by previous administrations that had to confront the Soviet Union. Prepared to reassert important ideals, such as human rights, and new ideas about material power, such as 'economic' security, the Clinton team began its first term with a dramatically broadened definition of security and foreign policy interests. The problem was, however, that there was no unifying strategy. Rather than articulate a cohesive and comprehensive security agenda, the Clinton administration opened the door to a plurality of unconnected definitions of security. The constraints of the Cold War were lifted, but the discipline it imposed was not replaced. This caused particular confusion for US regional strategy toward East Asia.

At the core of the Clinton administration's expanded definition of security were economic objectives. The National Economic Council (NEC) was established to ensure that economic security priorities received equal consideration to 'traditional' security concerns in foreign policy. The effect, however, was often to bifurcate decision-making and undermine precisely the kind of comprehensive approach originally intended. NEC staffers vied with the US Trade Representatives Office (USTR) for leadership in trade negotiations or championed pet projects aimed at specific hi-tech sectors of the domestic economy, but the NEC was rarely able to become the cockpit of economic development promised during the campaign.

In the one area where an attempt was made to form a comprehensive economic security strategy – towards Japan – the Clinton administration essentially put the political and security dimensions of the alliance on hold in an effort to squeeze results-oriented trade agreements out of Tokyo. This experiment with tough reciprocity toward Japan was also an attempt to verify more general assumptions the Clinton team had made about the role of government in establishing strategies for economic development. The focus of the 1993–95 Economic Framework Talks was on a basket of sectors and issues (insurance, autos, etc.) where the US side wanted 'indicators' of progress. By negotiating with the Japanese Ministry of International Trade and Industry (MITI) for results-oriented agreements, the administration was working on the assumption that sectoral intervention and managed trade were legitimate instruments of economic security policy. This assumption was carried into the administration by academics and consultants who had been impressed with MITI's role in Japanese economic development and wanted to establish a comparable function in the United States.[4]

While negotiating with Japan, the NEC was also implementing ambitious plans for defense conversion and technology investment at home, such as the Technology Reinvestment Project (TRP), the Advanced Technology Program (ATP), and the Flat Panel Display Initiative (FPDI). This Japanese-inspired technonationalist focus extended to the Pentagon, where officials announced a Technology-for-Technology Initiative (TfT) in 1994 that was designed to achieve greater reciprocity in the transfer of military-related technology to Japan.

Liberated from the bipolar structures of the Cold War, the Clinton administration also heightened the government's focus on global threats such as the proliferation of weapons of mass destruction (WMD). While concern about WMD was no less significant during the George H.W. Bush administration, the Clinton foreign policy team allowed its non-proliferation agenda to crowd out the traditional regional security and alliance-management priorities that containment of the Soviet Union had required. Thus, in responding aggressively to the North Korean nuclear crisis of 1994, the White House created fears in Seoul and Tokyo that the United States was willing to risk war in Northeast Asia in order to maintain the Non-Proliferation Treaty (NPT). The leadership in Tokyo and Seoul (the likely targets of North Korean nuclear weapons, after all) felt that regional stability was at least as important as preserving global non-proliferation regimes. In the end, the Clinton administration won the full support of Seoul and Tokyo, but the apparent devaluation of alliance coordination was disturbing to the region and to regionalists in the Departments of State and Defense.[5]

Human rights and democracy were also thrust to the center of the Clinton administration's definition of national security. Early plans to create the post of assistant secretary of defense for democracy were dropped after intense Congressional criticism, but the post was temporarily replicated in the National Security Council where it would not require Senate confirmation. After a brief period of soul-searching, the administration supported Most Favored Nation (MFN) status for China, but Clinton had to battle the same constituencies to pass MFN that had been emboldened by his promise as a candidate to link human rights to trading privileges.[6]

The lack of a strategic framework for the first Clinton administration's foreign policy agenda was particularly disorienting because of the crumbling base of foreign policy interest in the public, the media and Congress. The amount of time dedicated to international affairs on the major networks' evening news declined by nearly 50 per cent in the first half of the 1990s. Centrist/internationalist members of the House and Senate also retired or were defeated in large numbers in both the 1994 and the 1996 elections.[7] Without an elite foundation for international engagement, other ethnic, humanitarian or labor interest groups from the Democratic Party base filled the void. Thus, in his first term Clinton only used force in pursuit of humanitarian or democracy goals where absolutely no other critical US interest was at stake (Haiti and Somalia) and where domestic pressure groups and CNN commentators pressed for action.

In Asia the confusion of interests and ideals could be at least partly understood because of what Robert Manning at the time called post-Cold War Asia's 'three contradictions'. As Manning noted in 1993, the region was (1) more peaceful than ever, yet haunted by its checkered history and uneasy about the future; (2) absent any immediate security threat (other than the Korean peninsula), yet featuring some of the world's largest military powers; and (3) moving toward global and regional economic integration, yet plagued with territorial disputes and rising nationalism.[8]

The Clinton administration focused on only the first halves of these three contradictions. Washington defined US economic security based on an outdated model of Japanese economic development. They bet that liberal ideals and economic power would define power relations in Asia in the future. They assumed that the measures of American commitment and credibility could be redefined in these terms. In part they were right, but mostly they guessed wrong.

Signs that American credibility was hemorrhaging came early. Yoichi Funabashi captured the attention of many when he wrote in *Foreign Affairs* in 1993 that most Asians expected the United States to withdraw from the region.[9] The Japanese Advisory Panel on Defense established by Prime Minister Morihiro Hosokawa in 1993 to review long-term defense policy focused on multilateralism, independent capabilities, and other hedges against the prospect of US withdrawal.[10] Then in the spring of 1994 Assistant Secretary of State for Asia Pacific Affairs Winston Lord circulated a memorandum in the department warning that the cacophony of conflicting priorities in US policy were leading to a 'malaise' in US leadership in the region.[11]

Around the same time the spiraling crisis over North Korean nuclear ambitions revealed how unprepared American alliances were for conflict. Then the political crisis created by the rape of a young Okinawan girl in September 1995 demonstrated just how vulnerable the US-Japan alliance had become on political grounds. After exploring economic and neo-Wilsonian definitions of security, the Clinton administration was pulled back to the more traditional formulation of the three-chord note, with power considerations again the first priority.

The Pentagon spearheaded the effort to reverse the malaise in American regional leadership with the publication of the February 1995 East Asian Strategic Report (EASR). The EASR telegraphed American staying power by declaring that the United States would maintain approximately 100,000 troops in the region for the foreseeable future.

The EASR was followed by a deliberate and intensive 18-month bilateral review of the US-Japan alliance with Tokyo, which culminated in the April 1996 Tokyo Joint Security Declaration, reaffirming the alliance and opening a series of initiatives to strengthen bilateral security cooperation in a regional context. A formal reaffirmation of the US alliance with Australia followed shortly thereafter.

United States' willpower was further demonstrated by the high-profile dispatch of two US carrier battle groups to the area of the Taiwan Straits during the Beijing's attempts to intimidate Taiwan with a series of aggressive missile tests in March 1996. The Taiwan Strait crisis only deepened the administration's refocusing on balance of power considerations.

Meanwhile, certain high profile economic and human rights issues were accorded a comparatively lower priority in overall US policy toward the region. By the summer of 1995 the administration had either moved to settle its most intensive trade disputes with Japan, or to refer them to the World Trade Organization. Domestic 'industrial policies' such as the ATP, TRP and TfT had their funding taken away by the new Republican-controlled Congress. The Clinton administration formed a new alliance with the same Republicans to pass NAFTA and the WTO and return to a globalist, *laissez-faire* model of economic policy more consistent with the philosophy of the founders of Bretton Woods than than of the founders of MITI.

The degree to which the Clinton administration moved back to the general trajectory set by Bush was most evident in candidate Bob Dole's failure to draw a clear distinction for himself on Asia policy during the 1996 presidential campaign. In his major speech on Asia at the Center for Strategic and International Studies (CSIS) on 9 May 1996, Doe virtually endorsed the Clinton administration's emerging Asia policy, with the exception of tactical disagreements over engagement of North Korea and China, and a call for a region-wide missile defense system.[12]

Writing at the beginning of the second Clinton administration, Barry Posen and Andrew Ross concluded that 'ironically, the Clinton administration grand strategy has already evolved to a point where it has many of the trappings of primacy.[13] Indeed, Clinton's foreign and defense policy team has discovered that considerable US leadership and major commitments of US power are necessary for the pursuit of the transformed world order they seek.'[14]

Even as the second Clinton administration settled on a strategy of primacy, however, differences with the Republicans emerged over tactics and underlying assumptions about the future trends in East Asia. As Posen and Ross argued, 'The Republicans would probably follow a somewhat purer version of primacy, and move even further away from cooperative security ...'.

In fact, when Governor George W. Bush organized his foreign policy strategy in his 2000 campaign against Al Gore, this shift away from cooperative security was pronounced. Bush and his advisors promised to use the US military only for narrowly defined US national interests, to place a greater emphasis on national security (and particularly national missile defense) than international arms control regimes, and not to sacrifice alliance relations when dealing with states like China or North Korea. In Asia the Bush team took particular exception to the Clinton-Gore declaration of a new 'strategic partnership' with China. Gore, in contrast, emphasized cooperative security and the expansion of the community of like-minded states through engagement of transitioning nations like China or even North Korea. The Gore and Bush approaches differed, but only within parameters that were essentially the same. Both focused on the maintenance of US primacy, with Gore emphasizing cooperative security and Bush the balance-of-power in relative rather than absolute terms. The biggest difference between the two really rested in their assumptions about the conflicting trends of rivalry and interdependence in Asia. The Gore team placed relatively more faith in the trend of economic growth leading to interdependence, while the Bush team placed relatively more faith in the need to maintain alliances and deterrence in case power rivalry (particularly with China) gained more momentum.

Wild Cards and Competing Definitions of Security

For mainstream Republicans and Democrats, power still trumps ideals, though ideals remain an indispensable element in American foreign policy. Primacy remains the driving theme in US foreign policy toward Asia. There is a debate outside of government about the sustainability of the primacy, to be sure. Charles Kupchan, for example, argues that this unipolar moment is not sustainable and that the United States should seek accommodation with emerging friendly regional powers, devolving more power to the EU and encouraging regional integration and greater self-sufficiency within Asia.[15]

Others, like John Ikenberry, argue that it is ultimately the ideals behind American foreign policy that will sustain unipolarity – precisely because these ideals, as embedded in the UN, WTO, and other international institutions, constrain the United States and make its hegemony less threatening.[16]

Still others, such as William Wohlforth, argue that unipolarity and primacy have faded from official US rhetoric, but remain the core unifying theme of American security policy.[17] Whether or not Wohlforth is right about the stability of a unipolar system can be debated (although this author thinks he is correct), but there can be little debate that in the transition from the Clinton to the Bush administration – despite the ideological differences and the relative change in emphasis from ideals to power – primacy remains the central and consistent unifying theme for US strategy in Asia.

That said, it must be recognized that there is also a greater pluralism in the foreign policy process and that this complicates the formation of coherent regional strategies for both political parties. There are also new trends in technology and uncertainties about the duration of American internationalism that might cause a more fundamental change in the thrust of US foreign policy in East Asia. Before projecting how US foreign policy toward Asia will likely unfold in the next century, it is important to address these wild cards.

What might erode the internationalist consensus in the United States? The mainstream consensus behind the pursuit of primacy could be most easily disrupted by actual or perceived shifts in the balance of power. These shifts could result from American defeat in battle. Wargamers at the Naval War College, for example, concluded that the loss of capital ships in a conflict in the Taiwan Strait, followed by Japanese neutrality, might lead to a general US retrenchment from Asia.[18] The internationalist consensus could also be undermined by a perceived or actual loss of primacy through the 'death of a thousand cuts' as niche players gain asymmetrical weapons of mass destruction or alternate economic capabilities that allow them to ignore or challenge US hegemony with impunity.[19] The foreign policy consensus could also be disrupted by a dramatic economic downturn.

At this point there are compelling counterfactuals to all of these points, though. The United States response to defeat in battle could be retrenchment, but historical precedents (Pearl Harbor, for example) suggest that the response would more likely be resolve and retaliation. Similarly, 'death by a thousand cuts' could lead to more selective engagement or new coalitions, but not automatic isolationism. And an economic downturn could lead to an abandonment of primacy, but only if other economies surpass the US economy's hegemonic position – an unlikely prospect for Japan, China or any other state in East Asia for some time to come.

Nevertheless, the possibility of these exogenous shocks transforming the US foreign policy debate cannot be completely dismissed. Indeed, within the United States there are competing schools of thought that would seize upon these shocks to turn the nation away from the mainstream internationalist and primacy consensus. These anti-mainstream schools include:

1. *Offshore balancing.* Some scholars argue that the United States cannot sustain primacy and only decreases its own security by remaining forward deployed in entangling alliances in Asia. They argue that a better strategy would be withdraw forces from the region and act as an

'offshore' balancer in the same way that Britain did in Continental Europe throughout the nineteenth and twentieth centuries. By selective use of force, they maintain, the United States could maintain a stable balance in the region with far less of a commitment.[20]

2. *Elegant presence.* Beginning in the early 1990s, some US Air Force planners began arguing for a strategy that would reduce US military presence and exposure in Asia, but sustain US primacy through the clean, quick and decisive application of air power based primarily in the United States. This notion of 'elegant' or 'virtual' presence did not survive the 1995 Defense Department Commission on Roles and Missions, but it could gain support if the threat to US bases or naval power in Asia increases.[21]

3. *Economic populism.* As we noted, the Clinton administration's effort to institutionalize economic security faded by 1996 because (a) the new Republican Congress cut funding for high-profile economic security programs; (b) the administration put more energy into passing free trade agreements like NAFTA and the WTO; (c) the Treasury Department returned to its traditional free trade orientation; and (d) new security challenges in East Asia emerged to grab the administration's attention; and (e) the new 'dot.com' economy exploded entirely outside of governmental funding and guidance. As a result, economic populism, protectionism and mercantilism barely figured in the 2000 presidential election. Both Bush and Gore ran as almost pure free traders and internationalists. It is striking, however, that Ralph Nader gained a portion of the national vote by running against free trade, in much the same way that Pat Buchanan did in 1996. A prolonged economic crisis could conceivably fuel the candidacies of future presidents or Congresses that oppose US forward presence and open trading regimes.

4. *Human rights.* The United States has generally avoided conditioning important strategic relationships in Asia on human rights or democratic principles alone. The Carter and Clinton administrations both eventually moved to decouple strategic dialogue and human rights in relations with China, despite campaign promises to the contrary. However, no administration, and particularly no Democratic administration, can ignore the demands for idealism in US foreign policy. As Richard Haass warns, domestic lobbies for human rights are ever vigilant for chances to advance their agenda. Thus, 'when the White House fails to articulate

its foreign policy objectives – and public apathy is high – it leaves the door open for special interest groups and lobbyists to shape the agenda'.[22] The impact of human rights on US foreign policy in Asia has also increased as state legislatures and local governments have begun imposing their own economic sanctions on countries such as Burma. Combined with other trends, such as economic populism, it is possible that the idealistic human rights agenda in the United States could conceivably trump power considerations in the future. Indeed, human rights principles should always guide US foreign policy and the challenge is therefore one of relative weight and importance – a difficult thing for governments to calibrate when overall strategy is weak.

5. *The budget debate.* One final challenge to the mainstream view of US interests and strategy in East Asia comes from the 'budget hawks'. Tax-cutting, budget-balancing Republicans in the Congress made thinly veiled threats against the foreign policy and defense budgets of the Departments of State and Defense. Defense procurement has fallen by over 60 per cent since 1987 and the foreign affairs budget by close to 40 per cent.[23] Foreign Service Officers and US military personnel are already badly overstretched and need more resources. While engagement and forward presence in Asia will be sustainable given current economic and budget projections, they could not withstand a reduction in resources without major impact on their capabilities. It is also possible that further pressure to reduce taxes or balance the budget – or unanticipated increases in entitlements as baby boomers retire – could lead to a supply-side re-evaluation of US security policy in Asia.[24]

These various schools of thought all compete with the mainstream impulse in American foreign policy – which is to remain forward engaged and militarily committed in East Asia. These anti-mainstream schools of thought add dynamism to the debate about US interests in East Asia and capture a disproportionate and unrealistic amount of attention from the media – and particularly the East Asian media. It would require a confluence of traumatic events for US foreign policy to shift towards any one of them. Indeed, there are three other trends that are emerging to reinforce the US forward engagement in Asia and to sustain the US unipolar moment. These are:

1. *The growth of US economic interests in Asia.* There is not a state among the 50 United States that does not have a significantly greater level of

investment from Asia than it did two decades ago (except perhaps Hawaii, which always had it). Similarly, there is not a major American manufacturer or agricultural exporter who does not see Asia as one of its fastest growing markets over the next decade. United States' investment in China continues to grow, and in Japan – which is itself in economic stagnation – US investment has increased dramatically. In the nineteenth century, strategists argued that 'trade follows the flag', but in the twenty-first century 'the flag will follow trade'.

2. *The revolution in military affairs (RMA).* After the 1991 Gulf War, US strategists realized that the information revolution was transforming warfare and the definition of military power in some fundamental ways. Increasingly, it appeared that dominant military power rested not in weapons systems themselves, but the information technology that creates a networked 'systems-of-systems'. Strategists recognized that such a 'system-of-systems' would allow US forces to see the entire battlefield and strike with precision, while simultaneously blinding the enemy. Even as strategists debated the practicality of such a 'revolution in military affairs', the 1999 Kosovo campaign gave further evidence that US information-based warfare was outstripping the capabilities of allies and adversaries alike. There is no shortage of debate about whether the conservative US military is capable of such a transformation; whether countervailing 'cyber' and bio/chemical threats would undermine such capabilities; or whether the technologies are really so impressive. Nevertheless, there is no question, judging from the difference between the Gulf War and Kosovo, that the US military is developing increasingly effective coercive instruments.[25]

3. *Democracy.* Despite the core importance of material power in US security policy in East Asia, it is clear that American power also rests on the growing universality of American ideals. Democracy is strong today in South Korea, the Philippines, and Taiwan – three places that had authoritarian regimes two decades ago. In Japan liberal democracy (and its attendant fluidity) is taking ever firmer root. Civil society is growing in these countries also. Indonesia, despite its ills, is moving away from authoritarian control of government. China has begun experimenting with carefully controlled local elections. Indeed, the trend throughout the region is toward greater pluralism and democracy, and those countries that have chosen the opposite path – Burma and North Korea – are in the deepest economic trouble.

In sum, there are both schools of thought challenging the US strategy of primacy and countervailing trends that reinforce US unipolarity. Having considered what these might be, we now return to the major themes that will animate US strategy in the region over the coming years. We will assume a continued focus on primacy, but discuss how each regional theme and bilateral relationship could change with different US strategies.

US STRATEGY FOR EAST ASIA IN THE TWENTY-FIRST CENTURY

Regional Themes

In 1991 Secretary of State James Baker wrote an article in *Foreign Affairs* arguing that the United States accepted the growth of regional dialogue and identity in East Asia, but that these broader regional themes would be like the rim on a Conestoga wagon wheel. The hub and spokes – which ultimately hold the wheel together – would remain American bilateral alliances in East Asia and the forward presence of US military forces.[26] There is no doubt that the administration of George W. Bush will reassert this focus on bilateral alliances in East Asia, but the challenge of defining a US policy towards regional security remains.

In some respects a great deal has changed in East Asian regionalism in the 1990s. In 1991 there were only unofficial, second-track regional forums. Since 1993, however, the region's heads-of-state have gathered annually for the Asia Pacific Economic Cooperation (APEC) summit – ostensibly to talk about regional economic themes, but increasingly with an informal focus on security problems. Today the region's foreign ministers gather annually for the ASEAN Regional Forum. In 1991 Malaysia's Mohammed Mahathir was proposing an 'Asians only' East Asian Economic Caucus (EAEC) that the United States, Australia, Canada, New Zealand and Japan strenuously opposed. Since 1999 Japan, China, South Korea and ASEAN have begun meetings of the so-called 'ASEAN Plus Three' – yet this move has barely caused a yawn in Washington.

In short, there is a great deal more regional identity and dialogue in Asia than there was a decade ago. But the contents of the dialogue remain profoundly dissatisfying and unimpressive to most American policy makers. The veiled warning against excessive multilateralism and regionalism in Baker's 1991 *Foreign Affairs* article proved unnecessary. The ARF plods along with ASEAN rules requiring unanimity and rejecting interference in internal affairs. The ARF has barely moved beyond the status of 'talk shop' as a result. APEC made great progress in the early

1990s as a stimulus for global trade negotiations, but when the United States and Japan fought a major battle in Kuala Lumpur in 1998 over how much trade liberalization APEC should mandate, the Japanese won and sucked the life out of APEC in the process. The ASEAN Plus Three and Asia-Europe Summit (ASEM) have ominous undertones of excluding the United States, but the substance of the discussions is fairly benign and superficial. The symbolism of 'counterbalancing' US hegemony only counts when the United States is itself unilateral in trade policy, and much of the objective of these meetings is to constrain emerging Chinese regional power.

How then to approach regional security? The clear preference in Washington is for functional multilateralism; that is, multilateralism that achieves finite and clear objectives. One example is the Korean Peninsula Energy Development Organization (KEDO), which was established in 1995 to provide North Korea with peaceful nuclear energy in exchange for compliance with the non-proliferation regime. KEDO is funded and managed by the United States, South Korea, Japan, and the EU, with lesser participation from some other Asian states. Another example is the array of what the 1998 Pentagon East Asian Strategic Report calls 'overlapping plates of armor' – that is *minilateral* meetings with a finite agenda, such as the US-Japan-ROK Trilateral and Oversight Group (TCOG), created after the 1998 North Korean Taepodong missile launch to improve coordination on diplomacy toward Pyongyang. Similar 'minilaterals' include the second-track US-Japan-China dialogue at Harvard University or the US-Japan-Russia dialogue at SAIS, Johns Hopkins University. These minilaterals and functional multilateral institutions could conceivably expand in the future. Perhaps the next most significant development would be the establishment of a six-party forum for Northeast Asia to complement the Four Party Talks (China, ROK, US, DPRK) aimed at replacing the Korean War armistice with a permanent peace treaty.

The US preference for minilaterals and functional multilateralism is quintessentially pragmatic. They allow the United States to shape the agenda – something that it could not do in broader multilateral forums without provoking a backlash. They allow the United States to assemble coalitions of willing states to solve real security problems. And they complement rather than challenge the American system of bilateral alliances in the region.

It may be that minilateralism and functional multilateralism are not enough, however. The growing Asian sense of identity, unease with American unipolarity, and the emergence of common transnational security problems such as piracy and drugs – all provide a compelling case for the

United States to support broader security policies that go beyond bilateralism. Towards the end of the Clinton administration, the Pacific Command under Admiral Dennis Blair became particularly enthusiastic about an Asian 'security community'.[27] Their goal was to shape an Asia in which states view security problems as common challenges and move away from a balance-of-power, zero-sum view of their neighbors. The concept was a useful balm for Asian insecurities about US intentions, even if the United States itself continues to view the region in balance-of-power terms. The Pacific Command's security community concept also had the advantage of concrete operational elements, such as joint multinational humanitarian relief exercises and common training in confidence- and security-building measures.

It has often been suggested that there is an inherent tension between the United States' emphasis on bilateralism and the region's emphasis on multilateralism. However, it would be wrong to assume that there is such fundamental tension. The tension arises only when the regional multilateral institutions or forums fail to support the global agenda of the United States. And while alliances remain at the core of US strategy in Asia, over the next decade they will require broader multilateral complements to remain vibrant. How such multilateral arrangements emerge will depend in large measure on China. On the one hand, China's worldview might move towards interdependence, openness, and the concept of a regional security community. This stance would make inclusive multilateralism possible. On the other hand, if China's worldview becomes increasingly hegemonic and confrontational, the result might be exclusive multilateral bundling to constrain or contain Chinese power.

China

The future of the Sino-US relationship will be the most important determinant of East Asian security in the decades to come. Many observers focus on the US side of this relationship as the most uncertain variable. They argue, for example, that a US decision to move forward on National Missile Defense (NMD) threatens China's small nuclear deterrent and would discourage China from joining international arms control regimes while expanding its nuclear arsenal to compensate. They warn that US arms sales to Taiwan violate the spirit of the 1982 Shanghai Communiqué and force China towards a more hostile stance in the region. They lament the United States' slow approach to bringing China into the WTO.

In most of these cases, however, it is the Chinese side that is the uncertain variable. The United States, after all, is the status-quo power, and it is China that is going through the difficult process of transforming its economy and defining its role in the region and the world. China has been modernizing its nuclear forces to make them more survivable – not just because of NMD – but because Beijing now believes that its missiles could be critical in regional confrontations. These missiles would not just be symbols of Chinese power as they were in the past (after all, China's small nuclear deterrent was a vulnerable 'paper tiger' long before NMD came along). In the same vein, arms sales to Taiwan matter only because Beijing is no longer satisfied with Deng's willingness to let the cross-straits matter be resolved by the next generation. With its own legitimacy weak and the transition to a market economy perilous, the Beijing leadership does not have that luxury any more. Indeed, it was Beijing's deployment of 50 new ballistic missiles a year across from Taiwan that created sympathy in Washington for new arms sales to Taipei in the first place. And while the United States has not always followed through on its WTO negotiations with China, it is now conservatives in Beijing who drag their feet at completing the final stage of WTO accession, perhaps because of concerns that Taiwan would then be allowed to begin its own negotiations for membership.

None of these examples are intended to portray China as a hostile power to the United States. Only the most hawkish critics of Beijing argue that the United States should not encourage China's integration into the international community. Containment is simply not an option. But China is a rising power with colossal internal challenges and a carefully nurtured sense of wounded pride – and this combination creates far more uncertainty about China's ultimate direction than the contradictions and ideological debates that exist in US policy towards Beijing.

Ultimately, the traditional three-chord note of US foreign policy provides a clear framework for understanding how the United States will continue to approach China policy. If China's foreign policies aim at undermining or challenging American leadership, then Washington will respond with 'constrainment' if not outright containment. If China uses force against Taiwan, there is little doubt that the United States would respond diplomatically and militarily, no matter what the provocation from Taipei and regardless of a policy of 'strategic ambiguity' on what the response would be. But at the same time, because the United States is a status-quo power it will not encourage or support Taiwan's independence. As long as China does not threaten US leadership, the United States will focus on cooperation, particularly since the second of the three-chord notes, economic interests, dictates no less. American values will also intrude on the relationship – as they should – and this issue will rise or fall on Beijing's human rights record more than the politics of the issue in Washington. For the most part, however, American policy has operated on the assumption that China's embrace of market economic reforms will create the conditions for a democratic transition. That assumption may be wrong, of course, since Chinese nationalism may be further unleashed by the transition to democracy, but this dilemma is a reason to maintain strong US alliances rather than a reason to depart from the current policy. In short, it is China that is the question mark rather than the United States, but Washington has wisely bet that change in China will probably continue moving in a positive direction.

Japan

Japan is the cornerstone for American primacy in East Asia and, in many respects, the world. Japan hosts 45,000 US forces' personnel; provides the second-highest financial contribution in the United Nations, International Monetary Fund and most other critical international organizations; and shares with the United States a commitment to democracy, free markets, and regional stability. But Japan is changing in important ways. The Japanese economy has had virtually no growth in a decade. The pillars of 'Japan Inc.' are crumbling. The Japanese public is growing more sensitive to threats from North Korea and the rise of Chinese influence. And a new generation of Japanese political, bureaucratic and business leaders is less constrained by the war-guilt of the previous generation.

The United States has tended to be a status-quo power when it comes to Japan, too. When the Japanese economy was ascending rapidly in the late 1980s, Pentagon planners and CIA analysts quietly warned that our close ally could become a new techno-nationalistic peer competitor. These predictions were wrong, of course, primarily because the Japanese economic model was well suited for catching up, but not for maintaining an innovative economic lead (and unlike China, Japan never held a rival ideology to the United States). Ironically, it is the collapse of the Japanese economic model and not its continued success that is leading to changes in Japan's strategic culture. For now, Japan's leadership is paralyzed by indecision, but rapid changes are possible in the years ahead. United States' officials are beginning to notice this and explore ways to adjust and strengthen the alliance relationship accordingly.

The debate about Japan policy in the United States tends to focus on how to reduce asymmetries in the relationship – that is, how to decrease the burden of US forces in Japan while increasing Japan's share of the burden of international security. However, there are major barriers to this adjustment. The Japanese Constitution and regional apprehension make anything more than incremental changes to Japan's own military role difficult (absent a major external shock). The United States' requirement for regional deterrence and global power projection also makes it difficult to withdraw forces from Japan as well. Reducing asymmetry, in other words, may prove a less effective strategy than finding ways to share power in the broader sense. Power sharing requires more proactive strategic coordination with Japan and robust US support for Japan's diplomatic agenda in the region. Far from fearing Japanese leadership in Asia, the United States should encourage it. The danger, if there is one, is that Japan's difficult economic situation will cause Tokyo to retract from its current international role, which is often underestimated but indispensable to US leadership.

Again, the three-chord note explains the parameters of US policy toward Japan in the years ahead. United States' primacy and geostrategy rest on a strong and reliable Japan. United States' economic interests in the region require a Japan that is growing and open. And the promotion of US values is reinforced by the examples of our Asian democratic partners.

Korea

Before the Cold War the Korean peninsula was a footnote to US policy in Japan. Secretary of State Dean Acheson's famous exclusion of South Korea from the zone of critical US interests just before the North launched its attack in June 1950 is well known. Now, of course, South Korea is critical not just in the context of the lingering Cold War in Northeast Asia and the North Korean threat, but more importantly because it is our seventh-largest trading partner, an ally in the expansion of democracy and free-market principles, and – increasingly – the fulcrum in our complex relationship with China.

South Korean President Kim Dae Jung's 'Sunshine Policy' has yielded important results in terms of the diplomacy of the peninsula. After ignoring the South's overtures in 1998 and in 1999, the North suddenly agreed to a summit in April 2000 and hosted Kim Dae Jung in Pyongyang in June. That was followed by a marked absence of military provocations and hostile rhetoric towards the South and a more open reception for certain kinds of South Korean economic investment. And Pyongyang continues to abide by the 1994 Agreed Framework, which froze its known nuclear-weapons program, as well as a 1999 moratorium on testing of the long-range Taepodong missile (which is aimed at the United States).

The North's actions on the ground have been contradictory, however. After 1998 the North Koreans increased military training by one-third and deployed a range of new weapons, most troubling of all 100 Nodong ballistic missiles aimed at Japan. And while the Agreed Framework is still in progress, the North has yet to allow the inspections necessary to verify that it is plutonium-free. Indeed, in February 2001 Pyongyang threatened to withdraw from the Agreed Framework and begin test-launching Taepodong missiles again if the new Bush administration did not show better faith to improve relations and provide economic assistance.

The Korean peninsula is therefore a huge question mark for US policy in the region. North Korean provocations or internal instability resulting from its desperate economic situation could lead to chaos that spills across the North's borders in the form of refugees, artillery barrages, or missile launches. On the other hand, reconciliation with the South would remove the primary rationale for current US force structure in the region, potentially undermining the US leadership and unhinging the US-Japan alliance. And South Korea remains far more susceptible to any Chinese hegemony than Japan, meaning that a rapid disintegration of the North could pull the United States and China into a competitive relationship on the peninsula, where today there is at least as much cooperation as disagreement among the major powers.

The ultimate US interest on the Korean peninsula is stability and a process of reconciliation leading to eventual unification. Even if that reduced the rationale for US forces in the region, it would remove a serious material threat to the United States and its allies and represent a triumph of American values in the region. But the process could itself be destabilizing, and that is why the US-ROK alliance will not diminish in importance even if the North's hostility does. The United States and the ROK will have to determine how and when US forces can be deployed and what the command relationship will be bilaterally and trilaterally with US forces in Japan after reconciliation with the North. Nevertheless, there will be strategically compelling reasons for both Seoul and Washington to retain the US-ROK alliance and some level of US military presence on the peninsula. Even North Korean leader Kim Jong Il is said to have told Kim Dae Jung that he understands this point. The Korean peninsula will still be a 'shrimp among whales' and will need alignment with the geographically distant but supremely influential United States in order to manage relationships with Japan, China and Russia.

Russia

If Russia played no strategic role in East Asia, the region would probably not notice. In fact, Yeltsin gave Russia relatively little profile in the Far East for the first years of the post-Cold War era and the net effect was probably more positive than negative. However, when Russia chooses to be a spoiler, the region – and the United States – must take note. For that reason it is in US interests to maintain a cooperative and productive relationship with Moscow in an Asian context.

Vladmir Putin's approach to Asia has not been subtle. He has reinforced a symbolic 1996 Russian-Chinese 'strategic partnership' with substantive military cooperation. He has sold weapons such as surface-to-air missiles to North Korea (and Iran, of course). He has pressed South Korea and other states in the region to criticize US policies on national missile defense. These moves touch on US sensitivities about the rise of a Eurasian hegemonic rival and demand attention. Of course, the United States and its allies need not fear that Sino-Russian alignment would challenge US primacy. Neither country is strong enough and both are highly dependent on the United States and its allies for continued economic development. Nevertheless, these Russian geostrategic moves do complicate US leadership in the region. Moreover, Russia is a nuclear power and could do serious harm to US interests if it lost control of its WMD assets.

Much of Russia's new activism in the region is ideational – that is; it is motivated by the drive for respect as a great nation. In addition, Russia needs Japanese investment in its energy resources; South Korean debt forgiveness and investment in developing Kamchatka; as well as participation in the broader trade and investment opportunities the region has to offer. There are therefore arena where the United States can work with Russia as a cooperative partner in the region, such as APEC and any future Northeast Asia forum built around peace talks on the Korean peninsula. However, the United States will have to calibrate its Russia policy carefully, recognizing the limits on Russia's natural influence in the region and the risks of empowering Moscow diplomatically at a time when countering US hegemony appears to be a driving Russian ambition.

Southeast Asia

The United States has not focused on Southeast Asia with the same degree of interest as Northeast Asia. There are no major US bases, treaty commitments, or economic relationships as important as those in Japan and Korea. After the Vietnam conflict a consensus spread among strategic experts in the United States that even if a Southeast Asian nation became unstable or hostile to the United States in the future, that would not in itself jeopardize fundamental US interests. In part this consensus resulted from the declining threat of communist 'dominoes' spreading throughout the region. In part it resulted from the growing cohesion of the Association of Southeast Asian Nations (ASEAN), which prevented US, Chinese or Japanese strategic interests from coming into direct conflict in the subregion.

The myth of ASEAN cohesion and subregional stability may have contributed to complacency and inconsistency in US strategy after the Cold War. The Clinton administration pressed hard on human rights *vis-à-vis* Burma and Malaysia even at the cost of straining relations with other regional friends and allies like Singapore and Thailand. In addition, Washington was passive when the Thai baht collapsed in July 1997, sensing none of the danger of financial contagion or the kind of strategic implications that led to a rapid response when the Korean won collapsed six months later.

When Indonesia began to unravel in the first years of the new century, however, the United States could no longer take for granted ASEAN cohesion. Indonesia is the heartbeat of ASEAN and its continued weakness or collapse has the potential to open Southeast Asia to broader strategic competition among the major powers. How exactly this might happen no one can predict. It may be that instability on the Indonesian archipelago will be contained within certain islands; that China will not have the strategic reach to interfere; and that other Southeast Asian states will continue to prosper even if Indonesia does not. On the other hand, a weakened Indonesia and fractured ASEAN could also lead to expanding Chinese military presence and influence in Burma or Cambodia; the spread of economic instability even to Japan (which has tens of billions of non-performing loans exposed in the country); and the collapse of APEC, ARF and other multilateral fora. These material power considerations will force the United States to take a harder strategic look at the region than in the past and to forge proactive partnerships with Singapore, Japan, Australia and other like-minded states. However, even if Southeast Asia's problems drive geostrategy back to the top of the US priority list – subregional stability will ultimately be indispensable to the continued expansion of economic opportunity and democracy. The three-chord note of US interests will continue to set the agenda.

Australia

The United States and Australia share a common bond and an alliance relationship tested in war and peace over eight decades. The security relationship is crucial to the United States because it extends American military reach through extensive intelligence sharing, joint training, and access. Australia and the United States are not under pressure to redefine or restructure the security relationship because Australia already assumes responsibility for its own defense (except nuclear) and places a high emphasis on American weapons systems and interoperability, including a deliberate effort to keep up with the RMA. Thus, burden-sharing arguments rarely come into play in relations with Canberra.

Australia's approach to multilateralism in the region complements American strategy. Canberra helped to institutionalize both APEC and the ARF and often brings more enthusiasm and credibility to these fora than Washington can. At the same time, the Australian strategic priorities in these institutions match US interests – in particular Canberrra's push for trade-liberalizing open forums and resistance of closed regional economic groupings.

Australia's influence is vulnerable to the strategic changes quietly underway in the region, however. Australia was profoundly affected emotionally and strategically by the unraveling of Indonesia. Canberra took considerable risk and demonstrated real leadership when it organized the multinational response to the East Timor crisis in 2000. At the same time that Australian leadership is becoming conspicuous, however, Canberra is being excluded from many of the new regional groupings such as the ASEAN Plus Three and ASEM. For the United States exclusion from such groupings is not a serious threat, but for Australia it is. The United States needs Australia to have major diplomatic and security weight in the region, and will have to work carefully with Canberra, Tokyo and other regional players to reinforce Australia's credibility and initiative as an Asian power.

CONCLUSION

Despite eruptions over trade, human rights or missile defense – and perhaps a growing sense of strategic competition between Washington and Beijing – US engagement in Asia will long remain an indispensable source of stability in the region. It is not an exaggeration to say that every single regional actor – even North Korea – relies on the security and economic opportunity provided by US primacy.

At the same time it is not surprising that the region is somewhat uncomfortable with US primacy. Structural realists would expect American primacy to prompt counterbalancing. However, where there has been alignment against the United States, it has been limited, such as Russia's warming to North Korea and China – or it has been symbolic, such as the ASEAN Plus Three. Globalism and the spread of American ideals represent a threat to the legitimacy of many Asian regimes – even though the two are not always the same thing. Thus leaders in Beijing or Kuala Lumpur (or sometimes, even Tokyo) call for resistance to 'American standards' and a return to 'Asian values'. It is noteworthy, however, that this ideational conflict is most intense where the nation-state is youngest – in Southeast Asia or China rather than Japan, Korea or Australia. There is therefore some reason for hope that gradual convergence of ideas will eventually mitigate against ideological tension across the Pacific.

As Ikenberry points out, US primacy will be sustainable and counterbalancing minimal as long as the United States retains its relatively open style of hegemony. Sometimes unilateral action is unavoidable, but repeated and arrogant unilateralism will ultimately undermine American primacy and security. The United States will achieve its strategic, economic and ideational objectives in Asia only by leading or joining in coalitions of the willing. These begin with America's major allies in the region – Japan, South Korea, and Australia in particular. Washington must remain attentive to these allies' own strategic priorities so that when their assistance is required, they will be ready to act. Increasingly, coalitions will have to expand beyond traditional allies, though, and for this reason the United States will have to put energy into minilateralism and not give up entirely on broader regional multilateralism – even if the short-term pay-offs seem negligible. Sometimes leadership also requires following.

NOTES

1. See, e.g., Department of Defense Office of International Security Affairs, *United States Security Strategy for the East Asia-Pacific Region* (Washington DC: Department of Defense 1995).
2. For the classic realist critique of idealism, see Robert E. Osgood, *Ideals and Self Interest in America's Foreign Relations: The Great Transformation of the 20th Century* (Univ. of Chicago Press 1953).
3. Quoted in David Jablonsky, 'The State of the National Security State', in D. Jablonsky *et al.* (eds.) *US National Security: Beyond the Cold War*, Report of the National War College Strategic Studies Institute (Carlisle, PA: US Army War College 1997) p.11.
4. Laura D'Andrea Tyson, who eventually headed the Council of Economic Advisors and the NEC, for example, led a group at the Berkeley Roundtable on the International Economy that was profoundly influenced by the example of MITI and the concept of economic security. See Wayne Sandholtz, *The Highest Stakes: The Economic Foundations of the Next Security System* (NY: OUP 1992).
5. Don Oberdorfer, *The Two Koreas: A Contemporary History* (NY: Addison-Wesley 1997) pp.305–36.
6. Richard Haass, 'Fatal Distraction: Bill Clinton's Foreign Policy', *Foreign Policy* (1997) p.102.
7. Ibid. p.101.
8. Robert Manning, 'The Asian Paradox', *World Policy Journal* 10/3 (Fall 1993) p.55.

9. Yoichi Funabashi, 'The Asianization of Asia', *Foreign Affairs* 72/5 (Nov.–Dec. 1993) pp.75–85.

10. Patrick Cronin and Michael Green, 'Redefining the US-Japan Alliance', McNair Paper 31 (Washington DC: Institute for National Security Studies, National Defense University 1994).

11. Dan Williams and Clay Chandler, 'US Aide Sees Relations With Asia in Peril; Letter Is Sharp Departure From Optimism Clinton Expressed After November Summit', *The Washington Post* (5 May 1994).

12. For a comparison of the candidates' positions, see William Jefferson Clinton, 'Remarks by the President to the Pacific Basin Economic Council', Constitution Hall, Washington, DC (20 May 1996); and Bob Dole, 'America and Asia: Restoring US Leadership in the Pacific', Center for Strategic & International Studies Statesmen Forum, Washington DC (9 May 1996).

13. Primacy here means the maintenance of a US-centered international system and not US intervention in and maintenance of the internal affairs of other states per se. The interventions in Somalia, Haiti and other 'nation-building' exercises go beyond the strict definition of primacy and are arguably motivated more by idealism.

14. Barry R. Posen and Andrew L. Ross, 'Competing Visions for US Grand Strategy', *International Security* 21/3 (Winter 1996–97) pp.5–53.

15. Charles A. Kupchan, 'After Pax Americana: Benign Power, Regional Institutions, and the Sources of a Stable Multipolarity', *International Security* 23/2 (Fall 1998) pp.40–79.

16. G. John Ikenberry, *American Democracy Promotion: Impulses, Strategies, and Impacts* (NY: OUP 2000).

17. William C. Wohlforth, 'The Stability of a Unipolar World', *International Security* 24/1 (Summer 1999) pp.5–41.

18. Summarized in the *Proceedings of the United States Naval Institute*, Nov. 1995.

19. 'Death by a thousand cuts' is drawn from Posen and Ross (note 14) p.15.

20. See Chalmers Johnson and Barry Keehn Jr, 'The Pentagon's Ossified Strategy', *Foreign Affairs* 74/4 (June–July 1995) pp.103–15; Ted Galen Carpenter, 'Paternalism and Dependence: The US-Japanese Security Relationship', *CATO Institute Policy Analysis*, No. 244 (1 Nov. 1995); Earl Ravenal, 'The Case for Adjustment', *Foreign Policy*, No. 81 (Winter 1990–91) pp.3–19; Christopher Layne, 'The Unipolar Illusion: Why New Great Powers Will Rise', *International Security* 17/4 (Spring 1993) pp.5–51.

21. *Directions for Defense: Report of the Commission on Roles and Missions of the Armed Forces* (Washington DC: Department of Defense, May 1995) p.ES-5.

22. Haass (note 6) p.116.

23. Hans Binnedjik and Patrick Clawson (eds.) *1997 Strategic Assessment: Flashpoints and Force Structure* (Washington, DC: Institute for National Strategic Studies, National Defense University 1997) p.3.

24. Joshua Muravchik, 'Affording Foreign Policy: The Problem is Not Wallet but Will', *Foreign Affairs* 75/2 (March–April 1996) pp.8–13.

25. For a range of views on the pros, cons and feasibility of an RMA, see Eliot A. Cohen, 'A Revolution in Warfare: Technology Strikes Again', *Foreign Affairs* 75/2 (March–April 1996) p.44; Michael G. Vickers, *Warfare in 2020: A Primer* (Washington, DC: Center for Strategic and Budgetary Assessments, Oct. 1996); Stephen D. Biddle, 'Revolutionary Change in Warfare: A Review of Theories, Arguments and Policy Implications', IDA Paper P-3123 (Alexandria, VA: Institute for Defense Analyses, Sept. 1995); Michael O'Hanlon, *Technological Change and the Future of Warfare* (Washington DC: Brookings Institution 1999); and Bill Owens, *Lifting the Fog of War* (NY: Firrar, Strauss and Giroux 1999).

26. James A. Baker III, 'America in Asia: Emerging Architecture for a Pacific Community', *Foreign Affairs* 70/5 (Winter 1991) pp.1–18.

27. Dennis C. Blair and John T. Hanley Jr, 'From Wheels to Webs: Reconstructing Asia-Pacific Security Arrangements', *Washington Quarterly* 24/1 (Winter 2001) pp.7–18.

PART II

STRATEGIC AND SECURITY DYNAMICS

3

The Shift in Power Distribution and the Change of Major Power Relations

QUANSHENG ZHAO

This contribution attempts to analyze international relations in East Asia from the perspective of changing dynamics of power distribution. It will argue that the shift in power status is one of the most significant factors that changes perceptions among major powers, thereby effectively impacting upon international relations in the region.

One of the symbolic yet significant developments in the post-Cold War era since the early 1990s – particularly since 2000, is that one hears more labels such as 'partners', 'allies', 'competitors', or 'rivals' to refer to major powers and their relations. For example, US President Bill Clinton referred to China as a 'strategic partner' in his visit to the country in 1998. This debate intensified during the 2000 US presidential campaign, most noticeably due to Republican candidate George W. Bush's statement that the PRC should be viewed as more of a 'competitor' than a 'partner'. This play on words was elaborated upon by US Secretary of State Colin L. Powell in January 2001 when he stated 'China is a competitor, a potential regional rival, but also a trading partner willing to cooperate in areas where our strategic interests overlap'.[1] Powell later downplayed this statement in March 2001, indicating that '[w]e were not looking for a single word to describe this complex relationship, but ... acknowledge that it is a complex relationship'.[2] This gesture of downplaying the significance of labels was echoed by China-watchers outside the administration, such as former National Security Adviser Zbigniew Brzezinski, who stated that 'China is neither America's adversary nor its strategic partner'.[3] While one should indeed pay more attention to substance than labels regarding bilateral relationships, there are still symbolic implications for the terms that nations prefer to use to characterize their relations with others, and the shifts of labels may indicate a subtle but significant change of policy priorities toward another power.[4]

East Asian international relations have been greatly affected by the reconfiguration of power relations in the region since the beginning of the post-Cold War era. It is a common belief that the end of the Cold War in the late 1980s – especially with the collapse of the Soviet empire – significantly altered the configuration of major power relations in the Asian-Pacific region. The new global structure can be described, as some Chinese observers do, as *yi chao duo qiang* – meaning one single superpower faced with many strong powers – or, as Michael Green argues in his article in this volume, a 'unipolar' international structure, vis-à-vis multiple powers including European Union (EU), Russia, People's Republic of China (PRC) and Japan. This new structure replaced the so-called Beijing-Moscow-Washington 'strategic triangle' which prevailed in the 1970s and most of the 1980s. This study will concentrate primarily on the analysis of major power relations in East Asia – among China, Japan, Russia, and the United States. In addition, it inevitably will touch upon the roles and actions of small- and medium-sized actors, such as the two Koreas, Taiwan, and ASEAN states.

A 'TWO UPS AND TWO DOWNS' RECONFIGURATION

Tremendous changes with regard to power status have taken place in the post-Cold War era, which have brought a new order to major power relations in the region and redefined bilateral relations among China, Japan, Russia, and the United States. I would like to refer to this reconfiguration as 'two ups' and 'two downs', which have become apparent since the early 1990s. The 'two ups' concern the rise of the United States and China. The United States' rise to sole superpower status has given Washington a dominant role in all four dimensions of world affairs: political, strategic, economic, and technological/cultural. The American economic slowdown of 2001 is unlikely to lead to a major collapse or a depression such as that in the 1930s. It is therefore safe to say that the United States will retain its sole superpower status in the foreseeble future.

Meanwhile, China has achieved a spectacular economic performance since 1978 when China began its reforms and Open Door economic policy, sustaining high growth rates (even with the slowdown from 11–12 per cent to 7–8 per cent since 1998), and escaping the Asian economic crisis of 1997–98. This expansion has greatly increased China's influence in regional and global affairs.

The 'two downs' refer to the cases of Russia and Japan. With the collapse and dismemberment of the former Soviet Union in the early 1990s, Russia experienced major setbacks in all respects, and it will have a long way to go to return to its previous status and influence in the region. The nature of Japan's downturn is quite different as it is reflected in economic terms only, and is a result of consecutive economic recessions rather than the major financial crises that befell Korea and Southeast Asia.

The following four tables demonstrate the dynamics of these 'ups' and 'downs'. Since the Russian economic downturn is so obvious and some Russian-related data is inconsistent, the tables all focus on China, Japan and the United States. When we look at the most recent decade of available data on Gross Domestic Product (GDP) among the three countries (see Table 1), we will see that, whereas the United States maintained steady growth, China's lag behind both the United States and Japan was significantly reduced while Japan's gap with the United States grew. To be more specific, in a comparison of GDP in 1989, China's GDP is little more than eight per cent of the United States', while Japan's is roughly equivalent to 55 per cent of the United States'. However, ten years later in 1999, China's GDP has increased from eight to eleven per cent of the United States' and 23 per cent of Japan's. At the same time, Japan's GDP level relative to the United States decreased from roughly 55 per cent in 1989 to approximately 44 per cent in 1998, with a rebound to 50 per cent in 1999.

TABLE 1
COMPARISONS OF UNITED STATES, CHINA AND JAPAN
GROSS DOMESTIC PRODUCT (1989–99) ($ BILLION)

Year	USA	China	Japan
1989	5438.7	449.1	2897.3
1990	5743.8	387.8	2996.2
1991	5916.7	406.1	3413.9
1992	6244.4	483.0	3725.5
1993	6558.1	601.1	4292.8
1994	6947.0	540.9	4700.3
1995	7269.6	697.7	5144.1
1996	7661.6	815.4	4591.2
1997	8110.9	901.5	4187.6
1998	8511.0	961.0	3782.7
1999	8708.9	996.3	4395.1

Source: Economic Planning Agency, Japan (1998) pp.374–7; Economist Intelligence Unit, London, 4Q (1998, 1999); World Bank Annual Report 1999.

Similar trends may be observed in comparison with total trade during the same decade. China's gap with the US and Japan's levels of total trade reduced from seven times and four times respectively in 1988 to five times and two times in 1998. At the same time, Japan's total trade level relative to the United States decreased from roughly 60 per cent in 1988 to about 40 per cent in 1998.

TABLE 2
COMPARISONS OF UNITED STATES, CHINA AND JAPAN
TOTAL TRADE (1988–98) ($ BILLION)

Year	USA	China	Japan
1988	781.9	102.3	452.3
1989	856.7	111.7	483.7
1990	910.6	115.4	523.6
1991	930.1	135.7	552.4
1992	1002.1	165.5	573.2
1993	1068.2	194.1	603.9
1994	1201.8	236.7	672.3
1995	1355.6	277.9	779.2
1996	1447.1	290.1	760.1
1997	1555.3	325.0	759.5
1998	1592.1	317.7	625.7

Source: *Yearbook of International Trade Statistics, Vol. II*, United Nations (1997); Economist Intelligence Unit, London, 4Q (1998, 1999).

Similarly, the United States maintained its position as the top recipient of Foreign Direct Investment (FDI) from the late 1980s to late 1990s (see Table 3), helping fuel an economic boom. The United States experienced steady growth from $58.6 billion of FDI in 1988 to $70.8 billion in 1997. China and Japan, however, followed very different paths during the decade. The two countries began at roughly the same level in 1988 at $3.2 billion. By nine years later, China was receiving $45.3 billion in FDI, an increase of 15 times the original amount. In contrast, FDI in Japan only moved up to $5.4 billion in 1997 – far behind the United States and China. Although it can be argued that Japan and China followed different paths of economic growth in terms of need for FDI,[5] one can see, nevertheless, that China and the United States clearly are experiencing an upward trend in this regard.

When we analyze this 'two ups and two downs' power structure in the post-Cold War era, we have to bear in mind the following three points. First, China's rising position primarily is reflective of positive general trends.

TABLE 3
COMPARISONS OF UNITED STATES, CHINA AND JAPAN
FOREIGN DIRECT INVESTMENT (1988–97)
($ BILLION)

Year	USA	China	Japan
1988	58.6	3.2	3.2
1989	69.0	3.4	2.9
1990	48.4	3.5	2.8
1991	22.8	4.4	4.3
1992	18.9	11.0	4.1
1993	43.5	27.5	3.1
1994	49.9	33.8	4.2
1995	60.8	37.5	3.3
1996	79.9	42.4	3.2
1997	70.8	45.3	5.4

Source: Economic Planning Agency, Japan (1998) pp.314, 359; OECD, *International Direct Investment Statistics Yearbook 1997*, pp.177, 330; Economist Intelligence Unit, London, Q4 (1998).

TABLE 4
COMPARISONS OF UNITED STATES, CHINA AND JAPAN
GROSS DOMESTIC PRODUCT PER CAPITA (1988–98) (US $)

Year	USA	China	Japan
1988	20,606	364	23,843
1989	21,989	401	23,550
1990	22,983	342	24,273
1991	23,421	354	27,557
1992	24,450	415	29,979
1993	25,406	508	34,449
1994	26,658	427	37,632
1995	27,636	584	41,975
1996	28,863	670	36,521
1997	30,263	733	33,231
1998	31,488	773	29,900

Note: Figures are not adjusted for purchasing power parity (PPP).

Source: Economic Planning Agency, Japan (1998) pp.378–81; Economist Intelligence Unit, London, 4Q (1998, 1999).

However, when inspected more closely, the PRC's situation is far more fragile. There are widespread domestic difficulties such as state-owned enterprise reform, disparities between coastal and internal regions along with the problem of severe corruption, and many other problems that may not only slow down China's development but also plunge it into internal chaos if Beijing loses control of the pace of change.

Second, everything is in relative terms. Despite Japan's economic downturn, it remains the second-largest economy in the world. Furthermore, when we look at GDP per capita, China remains far behind both Japan and the United States (see Table 4). Although China more than doubled its GDP per capita from 1988 to 1998, China's $773 yearly GDP per person in 1998 *vis-à-vis* $29,900 in Japan and $31,488 in the United States is a clear indicator that China still is a developing country in this sense.

Third, Japan's slowdown is primarily reflected in economic terms, unlike Russia's total economic, political, strategic, and technological/cultural downturn is due to the collapse of the former Soviet empire. Despite its consecutive economic recessions, Japan has managed thus far to escape the major financial crises that beset Korea and Southeast Asia in 1997–98. Furthermore, since the end of the 1990s, some indicators suggest that the Japanese economy has begun to recover, as demonstrated by Japan's GDP growth from 1998 (US$3782.7 billion) to 1999 (US$4395.1 billion), despite some experts' more cautious assessment as to whether this is a true recovery. Indeed, some Japan observers have a bleak view of the prospect for recovery of the Japanese economy.[6] As a matter of fact, Japanese Economic Minister Taro Aso provided a gloomy prognosis in April 2001, indicating that Japan's economic recovery would not come soon because industrial output and corporate investment were deteriorating and the economy was 'weakening'.[7]

On the other hand, one has to recognize that Japan remains the second-largest economy in the world, and many analysts have speculated that Japan already has undergone an unprecedented 'economic revolution' and will rise again.[8] This sense of optimism was fueled by the election of Junichiro Koizumi as the head of the ruling LDP and prime minister of Japan in April 2001 as he pledged to take serious measures to conduct economic and political reform to reverse Japan's downward trend.

Therefore, the dynamic of 'ups' and 'downs' is relative and only a reflection of the past decade – from the early 1990s to the present time – namely, the early 2000s. It is difficult to say at this point how long the current trends will continue, and each country definitely will experience a variety of upward and downward trends in terms of its own development; that is to say, countries currently on the rise may face a downward trend, whereas debilitated countries may rebound. Nevertheless, the two 'ups' and two 'downs' structure has affected distribution of power in the region enormously, and has become a crucial factor in redefining major-power relations in East Asia along the lines of 'partners', 'allies', 'competitors', or 'rivals'. The impact of this change can be analyzed with reference to economic, political, and strategic factors.

ECONOMIC INTERDEPENDENCE AMONG MAJOR POWERS

Competition and cooperation are the two dominant modes of behavior among major powers in the economic dimension. East Asian international relations are no exception. An important element that characterizes post-Cold War international relations is the trend toward globalization, or economic interdependence. The shift in distribution of power and the rise of China in particular has placed major emphasis upon economic integration – take China, Japan, and the United States, for example. From Table 5, we can see that, in terms of top trading partners, each one of the three countries places the other two high on its list. Japan and the United States (excluding Hong Kong) were the number one and two top trading partners of China, respectively, together accounting for 33.8 per cent of China's total trade. Similarly, the United States and China are Japan's top trading partners, in combination counting for 36.3 per cent of its total trade in 1998. Meanwhile, the United States conducts most of its trading activities with its NAFTA partners (number one, Canada, number three, Mexico, collectively totaling 31 per cent of US trade) but Japan and China occupied a respective number two and number four position, together totaling 16.7 per cent of the US trade. Also notable is the fact that, in the case of China, Hong Kong's trade with the United States is not included in these statistics, which would increase the figures.

TABLE 5

TOP TRADING PARTNERS OF CHINA, JAPAN, AND THE UNITED STATES (1997) (%)

Rank	China	Japan (1998)	US
1	Japan (18.7)	US (27.7)	Canada (20.9)
2	Hong Kong (15.6)	China (8.6)	Japan (11.9)
3	US (15.1)	Taiwan (5.4)	Mexico (10.1)
4	Korea (ROK) (7.4)	Germany (4.5)	China (4.8)
5	Taiwan (6.1)	Korea (ROK) (4.1)	UK (4.4)
6	Germany (3.9)	Hong Kong (3.4)	Germany (4.3)
7	Singapore (2.7)	Australia (3.1)	Taiwan (3.3)
8	Russia (1.9)	UK (3.1)	Korea (ROK) (3.1)

Source: *Directions of Trade Statistics Yearbook* (IMF 1998); 'Japan 2000: An International Comparison', Keizai Koho Center (Japan Institute for Social and Economic Affairs, 15 Dec. 1999) p.60.

This extensive economic interdependency means that each bilateral relationship in the China-Japan-US triangle is considered to be of vital national interest to these countries. For example, the United States has long regarded the maintenance of the region's stability and prosperity as a top priority in its world strategy. Relations with China and Japan, the two most powerful countries in the region, are critical to American regional and global interests.

Similarly, China and Japan regard their bilateral relationship as second in importance only to the United States. Understandably, Japan will not change the foundation of its foreign policy, which is based on its alliance with the United States (discussed below).

On the other hand, Japan continuously has played a bridging role between China and the West. In 1990, for example, Japan was the first industrialized country to lift its economic sanctions imposed on China in the wake of the Tiananmen incident.[9] Similarly, Japan was the first industrialized nation-state to offer its approval, in July 1999, for China's entry into the World Trade Organization (WTO).[10] Obviously, Japan will continue to play a significant role in integrating China into the world economic system.

Additionally, Japan has a vital interest in China's development and stability because of its historical, cultural, and geopolitical proximity. It is a common belief that Japan's biggest nightmare would be China devolving into internal chaos as such a situation would disrupt regional stability and prosperity enormously. Were this scenario to unfold, Japan would be one of the first countries affected. Therefore, it is in Japan's interest to continue its cooperative and stabilizing relationship with China, and in particular to continue its official development assistance (ODA) program to promote China's modernization effort and help with the PRC's incremental development toward a more open and democratic society.

Nevertheless, Japan's ruling Liberal Democratic Party has decided to reassess its ODA to China due to concerns over China's increased military expenditures and its naval operations close to Japanese territorial waters.[11] Given such developments, Japanese ODA to China will likely be reduced in the years to come. Moreover, with generational change in Japan, younger politicians and foreign policy bureaucrats alike may feel less pressured by a sense of guilt surrounding its previous aggression toward China and the rest of Asia. At the same time Japanese nationalism has also been on the rise.[12] Nevertheless, despite although there is still a lack of proper recognition of its wartime behavior, Japan's nationalistic sentiment today is much different from that of World War II. This change primarily reflects Japan's pride in its achievements in the postwar period and its desire to play a greater role in the international community.

As for China, much has changed over the decades in terms of its immediate foreign policy concerns. In order to understand the importance China currently attaches to economic modernization, we need to look at how the priorities of Chinese foreign policy were altered as its leadership changed over time. Under the leadership of Mao Zedong and Zhou Enlai, Beijing's major concern was China's strategic position within the Washington-Moscow-Beijing triangle. China's primary concerns with Japan and the United States at that time were how to counterbalance the threat from the former Soviet Union and address the issue of Taiwan – a point perceived as crucial to the legitimacy of the Beijing regime.

In the subsequent period, the priorities of the Deng Xiaoping era were such that modernization became the major focus of Chinese foreign policy. Therefore, China came to view the United States and Japan, along with the European Union, as primary suppliers of capital, markets and advanced technology. Hence, economic cooperation with the United States and Japan became crucial to China. As a result of China's change in perception toward Japan and the United States, trade and investment between China and the other two countries increased rapidly and Japan became the largest donor of aid to China in the form of ODA.[13]

Although Russia is not included in Table 5, it is clear that Russia has increasingly integrated into the world economic system ever since the collapse of the old Soviet empire. The end of the Cold War has effectively removed a major barrier between Russia and the Western world as well as China in terms of bilateral relations in all fields. Moreover, Russia's efforts to conduct market-oriented economic reform has significantly increased its dependence upon the world market and major economic powers such as the European Union, United States, Japan, and China. Whereas business transactions with Russia only occupies a relatively minor proportion compared to Japan and the United States, China has noticeably increased its economic interactions with Russia.

In light of China's rising economic power, Western business circles have viewed China's enormous population and rapidly modernized economy as virtually the last untapped market. Regardless of whether the dreams of profits are fulfilled or not, the fact that China has moved up quickly to become a significant trading partner and a leading destination for foreign investment is a major factor in US foreign policy toward Beijing.

The powerful voices of the business community in providing Beijing a permanent normal trading relations (PNTR) status with the United States in

2000 and promoting China's entrance to the WTO offer two more examples of American economic interests in China at work. Furthermore, many people believe that China's economic modernization will help to create and enlarge an incipient middle class in China that will promote an enhanced civil society and democratization process in China. This mixed political-economic consideration became a foundation for the engagement policy advocated by the Clinton administration. In sum, in the economic dimension, one may sense more of a 'win-win' situation than the zero-sum game often reflected in the strategic and security fields. In this arena, one can see that the heated debate over the 'China threat' has created a significant policy shift toward China under the new Bush administration.

THE COMPLEXITY OF STRATEGIC CONCERNS

In terms of security perspectives, the old realist school of zero-sum games – namely, 'you win, I lose', and vice versa – has remained. Thus, with post-Cold War developments in the Asia-Pacific region, one can hear such arguments that if the United States' influence declines, China may enter into the power vacuum.[14] The major powers' respective strategic concerns can easily go in diametrically opposed directions – thereby promoting a polarized division of the world into enemies versus allies as was the case during the Cold War. At the same time, we also can see overlapping concerns over a variety of issues. Again, the new major-power configuration of 'two ups' and 'two downs' in the regions has had great impact on strategic concerns.

In general, both the United States and Japan view their alliance as the central point of their Asian policies. This position has been a clear landmark since 1945, the beginning of the American occupation of Japan, which was further confirmed in 1952 when the US-Japan Security Treaty was signed. According to Kenichi Ito, a Japanese professor of international relations, contemporary US-Japan relations can be divided into six stages: first, initial friendly relations (1853–1905); second, confrontation and conflict (1905–41); third, the war period (1941–45); fourth, the occupation period (1945–51); fifth, the Cold War alliance (1951–96); and finally, the post-Cold War alliance (1996–present).[15] Here we can see clearly that bilateral relationships sometimes can be so dramatically transformed as to change from arch rivals to close allies.

Nevertheless, it is not unusual for opposite trends to appear; that is, even when countries are in an alliance, problems may occur that lead to some kind of discomfort and misunderstanding between them. In addition to some troubling incidents which provoked outcry throughout Japan, such as high-profile Okinawa rape cases in the late 1990s that involved US servicemen, there are also differences in terms of strategic thinking. An example in point is the debate in Japan as how to respond to the American call for further cooperation in missile defense systems. Elements in Japan that oppose this move are concerned about constitutional disputes (in reference to Article 9, the so-called 'peace clause' of the Japanese constitution) and the likely negative outcry to such a change from China and Russia, not to mention North Korea.[16]

According to well-known Japanese journalist Yoichi Funabashi in his book, *Alliance Adrift*, although US-Japan relations have broadened and deepened, the political and social underpinnings of the dyadic relationship are frail.[17] While the two countries maintain close ties, each side has worried about the other country getting too close to Beijing. When President Clinton visited Beijing in 1998, he did not even make a stop in Japan, leading some Japanese observers at that time to worry that the United States had shifted from negative 'Japan bashing' to indifferent 'Japan passing' – considering it not worth the same attention as its troubled relationship with China.

The trend toward 'Japan passing', however, is obviously changing under the new administration since President George W. Bush entered the White House in January 2001. In the recent past, some American leaders had expressed concerns that China's growing power may force Japan to become 'neutralized' – thereby moving away from the US-Japan alliance, a cornerstone of American foreign policy in Asia. With the new Bush administration, however, one clear shift in American priorities in US foreign policy in East Asia is toward emphasizing its relationships with its allies there, most notably Japan. In fact, one of the original critics who argued that the US should pay more attention to the US-Japan alliance has become the Deputy Secretary of State, Richard Armitage.[18]

Indeed, US-Japanese cooperation has been so close that if 'one party coughs, the other gets sick'. An example in point is that the two countries have shared intelligence through a coded system. Together, the US and Japan will spend millions of dollars to change this communication system due to the Hainan incident of April 2001 in which the Chinese military examined the top-secret equipment of the US EP-3 surveillance aircraft.[19]

One other example of Japan's following America's lead is related to the controversial visit of Taiwanese President Lee Teng-hui to the United States in 1995 for the stated purpose of attending an alumni reunion at Cornell University. Similarly, there were extensive deliberations or preparations for Lee Teng-hui to visit Japan, also under the guise of attending an alumni event, since Lee also attended Kyoto University as an undergraduate. This plan did not get too far, since Beijing immediately gave a stern warning against such an action. However, Lee Teng-hui was granted a visa in April 2001 to visit Japan for heart treatment in a hospital in Okayama prefecture.[20] This situation can be viewed as involving close coordination between the United States and Japan as the United States also issued a visa to Lee Teng-hui at the same time.

As for the case of US-China relations, America's China policy is more contested than before. In creating his administration and implementing his new policy orientation, President Bush staffed his national security/foreign policy apparatus with some strong realist thinkers who advocate a tougher position toward Beijing and a more supportive policy toward Taipei. For example, Secretary of Defense Donald Rumsfeld, who was characterized by Chalmers Johnson as a 'classic old-time Cold Warrior',[21] is perceived as trying to place China in the position of former Soviet Union during the Cold War period.

As for China, the momentum of its rise has made its foreign policy leadership more assertive as well as more sensitive to the increasing nationalistic sentiment among the Chinese people. This new development has made the strategic calculations of Washington and Tokyo more complicated. On the one hand, this change may be viewed as a natural move for any rising power. In this view, China could legitimately claim greater influence over international affairs as long as it does not jeopardize regional stability and prosperity. On the other hand, however, the rising nationalism in China's populace places more pressure on the current Beijing leadership to address sovereignty issues such as Taiwan and attempt to redress negative historical legacies such as the Japanese wartime invasion.

Furthermore, with the decline of Russian influence in the region, China's strategic concerns have been increasingly focused on the United States and Japan. In regard to its relationships with Washington and Tokyo, a central locus of concern for Beijing is the issue of Taiwan. Indeed, Beijing regards the United States as a major obstacle to its goal of reunification with Taiwan. This issue can be traced back historically to the Chinese Civil War period (1946–49) when the United States supported the Chiang Kai-shek regime, and, when at the cessation of the Korean War in the early 1950s, the United States signed a Mutual Defense Treaty with Taiwan which effectively prevented the PRC from taking over the island. In the late 1960s and early 1970s, both Beijing and Washington were willing to normalize their relations due primarily to their mutual concern about the threat from the Soviet Union. Richard Nixon's historic visit to China in 1972 spotlighted the two countries' rapprochement, although seven years would pass before the PRC and the United States completed their normalization process in 1979.

However, while Washington has recognized Beijing officially and ceased its official relations with Taipei, there are two issues that Beijing still views as unwarranted 'intervention in internal affairs'. First, the United States continues to sell arms to Taiwan despite the 17 August 1982 Shanghai Communiqué which stipulates that the United States should reduce its arms sales to Taiwan both quantitatively and qualitatively. An example in point of this trend is the Bush administration's decision in April 2001 to sell Taiwan a large amount of advanced arms. The other issue relates to the Taiwan Relations Act – passed by the US Congress in 1979 – which, in addition to restricting the United States to non-official economic and cultural relations with Taiwan, requires American commitment to peaceful settlement of the Taiwan Strait conflict. Both actions, from Beijing's perspective, represent continued intervention in China's internal affairs.

Clearly, there are indications that the PRC views the United States as an arrogant rival and a threat and a major road block to China's rise toward greater power status.[22] Beijing's perception of United States' interference may have been enhanced by the February 2000 vote in the US House of Representatives that passed the Taiwan Security Enhancement Act by the vote of 341–70,[23] and, more recently, comments by President George W. Bush that the United States will defend Taiwan militarily in case of attack from China. China's deep concern is that America's arming of Taiwan may in fact prolong Taiwan's separate status, thereby promoting its eventual independence. Thus, the State Council of the PRC issued a Taiwan White Paper in February of 2000 that states:

> [I]f a grave turn of events occurs leading to the separation of Taiwan from China in any name, or if Taiwan is invaded and occupied by foreign countries, or if the Taiwan authorities refuse, sine die, the peaceful settlement of cross-Straits reunification through negotiations, then the Chinese Government will only be forced to adopt all drastic measures possible, including the use of force, to safeguard China's sovereignty and territorial integrity and fulfill the great cause of reunification.[24]

This passage indicates clearly that one more situation has been added which would prompt the PRC to use military force against Taiwan – that is, if Taiwan indefinitely delays negotiations with the mainland. Beijing's fears were fanned by the defeat of the moderately pro-unification Kuomintang (KMT) party in the March 2000 Taiwanese elections.[25] During the campaign, the successful Democratic Progressive Party (DPP) candidate Chen Shui-bian initially made statements that he disagreed with the unification of Taiwan with China into 'one country, two systems'.[26] Although President Chen made some conciliatory statements toward Beijing after the election,[27] there was no obvious progress in cross-strait relations.

In addition to the Taiwan and TMD issues, other actions by the United States such as sponsoring condemnation in the United Nations of China's human rights record, the passage of US Congressional resolution against China's sponsoring of the Olympic Games in 2008, and allegations that a Taiwanese-American, Wen Ho Lee, was a Chinese spy who stole top nuclear secrets, and so forth – all created an image that the United States was backing away from the 'strategic partnership'. Growing Chinese nationalist sentiment has lead many Chinese to question why such routinely unfriendly treatment should be responded to with friendly cooperation. Therefore, some China-observers argue that it may be a self-fulfilling prophecy for the United States to treat China as a rival or adversary as such actions and words may actually push China in this direction, further deteriorating bilateral relations.

Meanwhile, the issue of Taiwan has remained a problem also between China and Japan, who is a 'loyal follower' of the United States in international affairs. Beijing's main concern is the new security guidelines for the US-Japan Security Treaty announced in 1997.[28] Specifically, China's concern is over Part V of the 'Guidelines for US-Japan Defense Cooperation' as to whether 'surrounding areas' are meant to include Taiwan itself. Although the document specifically indicates that this term reflects the situation rather than geography, conflicting statements have been made by a variety of Japanese government officials, such as the announcement made by then-Chief Cabinet Secretary Kajiyama Seiroku in August 1997, that the guidelines indeed are considered to include Taiwan.[29] More typically, when asked about the inclusion of Taiwan, the standard informal answer from the Ministry of Foreign Affairs is that since this topic refers to joint guidelines, Washington will have to be asked for clarification. This apparent coordination of policy understandably alarms the PRC.

There are other problems between China and Japan, especially a territorial dispute over a chain of islands between Taiwan and Okinawa, called *Diaoyu* in Chinese and *Senkaku* in Japanese,[30] as well as the potential resurgence of Japanese militarism, memories of which stem from past

Japanese aggression.[31] The United States also played a significant role in the *Diaoyu/Senkaku* territorial disputes between China and Japan, at least at the initial stages. Even the current US position regarding this dispute remains ambiguously neutral. The historical fact is that when the United States returned Okinawa to Japan in 1971, the *Diaoyu/Senkaku* islands were included in the package.[32] There has long been speculation about the possibility of US involvement in the event of a military clash between China and Japan over these disputed islands.

China's primary claim has been that the *Diaoyu/Senkaku* islands are Chinese territory and should be returned. At the same time, Deng Xiaoping raised two points regarding this issue. First, he presented the idea of *gua qi lai*, meaning that the issue should be shelved for the time being, leaving it to future generations to resolve. Second, Deng suggested *gongtong kaifa*, which meant that China and Japan could develop the islands' natural resources jointly, thereby shelving the sovereignty dispute for the time being.[33]

Despite many discussions about the rising power of China and the potential threat to regional international affairs, the majority of China-observers have had the sober view that, in terms of military and strategic capacity, China is far from presenting a formidable force. Andrew Nathan and Robert Ross even call China's defense capacity merely 'an empty fortress', citing one of the master strategists, Zhuge Liang, during the Three Kingdoms period almost 2000 years ago in describing a strategy designed to promote the enemy's misperception of your strength and avoidance of military entanglement when you actually are weak.[34]

This line of thinking may well reflect reality. If we use Chinese-provided statistical figures in terms of comparative levels of defense spending, China is far behind other major powers. The United States spends more than 27 times the amount of China and six times the investment of Japan in military spending. One may, however, be aware that the Chinese figures are not necessarily as reliable as Western numbers due to a variety of reasons. Nevertheless, even with figures inflated two or three times the official Chinese numbers, as many foreign observers suggest, Chinese military spending still is significantly lower than American and Japanese levels.

On the other hand, one may also be alarmed by the recent increase in the Chinese military budget. Notably, China announced in March 2001 that it decided to increase defense spending by 17.7 per cent for the year, its biggest expansion in real terms in the past 20 years.[35] China's latest defense White Paper, however, argues that the 2000 Chinese defense budget is merely 5 per cent of the US defense budget, 30 per cent of Japan's, and 40 per cent of the UK's.[36]

Beijing and Tokyo also pay close attention to the other key players in the region, such as Russia and the two Koreas. For example, on the one hand, Beijing has been trying its best to be cooperative with the United States. On the other hand, Beijing also has prepared itself to face the strategic challenge presented by the new guidelines of the US-Japan Security Treaty, and discussions of a TMD system in East Asia. To counterbalance this perceived hostile environment, China has developed the following four strategies in its foreign policy:

First, China has further enhanced its cooperation with Russia and other former Soviet states, not only in economic and political areas, but more importantly in security matters. Second, Beijing has rekindled its interest in maintaining substantial influence over Pyongyang, so that China will have greater leverage in terms of political and strategic maneuvering in the Korean Peninsula. Third, China has moved to improve its relationship with its neighbors in Southeast Asia, that is, with ASEAN countries. Finally, China has increased its community-building efforts in East Asia, as demonstrated by the establishment of the China-Japan-Korea Forum in economic and technology areas. This three-way forum was decided in the summit meeting during the 'ASEAN Plus Three' Conference held in Singapore in November 2000[37] of Chinese Premier Zhu Rongji, Japanese Prime Minister Yoshiro Mori, and South Korean President Kim Dae Jung.[38]

An 'East Asian Vision Group' was established in 1999 to study future ways for the East Asian community to integrate as a region, thereby following the lead of other regional groups such as the EU and NAFTA.[39] Given the complex nature of political relations in the region, one suggestion for the group is to tackle economic and cultural issues first. Another idea is to focus on security confidence-building matters. Some also have suggested that the group concentrate on discussion of a code of conduct to avoid regional conflict and confrontation.[40] One of the examples in this regard is an international symposium entitled 'Cultural Conference Among Korea, China, and Japan', held in Seoul also in November 2000.[41]

Russia also is a major player in East Asian international relations despite the collapse of the Soviet empire in 1990. Beijing has worked very hard to bring Moscow to its side. At the same time, Russia is eager to secure China's support, as it has its own grudges – namely, the eastern expansion of NATO, the bombing of Kosovo, and the situation in Chechnya. Under these circumstances, with the two powers moving toward closer ties in political, economic and strategic dimensions, the most alarming development is Russia's willingness to help China modernize its military forces. In October 1999, for example, the two countries' defense ministries signed an agreement to conduct joint training and share information on the formation of military doctrine. Thus, as many as 2,000 Russian technicians were employed by Chinese military research institutes to work on advanced defense systems, such as laser technology, cruise missiles, nuclear submarines and space-based weaponry. In early 2000, China purchased two Russian-built destroyers worth $800 million each. The first destroyer was deployed and sailed through the Taiwan Strait in February 2000, en route to a Chinese naval base.[42] These developments have certainly raised concerns in Washington and elsewhere.

Meanwhile, Japan's concerns about the former Soviet Union during the Cold War era have greatly declined, and its attention has shifted toward China's potential military power and the Korean peninsula. Tokyo has its own agenda to improve its relations with Moscow. Japan took a positive position toward the major obstacle to bilateral relations – that is, the dispute over the northern four islands between the two countries.[43] Although the process for achieving a workable resolution has been slow, otherwise Japan's security concerns with Russia have almost entirely disappeared.

The Koreas represent two other crucial players in the region. The Korean peninsula can be considered a good example of overlapping interests among all major powers – China, Japan, Russia, and the United States. For instance, China holds a key to the security interests of the United States and Japan in the area – a core issue of northeast Asian security configurations. Indeed, China's positive contributions to peace and stability in the region can be demonstrated by its role in the four-party talks on the Korean peninsula. In 1995, South Korea suggested a four-party peace conference that included the United States, China, and the two Koreas for the purpose of working out a new peace agreement to replace the armistice and thereby bring a formal end to the decades-long Korean War. Initially, Pyongyang did not want Chinese participation.[44] After prolonged negotiations with the United States and South Korea in New York in July 1997, however, North Korea finally agreed to the four-party conference. The first preparatory talk was held in New York on 5 August 1997.[45] After several on-again, off-again negotiations among the four parties, the talks broke down once again on 19 September 1997, without even an agreed-upon agenda for further conferences to be held in Geneva.[46] A major previous obstacle was that the North Koreans insisted that conference participants agree in advance to discuss the removal of the 37,000 American troops stationed in South Korea.[47]

Japan and Russia were not included in the Korean four-party talks. Nevertheless, both countries would like to play an active role in any deliberations. In July 1997, Russian Foreign Minister Yevgeny Primakov visited Seoul and made a joint statement with South Korea on peninsula issues. The Russian side proposed that it hosted an international conference on the Korea issue parallel to the four-way talks.[48] A month later, Japan also resumed its negotiations with North Korea over the normalization of diplomatic relations. Although the four-party talks have not produced concrete results thus far, as proved by the most recent round of meetings in Geneva in summer 1999,[49] China's constructive role has been widely recognized.

As discussed earlier, strategic concerns in the region are also different among Beijing, Washington, and Tokyo. Due to widespread concerns over past and future North Korean missile tests, there has been a significant change of mood among the Japanese people which has led to the parliamentary approval in 1999 of revisions to the US-Japan Security Treaty. Among several steps that Tokyo has adopted, the most noticeable development is Tokyo's announcement that it will participate in the development of a ballistic missile defense system with the United States, known as Theater Missile Defense (TMD). Although the tension in the Korean Peninsula has appeared to be significantly reduced due to the Kim Dae Jung–Kim Jong Il summit in June 2000, the TMD plan is still ongoing. In addition, with the new Bush administration, the pace toward conciliation between Washington and Pyongyang may slow down or even be reversed. This development has alarmed Beijing, which fears not only a new US-Japan alliance to contain China but also this alliance's potential involvement in any future Taiwan Strait military crisis should Taiwan 'officially' announce its independence.[50] Let us now look at these issues from a political perspective.

THE DYNAMICS OF POLITICAL GAMES

When one examines the shift in power distribution and its impact on international relations in East Asia, one can see the ongoing dynamics of the political games played by major powers. Let us look first at the relationship between China and Japan, which has had its ebbs and flows since 1972 when the two countries normalized relations. For most of the 1990s, Sino-Japanese relations have been deteriorating and this trend has cast a shadow over regional and global affairs in the post-Cold War era. Given this concern, the two sides have worked hard to reverse the downward slide, as exemplified by the subsequent visits of the heads of state, namely Chinese President Jiang Zemin's trip to Japan in November 1998, and late Japanese

Prime Minister Keizo Obuchi's visit to China in July 1999.[51] Despite some positive results achieved from these visits, they have also highlighted the difficulties each side faces in handling this relationship.

The decline in Sino-Japanese relations began in the late 1980s. It was accelerated by the downfall of Chinese Communist Party Secretary General Hu Yaobang in 1987. Hu's removal was due largely to Beijing's domestic politics, but additional factors in his removal were criticisms that he was too 'soft' toward Japan and too personal in dealing with Japanese leaders.[52] This decline was compounded by the Tiananmen incident in 1989, when Japan followed the West's lead and imposed economic sanctions on China.

Unfortunately, there is a lack of true mutual understanding between the two countries. Although state visits occur virtually every year, there is a lack of in-depth discussion and multi-layered exchange. Neither country has a clear understanding of the nature of the other's domestic politics and foreign policy direction. Beijing may ask such questions as whether Japan has moved irreversibly down the path of a peaceful and democratic nation or might it still revert to militarism. By the same token, Tokyo's image of China also varies between that of a friendly and economically promising country, and that of a military threat.

China's policy toward Japan in the post-Deng era has primarily followed the previous lines of Mao and Deng, but some changes in policy priorities have become evident. While Taiwan and economic cooperation remain central aspects of Sino-Japanese relations, Chinese pressure on Japan to address the historical legacy of its wartime behavior as well as its potential for remilitarization has been strengthened. Indeed, sometimes it appears that wartime history has become a leading factor in China's Japan policy.

What both countries need to do to improve their ties is to conduct thorough studies of the contemporary history of the other country to gain greater insight into the nature of its politics and society. Tokyo must continue to learn lessons from its past wartime behavior since there will always be a small circle in Japan that ignores or denies its historical experience. At the same time, China should recognize that the overwhelming majority of the Japanese people do not want to repeat the mistakes of the past and that Japan has become a democratic society striving to cultivate a peaceful environment in the Asia-Pacific region. To ensure long-lasting and peaceful cooperation between the two countries, Beijing needs to educate and utilize more Japan specialists in formulating its policy toward Tokyo. Promoting mutual understanding should be a central position in bilateral exchanges, and educational exchanges should be further expanded and institutionalized.[53]

In the political dimension, a prominent problem between China and the United States is a difference of opinion and policy regarding human rights-related issues, and Japan, in general, sides with Washington in this regard. The issue of human rights has increasingly become a top priority of American foreign policy toward China. The central priority of Chinese foreign policy, however, has moved from 'revolution' under Mao to 'modernization' and economic development under Deng. In many ways, political considerations such as revolution or socialism have become much less prominent.[54] With these two opposite directions of foreign policy priorities, it is inevitable that there have been and will continue to be confrontations between China and the United States around the issues of democratization and human rights.

Another important background development regarding the human rights issue is the changing international environment. With the end of the Cold War in the late 1980s, US foreign policy has shifted away from containing communism to focusing on other factors. For example, Samuel Huntington has advocated giving increasing attention to the differences between civilizations and cultures. In his book, *The Clash of Civilizations*, Huntington argues that future conflicts in the international community will be largely derived from the confrontation of Western and non-Western civilizations. He has further singled out Confucianism and Islam as two key components of non-Western civilization.[55] While controversial, this notion of the 'clash of civilizations' has become a prominent factor among some academics and practitioners in their study of contemporary international relations. This emphasis on Western/non-Western differences has become a source of conflict regarding the process of China's democratization and its human rights record.

When we look at the human rights issue in major power relations, it is clear that Washington's China policy combines a variety of factors: strategic considerations, economic interests, as well as ideological elements such as human rights issues. In a pluralistic society such as the United States, there is a range of priorities regarding foreign policy within different sections of the society. Influential figures within the US Congress, human rights, religious, and other non-governmental organizations (NGOs) tend to put human rights as a top priority, whereas the White House and State Department have to calculate United States foreign policy primarily from the perspective of national interest, with such considerations as security and economic concerns.

Several important developments since the beginning of the 1990s may push Washington's China policy further toward strategic and economic considerations as a top priority rather than human rights considerations. The 1996 Taiwan Strait missile crisis over the issue of Taiwan, caused by the US permission of President Lee Teng-hui's unofficial visit to the United States the previous year, was regarded as the first 'wake-up call' in the post-Cold War era, indicating the necessity for both countries to avoid potential military confrontation. However, this event was followed by summit meetings between China and the United States, as may be seen with President Jiang Zemin's visit to Washington in October 1997, and President Clinton's China visit in June–July 1998, and Premier Zhu Rongji's trip to the United States in spring 1999. The second crisis in bilateral relations was the accidental bombing of the Chinese embassy building in Belgrade by NATO and the United States in 1999 that triggered large-scale demonstrations in several cities in China against the United States. The third 'wake-up call' was the US surveillance aircraft collision near Hainan Island in April 2001 and the subsequent stand-off between the two powers. In addition to the above direct encounters between the United States and China, the issues of nuclear development in North Korea, the economic crisis in Southeast Asia, and the increasing tensions between India and Pakistan caused by their respective nuclear tests, all require close cooperation and effective coordination between these two powerful states.

The United States, therefore, does not have the luxury of making human rights its top priority most of the time. First, the so-called 'big power' system was firmly established in the Asia-Pacific region after the two summit meetings between China and the United States in 1997 and 1998. This big power system has survived even one of the most severe tests – namely the tensions over the 1999 Chinese embassy bombing and the 2001 Hainan incident. Despite the escalation caused by nationalistic sentiments on both sides at a domestic level, cool heads prevailed in both Washington and Beijing. It is believed that, although the relationship may be damaged in the short term, it *may* facilitate better communication and more effective mechanisms to deal with crises in both bilateral and regional relations over the long run.

Second, as mentioned earlier, China has undertaken fundamental economic reforms that have significantly shifted its social and political system toward a more pluralistic direction. This progress has been confirmed by China's ratification in February 2001 of the UN-sponsored International Covenant on Economic, Social and Cultural Rights. Nevertheless, one may notice that the ratification was made with reservations as to providing workers with the right to strike and form labor unions.[56]

All of these developments, however, do not necessarily mean that the United States will take a lighter approach to human rights issues in its future relations with China. Domestic pressure from interest groups and lawmakers will remain a powerful force within the United States. One can expect Washington to continue to raise human rights issues with Beijing.[57] Also, it is important to note that China's human rights policy has always alternated periodically between the tightening and loosening of social controls. Needless to say, if there are negative developments in Beijing such as what happened in Tiananmen Square in 1989, there will be another major campaign from the United States to put pressure on China regarding human rights issues.

Meanwhile, China defends its position on human rights and has criticized US pressure by invoking sovereignty rights protected by the UN Charter, particularly 'The Declaration on the Inadmissibility of Intervention and Interference in the Internal Affairs of States'.[58] China argues that the UN Charter extends sovereignty to include human rights issues by citing provisions such as 'Every state has an inalienable right to choose its political, economic, social and cultural systems, without interference in any form by another state'.[59] The protection of human rights only becomes an international issue when a state violates treaties it has signed, commits 'large scale, gross' violations or endangers the peace and security of neighboring countries.[60] In the absence of these conditions, human rights are internal matters, according to China.

On the other hand, China has been willing to make concessions under certain circumstances. Partial concessions have been timed to coincide with levels of external pressure, the priority of human rights in the US' China policy and international debate on China's human rights conditions. These concessions, nevertheless, do not represent uniform changes in China's political system and have been made alongside continued arrests of dissidents.[61] Ultimately, the issues of democracy and human rights are still regarded as internal matters. Concessions and regressions coincide with each other and are employed strategically to influence debate between China's supporters and critics, undermine the overall efficacy of external pressure and maintain Beijing's ability to set its own human rights agenda. However, as China integrates further into world economy and international affairs, China's internal behavior norms, including the human rights issue, will inevitably be affected by external influences.

Having said that, China may become more alarmed by a hostile international environment, particularly a perceived 'encirclement' either by major powers such as the United States and Japan which has constituted a 'two against one' game, or by regional players such as India and Vietnam.[62] Thus, these countries – the United States and Japan in particular – should recognize that China's fear of being 'ganged up upon' by outside powers is not without cause, and they should be more sensitive regarding this concern so that their efforts do not backfire.

CONCLUSION

The 'two ups and two downs' dynamic presented here represents a major shift in power distribution in the Asia-Pacific area. It seems that these recent developments have demonstrated the conventional wisdom that a shift in power distribution will bring a new configuration in power relations. The following points, nevertheless, deserve further consideration. First, a shift in power distribution may indeed change perceptions among major powers, and may subdue other key factors in international relations such as ideological considerations. For example, Japan has been an ally of the United States ever since the end of World War II, but a major change of perception toward Japan from friend to rival happened when Japan's status rose to a level in the 1980s at which it could replace the United States, thereby becoming 'the next superpower'. During the period of Japan's 'bubble economy', it was not unusual to hear discussion of a popular book, *The Coming War with Japan*, in Washington.[63] This argument has almost completely disappeared since Japan fell into a recession in the 1990s. Therefore, Japan's role in the alliance has been 'rediscovered' and reemphasized, and the labels of 'rival' and 'threat' have since been given to China instead, as can be seen with a parallel title which also became a bestseller, *The Coming Conflict with China*.[64]

This line of argument may lead to a question: How much of a role does ideological difference really play in international relations? Of course, no one denies that ideological differences are an important factor, but they cannot explain why China has been treated with more hostility when China actually adopted a market-oriented new developmental strategy under Deng as opposed as a total planned/command economy under Mao. Indeed, China has made notable progress even in its human rights record compared to the decade of the Cultural Revolution (1966–76). However, many outside observers cannot fully appreciate the depth of this change, thus China has received more condemnation and increasingly has been labeled as a threat. One reason for this dislike may come from the simple fact that the rise of China has effectively changed the distribution of power. Therefore, China has been more frequently perceived as a challenge to the existing international order. From this line of argument, one may understand why the new Bush administration claimed China is a competitor rather than a partner, and why the new theme in Washington is to re-prioritize its foreign policy agendas and stress its alliances with Japan and South Korea.

Obviously, the shift in power distribution has enormous impact on the perceptions of major powers. Therefore, any discussion of the future directions of major-power relations in East Asia first must analyze each country's perspective. To begin with Beijing's perspective, Chinese foreign policy toward Japan needs to be reexamined and Beijing needs to clarify its true national interests. Clearly, the emphases on strategic consideration and the Taiwan issue under Mao and the stress on economic modernization under Deng should continue to be priorities in China's policy toward Japan. Other issues such as territorial disputes and historical legacies should be addressed, but not at the expense of major strategic and economic goals. It is in Beijing's interests to recognize the extremely important role Japan could play in creating a healthy and conducive international environment for China.

One may expect that Beijing will view its relationship with Tokyo from an overall global-strategic perspective. China will continue to promote friendly and cooperative relations with Japan, not only to facilitate its modernization but also to limit its economic and strategic dependence on the United States. While focusing on economic exchanges between the two countries, Beijing is likely to begin regular consultations with Tokyo on regional strategic and security issues, including recognition of Japan's legitimate concern about strategically important areas such as the South China Sea, and to sensitive issues such as human rights. As long as Beijing's legitimacy and sovereignty concerns over such issues as Taiwan are not threatened, Beijing will work closely with Tokyo on a wide range of regional issues, such as stability on the Korean peninsula and the Asian economic crisis. In doing so, Beijing will not only enhance its relationship with Tokyo but also may also improve its position *vis-à-vis* the United States in dealing with global affairs.

While trying its best to be cooperative with the United States, the only superpower in the post-Cold War era, Beijing has also prepared itself to face the above-discussed challenge of a perceived 'two-against-one game', represented by the new guidelines of the US-Japan Security Treaty and the Taiwan Strait crisis of 1996.

As for Japan, it may slowly develop a national consensus over time acknowledging its wartime role in Asia, especially in relation to China and Korea. Japanese politicians are likely to be cautious about any move toward revising the Japanese constitution, particularly Article 9, known as the 'peace clause', since this issue is still a sensitive one among Japan's Asian neighbors. Based on this consensus, Tokyo may work out an official document with Beijing, specifically and precisely expressing its sincere remorse for its past behavior.[65] In return, Beijing may agree that this document will serve as a foundation to conclude – as much as is possible – the unfortunate history between the two countries and to move ahead toward a new relationship.

Ever since the Meiji Restoration period that began in 1868, Japan has had elements of the East and West in terms of its national identity and foreign policy. One can even see this tension from such daily activities as, for example, the recent Japanese trend of switching name cards from the Western order of family name last, to the Eastern style of having the family name listed first.[66] In a larger sense, although Japan has already clearly sided with the United States and the West, it remains conflicted as how to deal with its Asian neighbors – China and Korea in particular – and how to position itself in the East Asian community.

With regard to future directions of its foreign policy toward China, Tokyo probably will continue to stick to its 'one-China policy' regarding Taiwan. Beijing has been particularly sensitive to any Japanese involvement in the Taiwan issue, considering that Taiwan was ceded from China to Japan in 1895 and remained Japan's colony for the next half century. Many older generations of Taiwanese politicians, such as Lee Teng-hui, Taiwanese president from 1988 to 2000, have a special emotional tie to Japan. It is understandable that any move by Tokyo to perpetuate the separation of Taiwan from the mainland would be interpreted as a continuation of Japan's long-term regional ambitions and would not be tolerated by any leadership in Beijing. Therefore, Tokyo probably will continue to make clear it will not support Taiwanese independence, and its proposed theater missile defense system would not include coverage of Taiwan. Clearly, it would be dangerous for Japan to use Taiwan as a 'card' to play games with Beijing.

From the perspective of the United States, when dealing with the new configurations of power relations in the Asian-Pacific region, and particularly the sensitive relations between China and Japan, it is hoped that Washington will continue to play a balanced role in order to maintain stability in the Asia-Pacific. Nevertheless, Washington will promote its alliance and enhance its ties with Tokyo, which serves as the foundation for US policy in the region. There is no reason to believe that an anti-American 'Tokyo-Beijing axis' will develop in the foreseeable future. The US-Japan relationship is well-developed, deeply rooted, mature and solid. The US-

Japan alliance will continue for the decades to come, and will not be overtaken by encouraging the further development of Sino-Japanese relations, given the complicated historical, political and emotional factors involved between Beijing and Tokyo.

Meanwhile, the United States' interest in China has its roots in the two countries' ambivalent historical relationship. Over time, the character of the US-China relationship has shifted starkly from American missionary activities in the nineteenth century to the search for business opportunities in contemporary times. It has also involved a transition from being wartime allies in World War II, to Cold War rivals in the 1950s to the 1980s, a 'strategic partnership' in the 1990s, and now a competitive relationship under the Bush administration.

While the United States may continue to engage Beijing politically, strategically and economically under President George W. Bush,[67] Washington also may encourage Japan to enhance its relationship with China, particularly in the political and security realms. There are understandably different arguments regarding how to deal with the 'rise of China', such as implementing a Cold War-style containment policy similar to that used against the Soviet Union. Yet, while being fully prepared for potential conflict, it is in the best interests of all parties that a more cooperative rather than confrontational approach should be given first consideration in dealing with these complicated yet delicate relationships.

Other significant players also need close attention. Although it is a declining power, one may expect a gradual recovery of Russia in its economic, political, and strategic power. Meanwhile, the perceived unfriendly attitude of Washington may prompt Moscow to continue developing close ties with Beijing to counterbalance the 'hegemonic' behavior of the only superpower. Meanwhile, the two Koreas will continue to remain a focus of regional concern among major powers. The dynamics of the North–South interaction as well as the internal political-economic development in North Korea will continue to have noticeable impact on major power relations in the region. In addition, ASEAN countries may play a leading role in terms of regional community-building efforts, while trying to maintain neutrality in the disputes among major powers in the region, although it may be difficult to back away from such conflicts. Therefore, the future directions of Southeast Asia also will have a clear impact on major power relations in East Asia.

As this contribution argues, a shift in power status is one of the most significant factors that changes relations among major powers. Clearly, stability and prosperity in the Asia-Pacific are in the best interests of all actors in the region. Nevertheless, without properly handling shifts in power distribution, as demonstrated by the ongoing dynamics of the 'two ups and two downs', a peaceful international environment in East Asia will not be maintained. This ability to adapt to new power configurations will not only be crucial to major powers, but also will have tremendous impact on the medium and small actors in the region.

NOTES

The author would like to thank Elizabeth Dahl for research assistance.

1. Steven Mufson, 'U.S.-China Ties in the Balance: Rights Resolution Could Signal Harder Line Toward Beijing', *Washington Post* (17 Feb. 2001) p.A22.
2. Secretary of State Colin L. Powell, remarks at the National Newspaper Association's 40th Annual Government Affairs Conference, Hyatt Regency Hotel, Washington, DC (23 March 2001). See at >www.state.gov/secretary/rm/2001/index.cfm?docid=1666<
3. Zbigniew Brzezinski, 'Living With China', *National Interest* 59 (Spring 2000) p.9.
4. There are many ways to characterize a bilateral relationship between major powers. One may have to consider different dimensions – such as the political, economic, and strategic – as they may have different types of relationship. On the other hand, the terms of relationship be enshrined in treaties or other formal arrangements. With allies, the two countries' relations may be built upon concrete security arrangements against a third-party threat. The best examples in this regard are the US-Japan Security Treaty, and a similar arrangement between the United States and South Korea. The former was used primarily to deter the threat from the Soviet Union during the Cold War era, and the latter was designed in light of the risk of attack from North Korea. 'Partner' is a more neutral yet complimentary term used to emphasize cooperation between two countries, but not likely an alliance relationship. Meanwhile, 'competitor' refers to a relationship prepared for conflicts of interest between two specific countries, but not necessarily in strategically hostile circumstances. Lastly, 'rival' more often refers to intensified and hostile competition in strategic and ideological dimensions, as well as in many cases fighting over natural resources or influence over a certain issue or regional areas.
5. Comments raised by Professor Katsuji Nakagane during the Workshop on the Sino-Japanese Relationship organized by the European Institute of Japanese Studies and the Swedish Institute for International Affairs, 17–19 Aug. 2000, in Stockholm, Sweden.
6. Aurelia George Mulgan, 'Japan: A Setting Sun?', *Foreign Affairs* 79/4 (July–Aug. 2000) pp.40–52.
7. Gary Schaefer, 'Japan Says Recession "Possible" Near Term', *Washington Post* (14 April 2001) p.D12.
8. M. Diana Helweg, 'Japan: A Rising Sun?', *Foreign Affairs* 79/4 (July–Aug. 2000) pp.26–39.
9. See Quansheng Zhao, *Japanese Policymaking: The Politics Behind Politics: Informal Mechanisms and the Making of China Policy* (Hong Kong and NY: OUP 1995) ch.5.
10. Susan V. Lawrence, 'Prickly Pair: China and Japan Remain Civil–and Deeply Divided', *Far Eastern Economic Review* (11 July 1999) p.20.
11. 'Quarterly Chronicle and Documentation', *China Quarterly* No. 164 (Dec. 2000) p.1121.
12. Chester Dawson, 'Flying the Flag', *Far Eastern Economic Review* (12 Aug. 1999) pp.18–19.
13. Zhao (note 9) p.163.
14. For details on American and Chinese shifts of influence in Asia, see Mark Mitchell and Michael Vatikiotis, 'China Steps in Where U.S. Fails', *Far Eastern Economic Review* (23 Nov. 2000) pp.20–2.
15. Kenichi Ito, 'U.S.-Japan Ties Face New Challenges: Equal Partners in an Ever-changing World Environment', *Japan Times* (1 Jan. 2001).

16. Doug Struck, 'Japan Divided On U.S. Call for Missile Defense: Constitutional Bar Creates Anxiety', *Washington Post* (8 Feb. 2001) p.A18.
17. Yoichi Funabashi, *Alliance Adrift* (NY: Council on Foreign Relations Press 1999).
18. Steven C. Clemons, 'The Armitage Report: Reading Between the Lines', Japan Policy Research Institute Occasional Paper No. 20 (Feb. 2001) p.1.
19. Shigehiko Togo, 'Japan Fears Loss of Code From U.S. Plane to China', *Washington Post* (14 April 2001) p.A14.
20. 'Taiwan's Ex-Leader to Visit Japan', *Washington Post* (21 April 2001) p.A13.
21. Chalmers Johnson, 'If Eisenhower Could Apologize, Why Can't Bush?', *International Herald Tribune* (9 April 2001).
22. John Pomfret, 'U.S. Now a 'Threat' in China's Eyes: Security and Taiwan Issues Lead to Talk of Showdown', *Washington Post* (15 Nov. 2000) p.A1.
23. Robert G. Kaiser and Steven Mufson, '"Blue Team" Draws a Hard Line on Beijing: Action on Hill Reflects Informal Group's Clout', *Washington Post* (22 Feb. 2000) p.A1; Thomas Legislative Information webpage: >thomas.loc.gov/cgi-bin/bdquery/z?d106:h.r. 01838<
24. 'The One-China Principle and the Taiwan Issue', *Renmin Ribao* [People's Daily] (22 Feb. 2000) p.1. Previously, the conditions for China's intervention were the declaration of Taiwan's independence or foreign power occupation.
25. Julian Baum with Dan Biers, 'When a Giant Falls', *Far Eastern Economic Review* (6 April 2000) p.18.
26. 'Editorial: Taiwan Blows Raspberries at Beijing: Who's Afraid of the Mainland?', *Far Eastern Economic Review* (6 April 2000) p.58.
27. Julian Baum and Dan Biers with Susan V. Lawrence, 'Chen's Chance', *Far Eastern Economic Review* (30 March 2000) pp.18–20.
28. See Part V of 'Guidelines for U.S.-Japan Defense Cooperation' (US-Japan Security Consultative Committee release) as follows:

> V. Cooperation in Situations in Areas Surrounding Japan that Will Have an Important Influence on Japan's Peace and Security.
>
> Situations in areas surrounding Japan will have an important influence on Japan's peace and security. The concept, situations in areas surrounding Japan, is not geographic but situational. The two Governments will make every effort, including diplomatic efforts, to prevent such situations from occurring. When the two Governments reach a common assessment of the state of each situation, they will effectively coordinate their activities. In responding to such situations, measures taken may differ depending on circumstances.
> …
>
> When a situation in areas surrounding Japan is anticipated, the two Governments will intensify information and intelligence sharing and policy consultations, including efforts to reach a common assessment of the situation.

29. *Yomiuri Shimbun* (18 Aug. 1998), as quoted in Zhong Yan, 'Xin ri-mei fangwei hezuo zhizhen ji xiangguan lifa pingxi', ['An Analysis of the New 'Guideline for Japan-U.S. Defense Cooperation' and Its Related Legislation'] *Riben Xuekan* [Japanese Studies], No.2 (2000) pp.1–12.
30. Suisheng Zhao, 'China's Periphery Policy and Its Asian Neighbors', *Security Dialogue* 30/3 (Sept. 1999) p.340.
31. Thomas J. Christensen, 'Chinese Realpolitik', *Foreign Affairs* 75/5 (Sept.–Oct. 1996) p.40.
32. For an excellent and detailed discussion on the US role in the *Diaoyu/Senkaku* dispute, see Jean-Marc Blanchard, 'The U.S. Role in the Sino-Japanese Dispute Over the Diaoyu (Senkaku) Islands, 1945–1971', *The China Quarterly* 161 (March 2000) pp.95–123.
33. Li Qingjin, 'Deng Xiaoping gongtong kaifa sixiang yu diaoyudao wenti' [Deng Xiaoping's Thoughts on 'Joint Development' and Prospects for the Issue of Diaoyu Island and Adjacent Islands] *Japanese Studies* 4 (1999) pp.1–12.
34. Andrew J. Nathan and Robert S. Ross, *The Great Wall and the Empty Fortress: China's Search for Security* (NY: Norton 1997) p.25.

35. John Pomfret, 'China Plans Major Boost in Spending for Military', *The Washington Post* (6 March 2001) pp.A1, A20.
36. PRC State Council, '2000 White Paper on National Defense', *Renmin Ribao* [People's Daily] (17 Oct. 2000) p.4.
37. *Renmin Ribao* (People's Daily) (25 Nov. 2000) p.1.
38. *Renmin Ribao* [People's Daily] (25 Nov. 2000) p.1.
39. The East Asian Vision Group was established with the suggestion from President Kim Dae Jung of South Korea in May 1999. The first meeting was convened in Nov. 1999 in Seoul, with former Minister of Foreign Affairs Han Sung-Joo (now a professor at Korea University) presiding. The meeting was in the so-called '10+3' format, namely the ten ASEAN members plus Japan, China and South Korea. Each country has two representatives, one being a government official of foreign affairs at the ambassador level and the other a leading scholar of Asia-Pacific international relations, making a total of 26 participants. In the future, the Vision Group may potentially be expanded to a '13+2' format in which North Korea and Mongolia will join as participants.
40. Interview with Zhang Yunling, Director of Institute of Asia-Pacific Studies, Chinese Academy of Social Sciences, 2 Jan. 2001, in Beijing, China. Zhang Yunling was one of the PRC's representatives for the East Asian Vision Group.
41. *Renmin Ribao* [People's Daily] (24 Nov. 2000) p.6.
42. John Pomfret, 'Russians Help China Modernize Its Arsenal: New Military Ties Raise U.S. Concerns', *Washington Post* (10 Feb. 2000) pp.A17–18.
43. *Washington Post* (11 Feb. 2000) p.A32.
44. Selig Harrison, 'Promoting a Soft Landing in Korea', *Foreign Policy* 106 (Spring 1997).
45. 'Pyongyang Accepts Framework for Peace Talks', *Straits Times* (2 July 1997) p.21.
46. Steven Myers, 'N. Korea's Talks with U.S. Fail Over Demand for G.I. Pullout', *New York Times* (20 Sept. 1997).
47. Robert Reid, 'Korean Peace Talks Break Down', Associated Press (20 Sept. 1997).
48. 'South Korea, Russia Issue Joint Statement on Peninsula Issues', *Korea Herald* (25 July 1997).
49. Shin Yong-bae, 'Sixth round of four-way peace talks ends with little progress', *Korea Herald* (10 Aug. 1999), from >www.koreaherald.co.kr/cgi-bin/searched_word.asp?qstr=fourlpartyl talks&path=/news/1999/08/__02/19990810_0208.htm<
50. Frank Ching, 'A Tale of Two State Visits', *Far Eastern Economic Review* (20 May 1999) p.36.
51. Lawrence (note 10) p.20.
52. For further discussion, see Quansheng Zhao, *Interpreting Chinese Foreign Policy: The Macro-Micro Linkage Approach* (Hong Kong and NY: OUP 1996) p.192.
53. One such suggestion is to establish a new comprehensive and internationally oriented university in China, jointly developed by China and Japan with substantial financial and academic support from Japan. This university should be first-rate – comparable to Beijing and Qinghua universities, the two leading higher education institutions in China. An important function of this university would be to enhance China's understanding of international affairs with a special emphasis on Japan. In addition, each side could also send a certain number of university professors annually to conduct lectures on aspects of the social, political, economic, and legal environments of their own country.
54. For a detailed analysis of the changing priority of Chinese foreign policy, see Zhao (note 53) ch.3.
55. Samuel P. Huntington, *The Clash of Civilizations and the Remaking of World Order* (NY: Simon & Schuster 1996) p.20.
56. Philip P. Pan, 'Beijing Ratifies Rights Treaty, but Has Qualifications', *Washington Post* (1 March 2001) p.A14. Also see 'Regional Briefing' (30 Nov. 2000) p.13.
57. Murray Hiebert and Susan V. Lawrence, 'Trade Tightrope', *Far Eastern Economic Review* (24 Feb. 2000) p.22.
58. 'A Report Which Distorts Facts and Confuses Right and Wrong – On the Part About China in the 1994 'Human Rights Report' issued by the US State Department', *Beijing Review* (13 March 1995) p.21.

59. Ibid.
60. Andrew J. Nathan, 'Human Rights In Chinese Foreign Policy', *The China Quarterly* No.151 (Sept. 1997) p.629.
61. Ibid. pp.641–2.
62. Nayan Chanda, 'After the Bomb', *Far Eastern Economic Review* (13 April 2000) p.20.
63. George Friedman and Meredith LeBard, *The Coming War With Japan* (NY: St Martin's Press 1991).
64. Richard Bernstein and Ross H. Munro, *The Coming Conflict With China* (NY:Knopf 1997).
65. See, for example, Frank Ching, 'A Tale of Former Allies', *Far Eastern Economic Review* (2 March 2000) p.35.
66. Shigehiko Togo, 'Putting Last Name Forward: Japan Scrapping Way of the West', *Washington Post* (15 Dec. 2000) p.A51.
67. Former Deputy Assistant Secretary of State on Asia Susan Shirk mentioned in a speech that five issues would continue to be salient for the next administration's policy on China: Taiwan, human rights, TMD, trade, and the accidental NATO bombing of the Chinese embassy in Belgrade. *Asia Comment 2001* of 2001 Asia Pacific Media Network, Asia Pacific Executive Forum: 'Doing Business in a Changing Asia: A Strategic Vision', at the East-West Center, Honolulu, Hawaii, 16–19 Jan. 2001. >www.asiamedia.ucla.edu/ASIAComment 2001/EastWestCenter01.19.2001.htm<

4

The Second Nuclear Age: Proliferation Pessimism versus Sober Optimism in South Asia and East Asia

VICTOR D. CHA

There is probably no place else in the world today where proliferation concerns are more acute than in Asia.[1] Actors in the region either possess or have exhibited clear desires for developing nuclear weapons capabilities. These programs are being cultivated in the context of intense rivalries over power and territory, and embedded, in many cases, in a cauldron of unresolved historical hatreds. There are no regional arms control regimes, and participation in global ones is sporadic. The danger with regard to these programs is exacerbated by their lack of transparency, their illiberal political sponsors (in some cases), and their profiles as small, unsafeguarded programs. For 'proliferation pessimists', Asia therefore represents the worst of two worlds: small nuclear powers operating under conditions of security-scarcity, where fierce animosities and rivalries do not bode well for rational or stable deterrence.

How accurate is this assessment? Is the first use, intentional or accidental, of a nuclear weapon since 1945 fated to be in Asia? More broadly, how should we be thinking about proliferation and the 'second' nuclear age in East Asia and South Asia in the twenty-first century? What are the prospects, if any, for regional arms control? If these prospects are poor, what is to be the ultimate form of order with regard to nuclear proliferation in the region?

This contribution makes two arguments with regard to the causes and consequences of the second nuclear age in Asia. Regarding causes of proliferation, I argue that these are *overdetermined* in Asia. As was the case in the first nuclear age, proliferation derives largely from the intersection of security-scarcity and resource constraints. However, in addition to these basic security drivers, there are a plethora of secondary drivers ranging from domestic forces, political currency (insurance and bargaining), prestige, and a healthy dose of skepticism regarding first world hypocrisy that explain the region's proliferation. The combination of these primary and secondary drivers not only ensures that proliferation is overdetermined in Asia, but also means that rollback of these capabilities, though desirable, is not likely.

The second part of the study addresses the consequences of proliferation. Contrary to the pessimistic assessment regarding the causes of proliferation, I make a case for 'sober optimism' regarding the prospects for stability. Asian nuclear and missile proliferation are certainly dangerous but not nearly as disastrous as has been popularly predicted. Swaggering, competitive testing, crises, accidents, and outright conflicts may certainly occur, but there is no reason to expect that the likelihood of this behavior escalating to a nuclear exchange is any more probable than was the case for the first nuclear age. Deterrence (albeit in a different form than the superpower experience) is likely to continue, augmented by an appreciation of the taboo on nuclear first-use.

An argument for 'sober optimism' with regard to Asian proliferation is *not* meant as an argument against nonproliferation. Stemming the spread and appeal of nuclear weapons and missile technology to 'rogue regimes' as well as to other potential proliferators remains extremely important. However, I argue that there is no necessary connection between an enthusiasm for nonproliferation and pessimistic assessments of proliferation consequences for the region. The two have been conjoined in almost stereotypical depictions of the agents of second nuclear age as irrational, maniacal, and irresponsible. In some cases such a characterization may be true, but I argue that there is no reason *a priori* to assume this as a hard and fast rule for the entire region. In short, one can still be an advocate of nonproliferation and remain soberly optimistic that the consequences of proliferation (should it occur) for the region are not unequivocally disastrous. Moreover, given the understanding of what drives proliferation behavior in the region, some specific recommendations emerge for the nonproliferation effort. I open with a brief empirical overview, followed by the arguments regarding the causes and consequences of proliferation in the region. I conclude with a short discussion on the role current and new nonproliferation institutions can play in reinforcing and enhancing the non-use outcome in Asia.

THE SECOND NUCLEAR AGE IN ASIA

The second nuclear age is substantively different from the first. In the first nuclear age, whether this term referred to the United States and the Soviet Union or the next tier of nuclear powers (Britain, France, China), there were fewer agents and, generally speaking, greater uniformity among them.[2] By contrast, the second nuclear age is like comparing apples and oranges. Not only are the levels of proliferation greatly varied, but they differ on a whole range of dimensions. China, the South Asian states, the two Koreas, Japan and Taiwan display a range of extant and recessed nuclear and ballistic missile (BM) capabilities that vary in terms of quantity and quality of systems, accuracy, range, infrastructure, and transparency. These capabilities are accompanied by varied degrees of commitments to nonproliferation regimes; moreover, they operate or are cultivated in an international structure no longer defined by bipolarity and one in which fears of abandonment, local threats, and uncertainty are brought into higher relief. A brief empirical overview makes clear these differences.

China possesses the most advanced nuclear weapons and ballistic missile programs in Asia. Its ballistic missile (BM) infrastructure offers a wide variety of land and sea-based systems (see Table 1 for details).[3] China's nuclear arsenal consists of 400–450 devices. Beijing relies largely on the land-based leg of the triad, reserving nearly 250 of these 'strategic' warheads for medium and long-range strike missions mated with the BM program.[4] Chinese efforts to modernize this arsenal were manifest in a series of tests completed in 1996, the information of which enabled finalizing weapons designs (China has conducted 45 tests over 33 years against 1,030 by the United States).[5] China is not currently producing more fissile materials for nuclear weapons but has a stockpile sufficient to increase or improve its weapon inventory. In addition, it is in the midst of a wide-ranging modernization program that aims to improve range, payload and accuracy of delivery vehicles (through development of solid propellants, improved rocket motors, and targeting technologies) to replace older DF systems deployed in the 1970s and the 1980s (see Table 1). Improvements are also being sought regarding the survivability of its nuclear and BM forces, command, control and communication capabilities, stealth technologies, as well as countermeasures to ballistic missile defense (decoy warheads, multiple reentry vehicles, electronic and infrared jammers).

At the next tier in terms of demonstrated capabilities are India and Pakistan. The South Asian rivals have two of the more advanced ballistic missile programs in the developing world. India's program, in particular, is

TABLE 1
THE SECOND NUCLEAR AGE

Country	Ballistic missiles	Range (km) Payload (km)	Nuclear	Comments
China	Dong Feng-3/3A (CSS-2)	2800 km 2150 kg	Nuclear warhead 1–5 MT	1-stage, liquid propellant; surface–surface. 50–120 missiles. Deployed 1971
	DF-4 (CSS-3)	4750 km 2200 kg	Nuclear warhead 1–5 MT	2-stage, 20–30 missiles. Deployed 1980
	DF-5/5A (CSS-4)	12,000–15,000 km 3200 kg	Nuclear warhead 1–5 MT	2-stage. Storable liquid fuel. 7–20+ missiles. Deployed 1981. Possible MRV
	DF-21/21A (CSS-6)	1800 km 600 kg	Nuclear warhead 200–300 KT	2-stage. Solid propellant. Replacing DF-3. 10–36+ missiles. Deployed 1986
	DF-15/M-9 (CSS-6)	600 km 950 kg	Nuclear warhead 50–350 KT	1-stage. Solid fuel. Dual capable. M-9 version for export. 100+ deployed (1995)
	DF-11/M-11/RDF-11S (CSS-X-7)	300 km 500 kg	Nuclear warhead 50–350 KT	2-stage solid fuel. Dual capable. M-11 version designed for export. 40+ (1995)
	M-7/8610 (CSS-8)	160 km 190 kg	Conventional warhead	2-stage. Solid fuel
	DF-31	8000 km 700 kg	Nuclear warhead 200–300 Kt	Tested 1999, under development; 3-stage, solid propellant; to be deployed 2000 to replace DF-4; possibly MIRV/MRV

TABLE 1 (Contd)

Country	Ballistic missiles	Range (km) Payload (km)	Nuclear	Comments
DF-41	12,000 km	Nuclear warhead 800 kg	In development, will replace 200–300 KT	DF-5 2010; 3-stage solid propellant. Possibly MIRV
	JL-1 (CSS-N-3)	1700 km 600 kg	Nuclear warhead 200–300 KT	2-stage SLBM; solid fuel. 12–24 missiles. Deployed 1986
	JL-2 (CSS-NX-4)	8000 km 700 kg	Nuclear warhead 200–300 KT	3-stage SLBM; solid fuel, same as DF-31; under development
India	Prithvi-150	150 km 1000 kg	1974 PNE	Operational, from Russian SA-2
			May 1998 tests	
	Prithvi-250	250 km 200 kg		Operational, from Russian SA-2
	Prithvi-350	350 km 500 kg		In development, from Russian SA-2
	Dhanush	250 km 500 kg		In development, from Prithvi
	Sagarika	300 km 500 kg		In development, from Prithvi
	Agni	1500 km 1000 kg		Tested 18 Feb. 1994, from Scout
	Agni-2	2000 km 1000 kg		Tested 11 April 1999, from Scout

TABLE 1 (Contd)

Country	Ballistic missiles	Range (km) Payload (km)	Nuclear	Comments
	Surya	1200 km ? kg		In development, from Polar Satellite Launch Vehicle and Agni-2
Pakistan	M-11	280 km 800 kg	May 1998 tests	In storage
	Hatf-1	80 km 500 kg		Operational
	Hatf-1A	100 km 500 kg		Operational
	Hatf-2	300 km 500 kg		In development, M-11 derivative?
	Hatf-3	600 km 500 kg		In development, M-9 derivative?
	Ghauri	1300 km 500–750 kg		Tested 6 April 1998, from Nodong
	Ghauri-2	2000 km 100 kg		Tested 14 April 1999, from Nodong
	Ghauri-3	3700 km 3500 kg		Engines tested 23 July 1999 and 29 Sept. 1999
	Shaheen-2	2500 km 1000 kg		Mobile, 2-stage, solid fuel, in development, from Nodong-2, unveiled at April 2000 Pakistan day parade. 'To be tested shortly'

TABLE 1 (Contd)

Country	Ballistic missiles	Range (km) Payload (km)	Nuclear	Comments
North Korea	Scud-B	300 km 1000 kg	weapons-grade plutonium reprocessing capabilities.	Operational, in production
	Scud-C	500 km 700 kg		Operational, in production
	Nodong-1	1000 km 700–1000 kg	2 LWRs (1994 Agreed Framework)	In development, tested
	Nodong-2	1500 km 770 kg		In development
	Taepodong-1	1500–2000 km 1000 kg		Tested 31 Aug. 1998, Combined Nodong and Scud
	Taepodong-2	3500–6000 km 1000 kg		In development
South Korea	Nike-Hercules-1	180 km 300 kg	Civilian nuclear energy	Operational, modified SAM
	Nike-Hercules-2	250 km 300 kg	Reprocessing capability	In development, modified SAM
Taiwan	Ching Feng	130 km 400 kg	Civilian nuclear energy	Operational, from Lance, from Green Bee
	Tien Ma	950 km 500 kg		In development, from Sky Horse

TABLE 1 (Contd)

Country	Ballistic missiles	Range (km) Payload (km)	Nuclear	Comments
	Tien Chi	300 km 500 kg		In development, modified SAM
Japan	M-3 (SLV)	4000 km 500 kg	Civilian nuclear energy	Capability
	H-1 (SLV)	12,000 km 550+ kg	Reprocessing	Capability
	H-2 (SLV)	15,000 km 4000 kg		Capability (program cancelled?)

Source: Compiled from Center for Nonproliferation Studies >http://cns.miis.edu/cns/projects/eanp/pubs/chinanuc/nstock.htm<; >http://cns.miis.edu/cns/projects/eanp/pubs/chinanuc/bmsl.htm<; Joseph Cirincione, 'Assessing the Assessment: The 1999 National Intelligence Estimate of the Ballistic Missile Threat', *Nonproliferation Review* (Spring 2000); William Carpenter and David Wiencek (eds.) *Asian Security Handbook* (NY: M.E. Sharpe 1996) p.67; *Jane's Defense Weekly*; and Robert Manning, Ronald Montaperto and Brad Roberts, *China, Nuclear Weapons, and Arms Control* (NY: Council on Foreign Relations 2000) pp.22–3.

capable of design and production of relatively advanced missiles (i.e., solid propellants, multi-stage, mobile, medium-range distances) with little foreign assistance.[6] Pakistan's missile program, although not as self-sufficient or deep in variety and range of missiles as India's, remains competitive in shorter-range missiles.[7] The object of much attention since the 1998 tests, India and Pakistan's nuclear programs mirror their missile programs in terms of levels of relative development. India's very active nuclear energy program has endowed them with the facilities to support a complete nuclear fuel cycle. The majority of Indian nuclear reactors are under International Atomic Energy Agency (IAEA) safeguards, however, those that are not have been the producers of weapons-grade plutonium and enriched uranium for weapons use (e.g., Bhabha Atomic Research Center). The nuclear weapons program started in the early 1960s, and after the 1974 peaceful nuclear explosion (PNE), India remained an undeclared nuclear power, its operational weapons capability limited to oversized bombs deliverable by airplane. From the mid-1980s they sought to modernize these capabilities in terms of miniaturization and accuracy, which was one of the purposes of the 1998 tests. Pakistan's nuclear weapons program originated in response to the 1971 war and accelerated after the 1974 Indian PNE. Like India, only a portion of its nuclear facilities are under IAEA safeguards;[8] however unlike its rival, Pakistan, while able to produce plutonium and highly enriched uranium, still remains dependent on foreign suppliers (China) for sophisticated materials and technologies to expand their program. While Islamabad has asserted its willingness to sign the Non-Proliferation Treaty (NPT) should India do so, both remain non-parties to the regime.

The Democratic People's Republic of Korea (DPRK or North Korea) stands in a separate category. Its ballistic missile program since the early 1980s has produced a range of missile systems, either deployed or tested, demonstrating progress beyond most expectations (see Table 1).[9] Mated with the missile program have been dedicated DPRK efforts at acquiring nuclear weapons capabilities. Deriving from atomic energy agreements with the Soviet Union in the 1960s,[10] Pyongyang's nuclear industry was capable of supporting a complete nuclear fuel cycle by the 1980s. Subsequent reactors (an operational 5-megawatt (MW) reactor and construction of 50 MW and 200 MW reactors) presaged an annual reprocessed plutonium production capacity that could sustain in excess of 10 nuclear weapons. While these activities remain frozen and are subject to dismantling as a result of the 1994 US-DPRK Agreed Framework, suspicions remain regarding the North's plutonium-reprocessing history, alleged covert activities outside Yongbyon, and possible crude nuclear devices.[11]

Finally latent or recessed capabilities are evident in the relatively advanced civilian nuclear energy programs in South Korea, Japan, and Taiwan. There are no explicit links between nuclear energy and weapons; however, the promotion of civilian power reactors (with safeguards on nuclear materials) encourages latent nuclear weapons capabilities by allowing states to develop the research reactors, industrial infrastructure, technology, and materials that could eventually be converted to bomb-making purposes.[12] In this vein, Northeast Asia is the only region in the world where nuclear energy is viewed as a substitute increasingly for fossil fuel resources.[13] As of the mid-1990s, nuclear power supplies 36 per cent of the Republic of Korea's (ROK) energy; 28.8 per cent for Taiwan, and 33.8 per cent for Japan (against 2 per cent for China), and by 2010 the US Department of Energy estimates that nearly half of global nuclear energy capacity will be in East Asia.[14] The Tokyo, Taipei and Seoul governments have all forsworn nuclear weapons and acceded to the NPT regime; nevertheless, the increasing reliance on nuclear energy in combination with the lack of storage space in Asia creates strong incentives for reprocessing spent fuel.[15] Moreover, connected with this dynamic is the vision of energy self-sufficiency through the development of fast-breeder reactor technology (e.g., Japan) which creates additional incentives for reprocessing and stockpiling plutonium. Hence latent nuclear capabilities are present in Asia's nuclear energy activities as are insecurity spirals deriving from the longer-term proliferation dangers of plutonium stockpiles.[16]

CAUSES OF PROLIFERATION

The causes for nuclear proliferation in Asia are *overdetermined*. Three sub-arguments substantiate this claim. First, despite the asymmetry of nuclear capabilities within the region, states in Asia proliferate for similar reasons. Second, these causes are generally similar to those that drove proliferation in the first nuclear age. Third, while the causes for proliferation are similar across the first and second nuclear ages, what distinguishes the Asian cases is that the entire spectrum of domestic and international factors cited by experts as highly potent drivers of a state's need for nuclear weapons and delivery systems are salient to Asia. Moreover, these drivers are both abundant and long-lasting.

The Security Rationale

The first cause relevant to all cases of proliferation in Asia operates at the intersection of security needs and material constraints. States seek security against perceived threats and seek to close gaps with rival competitors within very real resource limitations; moreover, the self-help imperatives of anarchy render reliance on allies for security an unattractive proposition (when abandonment fears are high) or an unfeasible one (when allies do not exist).[17] As Goldstein argues, nuclear weapons therefore offer the most efficient means by which to optimize across security needs, abandonment fears, and resource constraints.[18] Internal balancing against an adversary with conventional forces is less useful for these purposes for various reasons, the most important of which is if the gaps are too large to overcome. Nuclear weapons are also more 'fungible' than conventional forces in the sense that they remain relevant security assets in most cases regardless of wholesale changes in future adversaries or contingencies.[19] In sum, nuclear weapons offer the most robust means by which threatened states protect vital interests.

> National nuclear weapons enable states to satisfy basic security requirements self-reliantly and relatively economically. They are not cheap but when married to deterrent doctrines nuclear weapons can dissuade even much more powerful adversaries without incurring the high costs of comparably effective conventional defenses.[19a]

This security/cost/fear calculus of allied abandonment-based logic is common to all proliferation cases in Asia. In the most well-analyzed case of China (well analyzed relative to the new proliferators), there is general agreement that the Chinese sought nuclear weapons dating back to January 1955 as a direct function of perceived US nuclear threats against China during the Korean War and offshore islands crises in the mid-1950s; the security alliance with Taiwan; superior American conventional capabilities; and the turn to 'New Look' and massive retaliation in US strategic doctrine. Absence of confidence in the Soviet security commitment in a potential Sino-American conflict also weighed heavily in Beijing's decision to seek an independent nuclear capability.[20]

In the case of India, multiple external threats, resource constraints, and alignment uncertainties caused a shift away from its earlier adherence to disarmament norms. The 1962 Sino-Indian border war and 1964 Chinese nuclear test gave the initial impetus to India's nuclear program.[21] The ensuing 1965 Indo-Pakistani conflict over Kashmir and in particular, veiled Chinese threats to open a second front on the Himalayan border forced the Indians to contemplate seriously the inadequacy of their conventional deterrent and re-think the traditional emphasis on disarmament. The absence of external support also mattered in India's decision making. In particular, the reluctance of the British, Americans or Soviets to answer New Delhi's entreaties for nuclear guarantees informed the Indian decision to test in 1974.[22] In addition, larger superpower security dynamics in Central Asia created alignment patterns that heightened Indian threat perceptions. The Soviet invasion of Afghanistan in December 1979 led to a consolidation of US-Pakistani relations during the Reagan administration (e.g., $3.2 billion assistance package, F-16 sales, and CIA training of Afghan resistance fighters in Pakistan), which in turn, supplemented Indian concerns about Chinese support of Pakistan. These threat perceptions led India to develop (under the Defense Research and Development Organization (DRDO) Integrated Guided Missile Development Program [IGMDP]) and test fire India's first intermediate range ballistic missile (IRBM) (Agni) in 1989.[23] With regard to the most recent tests, the Chinese threat still remains the permissive condition for the Indian nuclear capability (in that one cannot imagine caps on the Indian program without retaining a minimum deterrent against China), however, the specific cause of the 1998 test was related to Pakistan.[24] In particular, Pakistan's test of the IRBM Ghauri in April 1998 demonstrated a more robust capability to target Indian cities (up to 26 cities) to which India had to respond.[25]

Like India and China, a similar mix of threats and resource constraints determined Pakistani nuclear and missile proliferation. From the late 1950s, Islamabad exhibited little interest in a nuclear program, but after the 1965 war with India, the government became more concerned about growing Indian conventional force superiority. Following that war, Pakistan's defeat in the 1971 war, the Indian 1974 test, and the Prithvi missile program (which was perceived to be designed specifically for targeting Pakistan), Pakistan set itself firmly on the path of acquiring nuclear weapons as the only equalizer to Indian conventional and nuclear capabilities.[26] Exacerbating the need to proliferate were unsettling variations in the level of aligned support for Pakistan from outside parties. One of Islamabad's justifications for the nuclear program was that it could not rely on the United States for its security. American support of Pakistan has varied widely, the low points being the end to arms transfers after 1965, cool relations during the detente years, and the imposition of sanctions during the Carter administration. Relations improved during the Reagan years largely as a function of Soviet actions in Afghanistan but with the end of the Cold War, Pakistani confidence in the United States plummeted. Islamabad saw a growing American alignment with India as a counterweight to China. This dynamic was manifest among other things in US unwillingness to provide security guarantees in the face of India's May 1998 tests, ultimately spurring the Pakistani decision to test.[27]

Although North Korea's nuclear program is by far the most opaque of those in the second nuclear age, an argument could be made that the drivers are not too dissimilar from other cases of proliferation. As noted above, Pyongyang's interest in atomic energy dated back to the 1960s, but serious endeavors really did not begin until the late-1980s (i.e., when the nuclear industry was capable of supporting a complete fuel cycle and construction of 50 MW and 200 MW reactors began). This interest coincided with a time when the North's political-military and economic situations took serious turns for the worse. Pyongyang watched helplessly as China and the Soviet Union normalized relations with South Korea (1992 and 1990 respectively). This situation became even more acute when Beijing and Moscow subsequently abrogated their Cold War security-guarantees (and patron aid) to the North. Almost contemporaneously, the North suffered successive years of negative economic growth; acute energy and food shortages; and deteriorating conventional force supplies and readiness. Arguably this combination of security scarcity and resource constraints made nuclear weapons appealing as the most fungible and robust security equalizer.[28]

This causal dynamic is relevant to the cases of Japan, South Korea, and Taiwan. Even though all are committed non-nuclear weapons states (NNWS) and supporters of the nonproliferation regime, all have latent capabilities and face salient external threats. For the most part, what obviates the perceived need for any of these countries to seek extant capabilities and delivery systems is American security guarantees (explicit in the former two cases and implicit in the third). The likelihood of any of these states proliferating would grow measurably if credibility in the American commitment waned. South Korean pursuit of an independent nuclear weapons capability in the late 1960s and the 1970s was not a function of heightened external threats, but directly a function of fears of American abandonment deriving from the Nixon doctrine and the withdrawal of the US 7th Infantry Division in 1970–71.[29]

In this regard ironically, the *success* of US alliances in East Asia is another factor that might contribute to future proliferation. A stabilization of the security situation on the Korean peninsula for example would lead to some drawdown of the American forward presence. For the allies, US extended nuclear guarantees in the absence of this presence would not be very credible, prompting greater interest in autonomous capabilities.[30] An even more radical interpretation would question the credibility of the US nuclear umbrella to Asian allies *today*. This argument is largely because the end of the Cold War structurally renders extended nuclear deterrence less credible to allies. During the Cold War bipolar conflict, what rendered credible the notion that the United States would respond to an attack on an ally and risk retaliation at home was the belief that this conflict would be decisive in terms of the wider geostrategic superpower competition. However, a similar nuclear exchange scenario (e.g., prompted by a DPRK chemical attack on Seoul in which the United States would respond and risk retaliation by the DPRK against Hawaii or San Francisco) would not carry the same stakes, and, logically speaking, should be less credible for the ally.

The Absence of Domestic-Political Obstacles

The second causal factor for proliferation in Asia is the absence of domestic-political opposition. This situation obtains either because the programs are covert and therefore not subject to public debate (e.g., the ROK clandestine program in the 1970s), or because there is proactive support among the general public and politicians. The latter dynamic is especially relevant in the South Asian cases.[31]

In India, domestic support for the programs took place at two levels. The first was at the level of politics and society in general where the nuclear program became interlinked with Indian status and prestige. The Bharatiya Janata Party (BJP) campaigned prior to its March 1998 victory on promises of restoring India to national greatness, and as a concrete act in this regard, 'inducted' nuclear weapons into the national security apparatus. Images were created regarding nuclear weapons status and being treated in the world as a first-class power which appealed not only to the conservative Hindu right but the population as a whole, such that as one analyst put it, '[i]n India today, there are very few votes to be found in a posture of dovishness on the nuclear issue'.[32]

The second domestic dynamic in support of proliferation occurred at the level of the bureaucracy. As Bracken argues, support and the drive for nuclear weapons-related research over the years became the means by which a young, rising, civilian technocratic sector circumvented and displaced the old, corrupt, and inefficient military bureaucracy.[33] This trend was especially the case in India where the Atomic Energy Commission, Defense Research and Development Organization (DRDO), and the Space Program formed a triumvirate of new influential technocratic bureaus that demanded respect in Indian society and developed powerful interests in self-perpetuation.[34]

Similar dynamics were evident in the Pakistani case. The government skillfully utilized the symbolism of nuclear weapons to rally support for the program. Throughout the evolution of the nuclear program, there was little public discussion. Instead, the government appealed to the public through skillful manipulation of the media, framing the issue in prestige and honor terms for Pakistan: '[T]he end result is that the majority of Pakistani citizens have no idea of the costs and consequences of the country's nuclear programme. Nor are they aware of the peace movements in various nuclear and non-nuclear states. Nonetheless, they have become innocent/ignorant converts of the value of nuclear weapons ...'.[35]

First World Hypocrisy: 'Do As We Say, Not As We Do'

A contributing factor on the domestic front for proliferation is widespread perceptions of First World hypocrisy. From the perspective of new proliferators, there are fundamental inconsistencies between statements and actions on the part of the nuclear weapons states (NWS). These states call for global nuclear disarmament, controls on technology transfer, a comprehensive test ban, and do not officially recognize any new nuclear powers, yet at the same time they do not consider a rollback of their own capabilities. On the contrary, NWS readily acknowledge in their own security doctrines the centrality of the nuclear deterrent.[36] In addition, if smaller nuclear powers such as Britain and France, for whom the Cold War was the primary driver of their acquisition of capabilities, do not willingly disarm, then why should others not acquire them?[37] This 'do as we say, not as we do' criticism pertains not only to NWS but also to NNWS states like Japan, Canada, Australia, and Germany whose commitments to nonproliferation regimes are seen to ring hollow because of the US nuclear umbrella and their plutonium stockpiles.[38]

First World hypocrisy reduces domestic constraints on new proliferators in two ways. It undercuts the legitimacy and dodges the arguments of domestic constituencies opposed to the weapons programs. Furthermore, it is easily manipulated by proliferation advocates to press forward with the program on normative grounds. As one expert noted

> Because of their discriminatory nature and the continued security value attached to nuclear weapons by the major powers, the non-proliferation treaties have been viewed by some as a mask for power play, to freeze the status quo in favor of the haves against the have-nots ... A large number of non-nuclear states have indeed accepted the NPT and CTBT ... This, however, does not imply that all – especially those that have the security concerns and the technical know-how, and who must or choose to rely on themselves for security – must or will accept it.[39]

In Pakistan, for example, the government portrayed the international nonproliferation norms as a First World conspiracy aimed at preventing Pakistan from attaining its rightful place in the world. In addition, US efforts to block Pakistan's acquisition of nuclear technologies (e.g., Kissinger's threats to Bhutto, pressuring France to renege on reprocessing deals with Islamabad in the 1970s) all had the effect of lionizing nuclear weapons in domestic politics as a symbol of national sovereignty.[40]

The hypocrisy arguments were heard most loudly in India where proliferation advocates could stymie the critics and keep the nation's nuclear option open by appealing to moralistic arguments about the inequities practiced by the First World's 'nuclear apartheid'.[41] New Delhi condemned the NPT in 1970 as an attempt by the nuclear club to prevent others from going nuclear (after China), but at the same time, not granting security guarantees to those NNWS countries left vulnerable.[42] India denounced the indefinite extension of the NPT on the grounds that, some half decade after the end of the Cold War, it was a travesty that the NWS could pull off such a feat while still relying on their nuclear deterrent.[43] First World hypocrisy drove proliferation not only by allowing virtually any regime to legitimize its drive for nuclear weapons in normative/equity terms, but also by counter-intuitively raising the incentives to test every time a new nonproliferation milestone had been reached. For example, the NPT extension and finalization of the CTBT in the mid-1990s actually prompted potential proliferators to consider testing sooner rather than later as First World-backed nonproliferation regimes were slowly closing the window of opportunity.[44]

Political Currency of Capabilities

An additional cause common to all cases of proliferation in Asia is the political currency of acquiring these capabilities. In addition to the strategic rationale for proliferating, states perceive various political benefits from becoming nuclear- and BM-capable. Of course, there are substantial political costs imposed by the nonproliferation regimes on new proliferators, but these costs are not seen to outweigh the benefits in terms of insurance, prestige, and bargaining position.

The bargaining and insurance motives are interlinked. On the one hand, nuclear and long-range BM capabilities, while sought for security and 'equalizer' purposes, can serve as tools of political coercion to gain bargaining advantages. Arguably, the DPRK through its fledgling BM capabilities was able to force international attention to its food problem as well as compel the engagement efforts by the United States, Japan, and South Korea. No one (except perhaps Pyongyang) intended for this coercion to be the case; nevertheless, it has been the net result; moreover, one that might not otherwise have been without the DPRK's missile program.[45] Similarly, Indian statements in the aftermath of the May 1998 tests hinted at diplomatic coercion based on its new, demonstrated capability. Home Minister Lal Krishna Advani stated after the tests that India had a new qualitative edge in solving the Kashmir problem and that Pakistan should 'realise the change in the geostrategic situation ..., and roll back its anti-India policy'. In a more blatant example, the Indian Army chief shortly after the tests made a symbolic visit to the Indian part of Kashmir to 'discuss the elements of a "new Strategy" with local commanders'.[46]

The flip side of the bargaining motive is the insurance motive. For fear of demonstration effects from cases like the DPRK, states choose to proliferate precisely to prevent becoming vulnerable to political coercion and nuclear blackmail. While security was certainly a driver of Pakistan's nuclear and missile program, an important motive was to avoid allowing its rival the political leverage to dictate its terms on significant political or sovereignty issues in a way unacceptable to Pakistan.[47] Similarly, after the test at Lop Nor in October 1964, voices within India called for a change in policy on nuclear capabilities to counter the political influence that China would gain with the nuclear advantage. As Indian diplomat Sisir Gupta said, '... without using its nuclear weapons and without unleashing the kind of war which would be regarded in the West as the crossing of the provocation threshold, China may subject a non-nuclear India to periodic blackmail, weaken its people's spirit of resistance and self-confidence and thus achieve without a war its major political and military objectives in Asia'.[48] India's insurance motive for proliferation was also evident in its behavior after the 1974 test. For nearly one decade thereafter, the nuclear program consisted of awkward, oversized, tactically challenged bombs that were not integrated into military operations. They served as a political hedge against Chinese nuclear blackmail, not as strategically relevant assets.[49]

Prestige

The political currency that derives from proliferation in Asia is also related to issues of prestige and status. As Sagan has argued, states acquire nuclear weapons not only to balance against external threats, but also for their symbolic power.[50] For many countries in Asia, nuclear weapons and ballistic missiles are today what national armies were in the postcolonial era.[51] They serve as marks of modernity and power. Many post-Cold War analyses of Asian security have drawn attention to the region's avid nationalism – a function of history, colonial legacies, and economic growth.[52] Inherent in this nationalism are aspirations to rise in the international prestige hierarchy and to be treated as a 'great' or 'major' power. Nuclear weapons and ballistic missiles have become an important indicator of this status. In extreme terms, these capabilities almost become like national airlines – countries seek to acquire them because of how they reflect on one's identity and level of development.

In the case of nuclear weapons, this boost in prestige is most certainly a function of their awesome destructive power.[53] Nevertheless, it is also a function of careful observation of precedents and examples of nuclear prestige set in the West. For France, for example, after the colonial defeats in Southeast Asia and devastation of World War II, becoming a NWS state was an important symbol of its return to historical great-power status.[54] Some argue that, without nuclear weapons, the UK would have no special reason for claiming a permanent seat today on UN Security Council.[55] Perhaps most important for Asian eyes were the perceived prestige precedents set by China's nuclearization in the 1960s. China became the last enshrined member of the hallowed nuclear 'club' in 1970 (with the NPT) after which all others could only be NNWS or illegitimate NWS. Subsequent events such as Nixon's decision to visit China in 1971 (and Sino-American rapprochement), the ousting of Taiwan from the UN, and the bestowing of a permanent security council seat to Beijing were all seen as tangible elevations to China's international stature directly related to its nuclear status. These lessons were not lost on India.[56] New Delhi's attitude toward nuclear and missile capabilities is strongly influenced, as acknowledged by prominent Indians, by ambitions to achieve 'great-power status'. As two Indians noted: 'The bomb is a currency of self-esteem.' Or, as K. Subrahmanyam said, 'Nuclear weapons are not military weapons. Their logic is that of international politics and it is a logic of global, nuclear order ... India wants to be a player in, and not an object of, this global nuclear order'.[57] Prestige factors also mattered for Pakistan. Not just in the sense of being perceived as India's equal in South Asia, but also as the first Islamic country capable of such technological feats despite severe resource constraints. *Izzat* (honor) or *sharam* (shame) constituted the language in which the country pursued its nuclear and Ghauri missile programs.[58]

Security or Symbols?

The argument here is not that prestige and political currency are the primary drivers of proliferation in Asia. The mix of security-scarcity and resource constraints are still the most compelling reasons for states to perceive nuclear weapons at the most robust and efficient means of 'equalizing' power disadvantages. At the same time though, prestige and political currency factors are not merely peripheral or causally insignificant factors. Status concerns are more than just the language with which proliferators embellish or justify their drive for nuclear and missile programs.[59] Prestige concerns are more than just afterthoughts; at times they are also the forethoughts that inform or cause proliferation decisions.

The causal significance of these factors derives from the fact that anomalies in some preeminent cases of proliferation in Asia cannot be explained by basic security arguments. For example, the 1998 South Asian tests do not make strategic sense, strictly speaking, in that they showed little value-added militarily. The Indian tests exhibited some ability to miniaturize and weaponize with missiles, but neither set of tests showed an ability for increased accuracy in weapons and delivery vehicles to the point of being able to demonstrate counterforce targeting capabilities. Thus, the South Asian balance still rested on mutual deterrence based on countervalue capabilities – which means that the tests in terms of their payoff were more for symbolic reasons. They represented both countries' declared nuclear status and the shift away from recessed nuclear deterrence.[60]

Similarly, more anomalies appear if one looks at either the India-China or Pakistan-India dyad. If the purpose of testing is for deterrence, then one wants to make certain that one has achieved a threshold deterrent capability, *before* testing. In other words, you must have the infrastructure and the ability to 'plus-up' in capabilities rapidly (e.g., in terms of stockpiles of fissionable materials, missiles, warheads, command and control, etc.) prior to taking an act that declares your capability. Otherwise, testing without the capabilities and infrastructure would leave you vulnerable to preemption. Neither the Indian tests *vis-à-vis* the Chinese in 1974, nor the 1998 Pakistani tests *vis-à-vis* India reflect this logic.[61] In the former case, New Delhi was a decade away from weaponizing their capabilities, and therefore by testing was actually putting itself in a more vulnerable position, raising Beijing's incentive to preempt.

An alternative line of argument against the importance of the prestige and political currency factors in proliferation says that what may have been true in the past is no longer true today. In other words, proliferation gave rise to some benefits in terms of status and bargaining power to countries like China; however, since the NPT in 1970, and given the ostracism imposed by the nonproliferation community, any benefits from proliferation are fleeting and negated by the costs.[62]

While this argument may hold true in the future (and indeed should be a goal of the nonproliferation effort), as yet there is not enough evidence to suggest its validity. For example, in the South Asian cases, the net result of the tests has been far from negative. The US imposed sanctions on the two countries after May 1998 as mandated by 1994 Nuclear Proliferation Prevention Act, and withdrew support for World Bank and IMF loans, but one month later reinstated agricultural exports because of pressures from the American farm lobby, and by early November only retained sanctions that covered high technology and military exports as New Delhi and Islamabad announced testing moratoria and pledged to sign the CTBT.[63] In addition, although other nonproliferation leaders like Japan followed suit, sanctions were largely ineffective as the Japanese government did not prevent private companies from operating in India. Neither the United Nations, Group of Eight, nor the European Union took actions going beyond a verbal statement condemning the tests.[64] For Pakistan, Islamabad understood that responding to the Indian tests in May 1998 would attract economic sanctions, but it calculated that enthusiasm for punitive actions would fade as the world could not indefinitely sanction one-fifth of the world's population.[65] For India, arguably, the 'benefits' of testing were a Clinton-Vajpayee summit in March 2000 which resulted in the Agreed Principles – this agreement institutionalized a regular summit-level dialogue, foreign ministers meetings, finance and commerce minister meetings with the United States. Some argue that the 1998 tests marked a watershed in US attention to the South Asian problem, moving from policies that were poorly conceived, reactive, and ambivalent to uncharacteristic focus and organization.[66]

The costs of proliferating will be higher the more embedded the states are in the international arena, hence skewing the cost calculations for regimes like Pakistan and North Korea in favor of proliferation. Finding ways to raise these costs is part of the solution to nonproliferation (discussed in the regimes section below), but this does not discount prestige and political currency as causally significant factors for proliferation. Again, they do not outweigh the security factors, but operate along side them, sometimes playing a more prominent role. Without these variables, proliferation behavioral anomalies cannot be explained.

CONSEQUENCES OF PROLIFERATION: SOBER OPTIMISM

For reasons of security-scarcity, resource constraints, political currency, and First World hypocrisy, nuclear proliferation is overdetermined in Asia. Two implications follow from this observation: (1) proliferation is not likely to decline in the future because of the abundance of these causal factors; and

(2) the likelihood of getting new proliferators to rollback their capabilities is low.[67] As long as the causal factors that drive proliferation remain in abundance in Asia, the potential for vertical and horizontal proliferation remains real. What then are the consequences?

Proliferation Pessimism

'Proliferation pessimists' see grave implications of these trends in Asia.[68] Three basic arguments inform this viewpoint. The first focuses on the exceptionalist nature of the Cold War nuclear deterrence situation. The US-Soviet nuclear confrontation was based on a unique set of circumstances (i.e., territorial separation, absence of previous history of hostility, status quo orientations, simplicity of the bipolar rivalry) that made for a balance of terror and stable deterrence.[69] This experience is the obverse of Asia where one sees close proximity, high levels of inter-state conflict, antagonistic histories, and non-status quo orientations among many of the regional powers. Contrary to Waltzian-type arguments for nuclear stability, the exceptionalist school therefore argues that differentiation among the units matters in terms of outcomes, and that the non-use outcome experienced in the Cold War US-Soviet dyad is not replicable in post-Cold War Asia.

A second school of thought focuses on dangers associated with accidents, organizational flaws, judgement errors, and failed fail-safe systems, and argues that the many problems evident in elaborate systems constructed by the Americans and Soviets would be exponentially worse in the rudimentary systems in Asia.[70] A third set of arguments draws from preventive/preemptive war logic, and draws attention to the asymmetric advantages created by proliferation and how these advantages, particularly when they are either temporary or vulnerable to attack, give rise to windows of opportunity for preemptive or preventive action.[71]

While proliferation is likely to continue in Asia, this trend may not, however, warrant such a pessimistic assessment. If states are proliferating for three basic purposes (i.e., security; avoiding blackmail; and prestige and political currency), then the outcome may not be nearly as dire as the conventional wisdom predicts. This proposition neither assumes nor implies that nonproliferation is a futile or wasted effort. Instead, it argues that, aside from individual cases of rogue regime proliferation, there is not an intuitively obvious reason to equate Asian proliferation and the pessimist school's predictions of disastrous outcomes as many nonproliferation advocates have done. The reasoning in this vein is far from air tight and actually does a disservice to the nonproliferation school by basing its arguments on weak analogies or inconsistent logic.

Ethnocentrism

Either explicitly or implicitly informing all of the proliferation pessimism views are 'First World socialization' presumptions that the dangers of US-Soviet proliferation were mitigated by the abhorrence of violence among the public and political leadership, an understanding of the high stakes involved with such destructive weapons, and rational calculations. In the Third World, however, a combustible combination of historical resentments, religious rivalries, and hypernationalism makes nuclear weapons use more likely. One of the key differences between the first and second nuclear ages is that latter is dominated by fierce nationalism and fanatic leaders, who embrace nuclear and ballistic missile technology as the great equalizer against hated, mortal enemies. 'Asian nationalism harnesses all the immaturity and energy unleashed by the French Revolution and by communism in its expansionist heyday.'[72] This mindset contrasts with the former world with the cool and calm (albeit intense) competition of sophisticated thinkers, rational deterrence models and responsible leaders. As Bracken puts it, 'The idea of budding defense intellectuals sitting around computer models and debating strategy in Iran or Pakistan defies credulity.'[73]

There is no denying that Asia has its fair share of conflicts steeped in peer competition, history, race, and religion. Moreover, *han* (or unredeemed resentment) characterizes many of the dyads in which proliferation potential exists or has already been realized. Nevertheless, there is no evidence to validate the assumption that the animosities are necessarily the most raw and vulgar in Asia.[74] Some have even argued that in broad historical perspectives, the level of bloodshed in Asia pales in comparison with that in Europe.[75] There is no reason *a priori* to assume that the animosity in Asia is any more base or any less informed by rationality than the animosity and emotions that reigned during the first nuclear age.[76]

Moreover, the causal link between hate and nuclear action is spurious. In other words, even if one were to accept that Asian hatred and enmity are inherently more intense and primordial than in the West, there is no necessary connection with the propensity to use nuclear weapons. The decision to wage nuclear destruction on another is not based on how much you loath the opponent but on how much you value the target of your opponent's retaliation, your own constituency.[77] Hence ethnocentric arguments about nuclear exchanges in Asia should focus not on hate but on the willingness to commit suicide as the primary cause.

These arguments also fail to comprehend how the bipolar superpower experience has greatly prejudiced our thinking on nuclear deterrence and stability. As Goldstein notes, the conventional wisdom demonstrates an insufficient appreciation of the uniqueness rather than generalizability of the superpower experience.[78] For example, organizational arguments assume that the profile of the Asian programs as small and underdeveloped make them more prone to accidents, 'loose nukes', or inadvertent use. However, if the arsenals are small in size and few in number, they are, as a general rule, easier to monitor and control. In addition, many of the organizational pathologies made famous by Sagan require complexity in the nuclear infrastructure and decision-making trees – a precondition that is irrelevant in Asia because the infrastructures are basic and in many cases, divorced from the military bureaucracy (another pathology often mentioned).[79] In a similar vein, poor command, control, and communications infrastructures in Asia empirically have not resulted in 'use-or-lose' mentalities but have bred more caution (e.g. Indo-Pakistan conflicts). Limited overhead and reconnaissance capabilities have not encouraged confidence in the ability to hide one's arsenals but have discouraged confidence in carrying out successful first strikes. In addition, many of these small fledgling programs, by virtue of resource constraints, remain at underdeveloped stages (i.e., de-alerted, de-targeting, disassembled weapons systems, separated warheads from delivery vehicles).[80] Therefore, until an accident or outcome confirms the organizational school's view in the second nuclear age, and given what is now being unearthed about the near-misses and near-disasters in the first nuclear age, there is no *a priori* reason to assume a necessary causal connection between small programs and de-stabilizing outcomes.

Existential Deterrence

Proliferation pessimists fixate on assured second-strike capabilities as the primary agent of deterrence and underestimate the validity of other forms of deterrence among smaller nuclear powers. The pessimist's assessment rests on faith in the 'use or lose' logic – that is, that when states do not have assured second-strike capabilities, they live in constant fear of being vulnerable to a debilitating first strike. Thus, in a crisis between adversaries with small nuclear forces, the incentive to preempt (as well as the fear of being preempted upon) becomes high, giving rise to a destabilizing 'use-or-lose' mentality.[81]

There are two problems with this argument. First, in deductive terms, there is no denying that assured second-strike capabilities can form the backbone of stable deterrence; however, it does not mean that the *absence* of this condition necessarily leads to instability. Second, the empirical record does not bear out the 'use-or-lose' argument. As Hagerty notes, in all of the crises involving smaller nuclear powers (Cuba 1962, Sino-Soviet 1969, Arab–Israeli 1973, Kashmir 1990), preemption has not occurred.[82] Instead what appears to operate among smaller nuclear powers is existential deterrence: '... the mere existence of nuclear forces means that, whatever we say or do, there is a certain irreducible risk that an armed conflict might escalate into a nuclear war. The fear of escalation is thus factored into political calculations: faced with this risk, states are more cautious and more prudent than they otherwise would be.'[83]

What therefore prevails in the second nuclear age in Asia may not be assured second-strike capability but 'first-strike uncertainty'. Stable deterrence derives from having just enough capabilities to raise uncertainty in the mind of the opponent that s/he cannot neutralize you with a first-strike. The precedent for this form of deterrence had already been set by the second-tier nuclear powers in the first age. As Goldstein's study shows, existential deterrent doctrines drove China, Britain, and France's pursuit of an independent but not second-strike assured nuclear deterrent against their respective superpower adversaries.[84] In the new nuclear age in Asia where cost constraints among new proliferators will be acute, smaller arsenals counter-intuitively will not incite attack. In addition, the opaque conditions under which programs in Asia develop enhance first-strike uncertainty, as worst-case assessments generally tend to err on the side of caution.

The South Asian case appears thus far to validate existential deterrent claims. Both countries will not be able to develop an assured survivable force because of resource constraints. Moreover, neither will possess the missile guidance and accuracy capability to move beyond countervalue targeting. However, both will have sufficient fissile material for a small number of atomic bombs on aircraft (Mirage, MiG-27, MiG-29, SU-30 and Jaguar for India or the A-5, F-16 and Mirage 3 for Pakistan); and the potential for weaponized warheads on some ballistic missiles (Prithvi 150 for India and Hatf 2 for Pakistan), but not to the level of a successful first-strike.[85] Neither country has attempted preemptive destruction of the other's nuclear facilities and both signed a Non-Attack agreement in 1991 based on their *de facto* nuclear status. The fact that these are now *de jure* capabilities should not make a difference.[86] India's draft nuclear doctrine makes reference to pursuing a triad, but most experts see this as 'grandiose', and contradictory with India's other stated and more realistic objective of a minimum deterrent.[87] Nuclear weapons have instilled a fear of escalation in bilateral conflicts that tempers actions on both sides. In the Indo-Pakistani crises of 1987, and especially 1990 and 1999, many site the dampening effect that New Delhi's explicit concern about rapid ascent up the ladder of escalation had on behavior.[88]

Nuclear Taboo

Another factor reinforcing the stability of first-strike uncertainty in the second nuclear age is the potential for new nuclear powers to become compliant with the norms against nuclear weapons use. As Russett argues, the first nuclear age recognized that such weapons were in fact unusable across much of the range of military and political interests. Despite the absence of restricting international laws or conventions and explicit threat of symmetrical retaliation, nuclear powers refrained from using such weapons in military situations where it could have altered a neutral or losing outcome. The United States did not use them in Korea or Vietnam, the Soviets did not use them in Afghanistan, and the Chinese did not use them in Vietnam.[89]

Proliferation pessimists do not deny the existence of the nuclear taboo; they do, nevertheless, see this taboo as shared only by First World proliferators. Is this a fair assessment? As Tannenwald argues, a taboo takes effect when the agent realizes (1) the exceptionalist nature of the weapon (i.e., in terms of its destructive power); (2) the absence of effective defenses (i.e., vulnerability); (3) and fears the political and social consequences of taking such an action. All of these conditions readily hold for new nuclear powers. Moreover, the revulsion against nuclear weapons use (first-use) has become so institutionalized in an array of international agreements and practices such that new NWS states operate in an environment that severely circumscribes the realm of legitimate nuclear use.[90]

Proliferation pessimists therefore underestimate the *transformative* effects of nuclear weapons on these new proliferators. They assume that the interests for aspiring nuclear powers remain constant in the pre- and post-acquisition phases. They do not consider that once states cross the nuclear threshold, they become acutely aware of the dangers and responsibilities that come with these new awesome capabilities. The likelihood of such a learning process occurring is even higher if nuclear weapons are valued for their political currency. As noted above, while security needs certainly drive proliferation in Asia, a predominant factor that cannot be disentangled from this dynamic is the striving for prestige and international recognition as an NWS state. Moreover, if the taboo equates the use of nuclear weapons with an 'uncivilized' or 'barbarian' state,[91] then those states that are status-conscious will be that much more attuned to the taboo. The effects of the taboo on Asian proliferators are therefore both regulative and constitutive. In the former sense, as these states further embed themselves in the international community (discussed below), this change heightens the costs of breaking any rules regarding nuclear use. The taboo's constitutive effects also are evident in that any use would undermine one of the primary purposes for which the capabilities were sought (e.g., prestige, badge of modernity).

Although it is still relatively early in the game, there is some evidence that the acquisition of nuclear capabilities has been accompanied by a change in preferences about what is acceptable behavior. While India has rejected any notions that it might roll back its newfound capability, it has readily admitted that as an incipient nuclear weapons state, it now has certain responsibilities that include a no-first-use policy and not sharing nuclear weapons technology with other irresponsible states.[92] Similarly, Pakistan previously placed little value and even resented nonproliferation norms as these were seen as inhibiting and degrading to the national character.[93] Otherwise, they might have been swayed by the *benefits* of not responding to the Indian tests as a shining example of a country adhering to nuclear nonproliferation norms. Arguably it is only after becoming an incipient nuclear weapons state that such arguments about nonproliferation gain value. Nowhere is this perverse dynamic more evident than in both sides' views of the CTBT. Previously perceived as an instrument intended to preempt nuclear spread beyond the first age, the CTBT is now arguably seen by India and Pakistan in less antagonistic terms, and even among some, as a responsibility to be borne as a nuclear state.

CONCLUSION: THE ROLE OF THE NONPROLIFERATION REGIME? MORE SOBER OPTIMISM

This contribution has made two points with regard to proliferation in Asia. First, proliferation is overdetermined, and hence rollback, though desirable, is unlikely. Second, while the likelihood of continued Asian proliferation in the future is real (given the abundance of causes), this tendency does not necessarily presage disastrous consequences for regional stability (contrary to proliferation pessimists).

What then are the implications of this argument for the nonproliferation regime? First, the argument does *not* connote the irrelevance or futility of nonproliferation. It does, however, imply that nonproliferation arguments based on an inherent equating of new proliferation with irrational and/or inadvertent nuclear use are spurious (and ultimately do a disservice to the objectives of the nonproliferation community). Second, the argument shows that the challenges faced by the nonproliferation advocates are formidable. The abundance of causes means that more states will likely try to proliferate, and that if they are successful, rollback, although ideal, will be difficult except in specific circumstances.[94] Moreover, the nonproliferation community's focus on rollback may actually be detrimental to stability because it fails to acknowledge the security factors that drove proliferation in the first place. Without addressing the former, one cannot have rollback of the latter: 'Non-proliferation is the means and security the end, not vice-versa.'[95] Rollback should not be a normative prescription but a pragmatic decision based on an assessment of the region's proliferation drivers.

Third, because rollback is problematic, where the nonproliferation community's efforts are at a premium are in terms of (1) stopping proliferation before it happens, and (2) maintaining and reinforcing a robust norm against nuclear non-use. Indeed, fostering the region's compliance with existing global regimes on the control of technology and materials, as well as building upon existing regional and bilateral institutions, can greatly reinforce the non-use outcome in Asia.

At first glance, the region's record of compliance with global conventions and international treaties appears weak and inconsistent.[96]

Moreover, the absence of leadership among the First World nuclear powers (particularly the US on failure to ratify the CTBT and discussions of NMD and revision of the ABM treaty) only reinforce perceptions of First World hypocrisy among the new proliferators.[97]

Despite these setbacks, there is still room for optimism. Even though key states like Pakistan, India, and the DPRK remain outside the NPT regime, the treaty's indefinite extension in 1995 sets an important precedent with regard to universal membership and compliance which these states cannot simply ignore or dismiss. Moreover, Chinese participation in arms control and nonproliferation regimes over the past 15 years has increased substantially. In addition to membership in the NPT, CWC and BWC, China became a Zangger Committee member in 1997. Despite earlier transfers of nuclear technology and missile parts to the Middle East and the South Asian subcontinent, Beijing has since committed to adhering to the NSG triggers list and to abide by the MTCR principles in a bilateral agreement with the US (see Tables 2 and 3). In addition, it announced a self-imposed testing moratorium in 1996 and has committed to upholding the CTBT despite the US failure to ratify. Beijing also acceded to the Rarotonga protocols in 1997 (see Table 4, p.120), and supports FMCT negotiations.[98] While not a perfect record, the situation still is far from hopeless.

In addition, at the regional and sub-regional level, one development that raises confidence in the region's ability to organize support for nonproliferation institutions are the nuclear weapons-free zones. Four exist today, of which two are in Asia.

TABLE 2
GLOBAL REGIMES

Country	IAEA	CD	NSG	ZAC	MTCR	AG	WAAS	Comments
US	Yes	Yes	Yes	Yes	Yes	Yes	Yes	
Russia	Yes	Yes	Yes	Yes	Yes	Yes	Yes	
China to join.	Yes	Yes	No – invited Declined Adheres in principle to NSG trigger lists	Yes (97)	bilat w/US	No – declined US offer 97 to join	No – urged to join by US but declined	ZAC member 1997; Bilat w/US on MTCR 1992
Japan	Yes	Yes – supports goal of total elim nukes	Yes	Yes	Yes – original member	Yes	Yes – original member	AG original member
DPRK	Yes	Yes	No	No	No	No	No	
ROK	Yes	Yes	Yes	Yes	No	Yes	Yes	AG member 1996
ROC	No	N/a	No	No	No	No	No	
India	Yes	Yes	No	No	No	No	No	

TABLE 2 (Contd)

Country	IAEA	CD	NSG	ZAC	MTCR	AG	WAAS	Comments
Pakistan	Yes	Yes	No	No	No	No	No	
Australia	Yes	Yes	Yes	Yes	Yes	Yes	Yes	
NZ	Yes	Yes	Yes	No	Yes	Yes	Yes	

Source: compiled from *Inventory of International Nonproliferation Organizations and Regimes: 1996–1997* (Monterey, CA: Center for Nonproliferation Studies 1997); 'Northeast Asian Participation in Arms Control/Nonproliferation Regimes', available on the Center for Nonproliferation Studies website at >http://cns.miis.edu/cns/projects/eanp/fact/nearegms.htm<; 'Japanese Participation and Positions Regarding Various Arms Control and Nonproliferation Agreements, Organizations, and Regimes, July 1999', at >http://cns.miis.edu/cns/projects/eanp/fact/japan.htm<.

Notes:
IAEA: International Atomic Energy Agency (established 1957). To encourage atomic energy usage for peaceful purposes and administer safeguards to ensure that not used for military purposes.
CD: Conference on Disarmament (established 1979). Primary multilateral disarmament negotiating forum of intl community.
NSG: Nuclear Suppliers Group (established 1975). Also known as 'London Club' ensure that nuclear exports made only under appropriate safeguards, physical protection and nonproliferation conditions. Requires IAEA safeguards as condition of supply of nuclear materials and restricts supply to countries with proliferation potential.
ZAC: Zangger Committee (established 1971). Trigger list of fissionable materials and equipment for purpose of processing, use or production of fissionable materials. Status is informal. Not legally binding on members.
MTCR: Missile Tech Control Regime (established 1987). Informal nontreaty association of governments with common interests in nonproliferation of missiles, UAVs and related technologies. Equipment and systems restricted are for missiles greater than 300 km, 500 kg payload, bio/chem capable missiles, and solid/liquid propellant engines.
AG: Australia Group (established 1985). Informal association works on basis of consensus. To limit spread of CBW through control of chemical precursors, equipment and BW agents and organisms (dual-use chemicals).
WAAS: Wassenaar Arrangement on Export Controls for Conventional Arms and Dual-Use Goods and Technologies (established 1995). Successor to COCOM.

TABLE 3
INTERNATIONAL TREATIES

Country	NPT	CTBT	PTBT	BWC/CWC	OST/SBT	Geneva/OPCW	IWC	Nuke material	Comments
US	Yes	Signed/no	Yes ratify	Yes/yes	Yes/Yes	Yes/Yes	?	?	
Russia	Yes	Signed/no	Yes ratify	Yes/Yes	Yes/Yes	Yes/No	Yes	Yes	
China	Yes	Signed/no ratify – unilateral moratorium on testing 1996	No	Yes/Yes	Yes/Yes	Yes/Yes	Yes	Yes	Working with Japan on joint project to clean up chemical weapons left in C
Japan	Yes – supported indefinite extension	signed/ ratify 1997	Yes	Yes/Yes	Yes/Yes	Yes/Yes – founding member OPCW	Yes	Yes	BWC ratified 1982; ratified CWC 1995
DPRK	Yes	No	No	Yes/No	No/No	Yes/No	No	No	Threatened NPT withdrawal 1996
ROK	Yes	Signed/no ratify	Yes	Yes/Yes	Yes/Yes	Yes/Yes	No	Yes	

TABLE 3 (Contd)

Country	NPT	CTBT	PTBT	BWC/CWC	OST/SBT	Geneva/OPCW	IWC	Nuke material	Comments
ROC	(Yes)	No	(Yes)	No/No	(Yes)/(Yes)	(Yes)/(No)	No	No	
India	No	No – tried to lock draft treaty because saw as NWS Discrimination	Yes	Yes/Yes	Signed and ratified	?/Yes	Yes	?	Clinton-Vajpayee joint statement 3/00 that withdrawl forgo nuclear tests
Pakistan	No	No – refused to sign 1996 unless India did	Yes	Yes/Yes	Signed and Ratified	??	Signed	?	
Australia	Yes	Signed and ratified	Yes	Yes/Yes	Signed and Ratified	?/Yes	Signed and ratified	?	
NZ	Signed and ratified	Signed and ratified	Yes	Yes/Yes	Signed and ratified	??	Signed and ratified	?	

Source: compiled from *Inventory of International Nonproliferation Organizations and Regimes: 1996–1997* (Monterey, CA: Center for Nonproliferation Studies 1997); 'Northeast Asian Participation in Arms Control/Nonproliferation Regimes', available on the Center for Nonproliferation Studies, website at >http://www.cns.miis.edu/cns/projects/eanp/fact/nearegms.htm<; 'Japanese Participation and Positions Regarding Various Arms Control and Nonproliferation Agreements, Organizations, and Regims, July 1999', at >http://www.cns.miis.edu/cns/projects/eanp/fact/japan.htm<.

TABLE 3 (Contd)

Notes:

NPT: Treaty on the Nonproliferation of Nuclear Weapons (1970). NWS do not transfer nuclear weapons. NNWS do not receive nuclear weapons. 187 member states of which 5 are NWS. Only 4 states remain non-parties: Cuba, India, Pakistan, and Israel.

CTBT: Comprehensive Test Ban Treaty (1996). Opened for signature. Bans any nuclear weapon test explosion.

PTBT: Partial Test Ban Treaty (Banning Nuclear Weapon Tests in the Atmosphere, Outer Space and Under Water): 1963. Bans nuclear weapon tests in atmosphere, outer space and underwater and anywhere where fallout spills outside of territorial borders. Precursor to CTBT. And if states cannot ratify CTBT, they are still under obligations of PTBT.

BWC/CWC: Convention on Prohibition of the Development, Production and Stockpiling of Bacteriological (Biological) and Toxin Weapons (entered into force 1975); Convention on Prohibition of the Development, Production, Stockpiling, and Use of Chemical Weapons (opened for signature 1993). BTWC - not to develop, produce, stockpile or otherwise acquire or obtain microbial or other biological agents or toxins for nonpeaceful purposes and to destroy or divert to peaceful uses any such items within 9 months of signing; CWC – same restrictions for chemical weapons. Signatories must destroy within 10 years all weapons and production facilities.

OST: Outer Space Treaty (1967). Prohibits use of outer space for military purposes. No weapons on objects that orbit the earth. Use of outer space for peaceful purposes.

SBT: Seabed Treaty (1972). Not to embed in seabed outside 12-mile territorial limit any nuclear weapons, or WMD and installations for such purpose.

Geneva Protocol: Protocol for the Prohibition of the Use in War of Asphyxiating, Poisonous, or Other Gases, and of Bacteriological Methods of Warfare (1925). Signatories reserve the right to exception if others resort to CW use.

OPCW: Organization for the Prohibition of Chemical Weapons (1997). Came into being after entry into force of CWC. Implementing and verification body for CWC.

IWC: Inhumane Weapons Convention (1983). Not to use weapons that create non-detectable fragments; not to mine against civilian populations; not to use incendiary weapons against civilians or air-delivered incendiaries.

Nuke Material: Convention on the Physical Protection of Nuclear Material (1987). For physical protection of nuclear materials during international transport (plutonium, uranium 235 and 233, irradiated fuel).

These generally entail a legal obligation to place all nuclear materials and installations under full-scope IAEA safeguards; clearly demarcate geographic limits of the NWFZ; and specify the obligations, rights, and responsibilities of parties with regard to disavowing nuclear weapons. For example, the South Pacific Nuclear Free Zone (Treaty of Rarotonga) of 1986 forbids the manufacture, acquisition, possession, or control by its member states of any nuclear explosive device inside or outside the treaty zone. It also forbids testing, stationing, dumping or transfer of nuclear materials or equipment to any state not subject to IAEA safeguards. In addition the regime has been relatively successful in getting the NWS to observe the three Protocols of 1996 barring them from similar activity in the region.[99]

Because nuclear and missile programs in Asia are not likely to disappear, embedding these programs in global nonproliferation regimes as well as encouraging the creation of new regional institutions can reinforce stability in Asia in two ways that support nonproliferation objectives. First, such institutions ensure that the barriers to entry regarding nuclear and missile capabilities remains high. If nuclear rollback is not a feasible option, then the next best option is to make acquisition of these capabilities as difficult and costly as possible. This factor contributes to the non-use outcome in Asia by at least slowing the pace of proliferation. It also lowers the danger of accidents as those that undertake the efforts to surmount these barriers are also likely to be the more responsible proliferators. Second, such institutions create normative pressures to forgo acquisition as parties deeply enmeshed in the regimes greatly discount the benefits of going nuclear by the reputational costs of violating the regimes. Moreover, for those that have already proliferated, the robustness of these regimes further socializes these states to the nuclear taboo.

Based on the region's current nonproliferation activities, two additional possibilities deserve mention. One is a limited nuclear weapons-free zone in Northeast Asia centered on the Korean peninsula and Japan (after moderation of the North Korean threat). The foundation for such an institution could be built upon a 'bundling' of events in the region that act as permissive factors to such a zone: the 1992 North-South De-nuclearization Declaration; KEDO; Japan's non-nuclear principles; the 1994 Agreed Framework and the 1991 US declaration regarding the removal of nuclear weapons from the region.[100] Track II groups have looked at various proposals in this regard.[101] In South Asia, there is little likelihood of a nuclear-free zone. The salience of unresolved conflicts renders rollback difficult and heightens the regional players' perceived need for deterrent capabilities. Nevertheless, this does not negate the potential for a no-first-use zone. Sucha zone could be 'bundled' around the India-Pakistan Non-Attack Agreement of 1988,[102] the South Asian Association for Regional Cooperation (SAARC),[103] and the Clinton-Vajpayee summit joint vision statement (in which India in principle supports forgoing of future tests; seeks support of starting talks on FMCT; and supports export controls).[104] Other possibilities include a Northeast Asia fissile material register and a North and South Asia technology control regime.[105]

Thus, an assessment of sober optimism with regard to the consequences of proliferation in Asia does not preclude the importance of current or future nonproliferation regimes. These regimes are not only critical to raising the material and reputational costs of proliferating, but also reinforcing norms of safety and taboos on non-use, once proliferation has occurred. For nonproliferation advocates, however, to focus on nuclear rollback in Asia without addressing the causes (of which there are many) is fruitless.

Finally, the case for sober optimism is not implying that all will be rosy in Asia. Nuclear weapons will not have an inherent pacifying effect on conflicts and rivalries in the region. On the contrary, such rivalries will continue and may even heighten. Indeed there may be more saber rattling and swaggering; attempts at political coercion, hostile rhetoric and threats, and even sub-nuclear conflicts in the new nuclear age in Asia. Nevertheless, there is nothing as yet that can lead one to argue conclusively that, relative to the first nuclear world, such conflicts are more likely to escalate and that this second nuclear age is more dangerous. Such conflicts are undoubtedly worrying, but they do not necessarily undermine the reality of a minimum deterrent Asian nuclear world bounded by taboos on nuclear use.

ACKNOWLEDGEMENTS

An earlier and different version of this contribution was presented as a paper at the Workshop on Security Order in the Asia-Pacific sponsored by the East-West Center and the Center for Strategic and International Studies, Bali, Indonesia, 29 May–2 June 2000. The author thanks Muthiah Alagappa, Barry Buzan, Sumit Ganguly, Avery Goldstein, Peter Katzenstein, and Aki Tanaka for comments on earlier drafts.

NOTES

1. In this contribution, Asia will include both Northeast and South Asia. I will focus mostly on China, Japan, and the two Koreas in Northeast Asia; and Pakistan and India in South Asia.
2. This is admittedly less the case for China. On second-tier nuclear powers in the first nuclear age, see Avery Goldstein, *Deterrence and Security in the 21st Century: China, Britain, France and the Enduring Legacy of the Nuclear Revolution* (Stanford UP 2000).
3. China remains the only power besides Russia with the ICBM capability to reach the United States and until a recent US-China non-targeting agreement (June 1998) was believed to have the majority of its long-range ICBM force of 20 missiles targeted on the US (it is believed to keep its missiles unfueled and without warheads separated).
4. The bomber leg of the triad are approximately 120 Hong-6 bombers (range of 3100km, each capable of delivering 1–3 bombs of 10KT–3MT); and 30 Qian-5A attack aircraft (range of 400 km, capable of delivering one nuclear bomb 10KT–3MT) deployed in 1965 and 1970 respectively. The sea-based leg consists of about 12 JL-1 SLBMs deployed in 1986 on one *Xia*-class submarine. Experts consider both the air- and sea-based legs of the triad less threatening. The bomber force is old, highly vulnerable to air defense, and incapable of reaching the US. The SLBM program has proved less successful despite the four decades of development invested in it. In addition, China is believed to possess about 150 tactical weapons made up of low-yield bombs, artillery shells, atomic demolition munitions and short-range missiles (although it does not officially acknowledge possession of tactical weapons). For a concise overview, see Robert Manning, Ronald Montaperto and Brad Roberts, *China, Nuclear Weapons, and Arms Control* (NY: Council on Foreign Relations 2000) pp.15–37.

5. China conducted its first nuclear test in 1964. It exploded a hydrogen weapon in 1966 and began production of nuclear weapons in 1968 and thermonuclear weapons in 1974.
6. India's most capable operational missile, the Prithvi-150, has a 1000kg payload and a range of 150km, although it has tested and developed longer-range systems (e.g., Agni). Modernization plans include the acquisition of submarine-launch capabilities. India also possesses an ambitious space-launch vehicle program for which the ready availability of guidance sets and warheads give them additional recessed BM capabilities.
7. Pakistan's most capable missile, the Hatf 2, has a 500kg payload and range of 280 km, although it has test launched longer-range missiles (e.g. Ghauri). The SRBM industry includes rocket motor production and test facilities. Substantial support for the Hatf series has come in the past from China (M-11 equipment transfers in the early 1990s). More recently, Pakistan has concentrated its efforts on testing and development of 1300–3500km range of the Ghauri and Shaheen series largely based on transfers of the North Korean Nodong missile series (see Table 1). Neither country is a member of the Missile Technology Control Regime (MTCR)
8. Three operating reactors are under IAEA safeguards (KANUPP power reactor in Karachi, PARR I and PARR II research reactors near Islamabad) Chashma nuclear power plant also is under IAEA safeguards. Pakistan also operates un-safeguarded reactors that are capable of producing weapons-grade plutonium
9. Despite its dire material constraints, North Korea accomplished this progress largely through reverse-engineering of Scud-B missile technology acquired from the Soviet Union. North Korea's first indigenous operational missile, the Nodong series, derives from Scud technology. The Aug. 1998 test flight of the Taepodong 1 over Japan demonstrated an unexpected leap in IRBM technology (albeit a failed 3-stage payload launch). In defiance of MTCR norms and often described as the agent that could single-handedly undermine the entire regime, North Korea has been the most active producer and provider of Scud missiles and missile technology to Iran, Syria and Pakistan; concerns abound regarding future proliferation of longer-range systems (e.g., Pakistan's Ghauri and Shaheen series are derivative of Nodong technology). For further discussions, see Evan Medeiros, *Northeast Asia in 1999: Current Threats to Nonproliferation Regimes*, CNS Occasional Paper 3 (n.d.), Center for Nonproliferation Studies (see >http://cns.miss.edu/ pubs/opapers/op3/ medeiros.htm<, p.4.
10. A peaceful uses of atomic energy agreement with the Soviet Union enabled North Korea to develop a small nuclear research reactor and a basic understanding of nuclear physics, engineering, and reactor operations.
11. Concerns abound regarding possible reprocessing activities in 1989 and May–June 1994, that would have provided the DPRK with enough weapons-grade plutonium for several nuclear weapons.
12. This transfer capability largely occurs through the capacity to produce highly enriched uranium (for reactor use early in the fuel cycle), and to reprocess plutonium and/or accumulate plutonium from the spent fuel. The former material forms the core of the atom bomb (used at Hiroshima) and the latter the implosion bomb used at Nagasaki. Crude implosion bombs require no more than 10kg of plutonium, which is a fraction of what can be extracted from the spent fuel of a civilian nuclear reactor (for the general point, see Scott Sagan, 'Why Do States Build Nuclear Weapons?', *International Security* 21/3 (Winter 1996–97) pp.56–7).
13. For resource-poor countries in Asia, nuclear electricity is price competitive with coal-based electricity (assuming stable capital costs for plant construction). Some argue that nuclear electricity is actually cheaper than coal-based energy because coast calculations for the former include cautionary expenses related to disposal, safety, and radiation protection, while the latter do not factor in the cost of pollution and other negative externalities (see Michael May, *Energy and Security in East Asia*, A/PARC Working Paper (Stanford University, Jan. 1998) p.20)).
14. By contrast, the US is estimated to reduce by ten percent its nuclear energy capacity by 2010. South Korea stands out as likely to experience the largest relative increase in nuclear energy capacity in the next decade, more than doubling its current capacity (not including

the additional power generation stemming from two 1000 MW reactors in North Korea as a result of the 1994 Agreed Framework implementation).

15. For further discussions, see Eiichi Katahara, 'Japan's Plutonium Policy: Consequences for Nonproliferation', *The Nonproliferation Review* 5/1 (Fall 1997); Selig Harrision (ed.) *Japan's Nuclear Future* (Washington DC: Carnegie Endowment for International Peace 1996); and 'Energy and Security in Northeast Asia: Fueling Security', IGCC Policy Paper No. 35 (La Jolla, CA: IGCC 1998) pp.20–1. For more general concerns also see Kent Calder, *Pacific Defense* (NY: William Morrow 1996) pp.62–74.

16. Regarding ballistic missiles, Japanese capabilities for ICBM arsenals deriving from their Space Launch Vehicle (SLV) program are well known, as are the normative and constitutional constraints to doing so. Gaining more recent attention have been ROK missile capabilities. These are modest based on a 1979 bilateral agreement with Washington that limited ROK missile ranges to 180km (the quid pro quo for this voluntary agreement was the transfer of US technology for the South's Nike-Hercules-2 missile). However, ROK intentions with the agreement's expiration (1999) and with the North's BM program have been for more independent development of longer-range missiles (pursuant to the DPRK Taepodong test flight in August 1998, the ROK tested a surface-to-surface missile [April 1999] demonstrating Seoul's capabilities and determination to develop a more advanced missile deterrent). US-ROK bilateral discussions center around an upgrading of ROK missile capabilities in line with MTCR guidelines, but Seoul's aspirations are for research and development of missile ranges in excess of this understanding. The South Koreans also have aspirations for an SLV program. While ROK BM capabilities are less advanced than Japan's, arguably they are also less 'recessed'. On the BM and SLV programs, see Victor Cha, 'The Economic Crisis, Strategic Culture, and the Military Modernization of South Korea', *Armed Forces and Society* (forthcoming).

17. See Sagan's 'security model', in Sagan (note 12); John Deutsch, 'The New Nuclear Threat', *Foreign Affairs* 71/41 (Fall 1992); and Goldstein (note 2).

18. Goldstein (note 2) p.57.

19. For further discussions on the relative advantages of nuclear over conventional deterrents, see Goldstein (note 2) pp.35–40, 54–5.

19a. Goldstein (note 2) p.225.

20. Manning *et al.* (note 4) pp.15–16; John Wilson Lewis and Xue Litai, *China Builds the Bomb* (Stanford UP 1988); Goldstein (note 2) ch.3, pp.62–7, 250–1; Paul Godwin, 'China's Nuclear Forces: An Assessment', *Current History* (Sept. 1999); and Chong-Pin Lin, *China's Nuclear Weapons Strategy* (Lexington, MA: Lexington Books 1988).

21. India was roundly defeated in the 1962 war over territorial disputes that remain unresolved today. As Hagerty claims, 'The national security roots of India's nuclear weapon programme lie in the 1963 [*sic*] defeat, and in China's 1964 nuclear explosive test. The programme's *raison d'être* is to deter another attack by China, which, while considered highly unlikely, cannot be entirely ruled out by any future leader.' Devin Hagerty, 'South Asia's Big Bangs', *Australian Journal of International Affairs* 53/1 (1999) pp.20–1; Muthiah Alagappa, 'International Response to Nuclear Tests in South Asia: The Need for a New Policy Framework', *Asia-Pacific Issues* 38 (15 June 1998) East-West Center, p.5.

22. Indian requests for such guarantees were raised at the UN Disarmament Conference (and after the 1965 Indo-Pakistan war) as a quid pro quo for British and American efforts to halt further proliferation in the aftermath of the Chinese test. The issue came up again in 1968 when the US, UK and Soviets sought India's accession to the NPT without offering credible guarantees to non-nuclear weapons. One could attribute at least partially the delay between Indian threat perceptions in 1965 and the decision to test in 1974 to Indira Gandhi's Aug. 1971 treaty of peace with the Soviet Union which Ganguly argues has been underestimated in terms of the security guarantees provided to India by Moscow (Sumit Ganguly, 'India's Pathway to Pokhran II', *International Security* 23/4 (Spring 1999) pp.153–7, 159).

23. Ganguly (note 22) pp.162–4; Alagappa (note 21) p.7.

24. Alagappa (note 21); Sandy Gordon, 'Capping South Asia's Nuclear Programs', *Asian Survey* 34/7 (July 1994) pp.662–73; and Hagerty (note 21) pp.20–1.

25. Indian perceptions with regarding to closing windows of opportunity with passage of the Comprehensive Test Ban Treaty (CTBT) in 1996 discussed below.

26. As Hagerty puts it, the 1971 war was for Pakistan what the 1962 war was for India. The core aim of Pakistani nuclearization from then on was to avoid a repetition of the humiliating defeat in 1971 (where Indian superior conventional capabilities enabled a successful intervention in the Pakistani civil war). See Hagerty (note 21) p.22; Samina Yasmeen, 'Pakistan's Nuclear Tests: Domestic Debate and International Determinants', *Australian Journal of International Affairs* 53/1 (1999) pp.43–4; also see Mohammad Aslam, *Dr. A.Q. Khan and Pakistan's Nuclear Programme* (Rawalpindi: Diplomat Publications 1989).

27. Proponents of this view also pointed to Secretary Albright and Undersecretary Pickering's visits to New Delhi in Oct. 1997 and Energy Secretary Bill Richardson's April 1998 visit as evidence of America's new embedding of South Asia policy in the larger Sino-American context. The US offered a variety of incentives to Islamabad not to respond to the Indian test (e.g., a high-level visit to Washington; repeal of the Pressler Amendment and release of previously suspended purchase of 28 F-16s; and $5 billion in World Bank and IMF loans over 5 years), but provided no concrete assurances against an Indian use of nuclear weapons (see Yasmeen (note 26) pp.43–4, 46; Samina Ahmed, 'Pakistan's Nuclear Weapons Program: Turning Points and Nuclear Choices', *International Security* 23/4 (Spring 1999) pp.180–90; and Hagerty (note 21) p.22).

28. This interpretation assumes some degree of deterrence-motivation with regard to DPRK intentions. An alternative interpretation that saw DPRK intentions as aggressive and revisionist would not assign such defensive motivations to North Korea's proliferation of nuclear and ballistic missile capabilities. For a discussion of revisionist intentions behind North Korea's proliferation, see Victor Cha, 'Making Sense of the Black Box: Hypotheses on Strategic Doctrine and the DPRK Threat', in Samuel Kim (ed.) *The North Korean System* (Palgrave, forthcoming). Also see Leon Sigal, *Disarming Strangers* (Princeton UP 1998).

29. See Victor D. Cha, *Alignment Despite Antagonism: The United States-Korea-Japan Security Triangle* (Stanford UP 2000) Ch.3.

30. On additional discussions regarding the link between the forward presence in Japan and Korea and attitudes toward the nuclear umbrella, see Narushige Michishita,'Alliances After Peace in Korea', *Survival* 41/3 (Fall 1999) pp.68–83.

31. The exception that proves the rule here is Japan.

32. Hagerty (note 21) pp.21–2.

33. Paul Bracken, 'Asia's Militaries and the New Nuclear Age', *Current History* 98/632 (Dec. 1999) pp.415–21.

34. See George Percovich, *India's Nuclear Bomb: The Impact of Global Proliferation* (Berkeley: Univ. of California 1999); and Bracken (note 26).

35. Yasmeen (note 26) p.44.

36. For examples of such contradictions in the US Secretary of Defense Annual Report 2000 and the 1999 NATO Strategic Concept, see Daniel Plesch, 'Anarchy in Action: Western Policy on Weapons of Mass Destruction', *Global Beat* (April 2000) >www.nyu.edu/ globalbeat/ nuclear/plesch0400.html<. Also see Hagerty (note 21) pp.27–8.

37. Goldstein (note 2) pp.228, 234–5.

38. On the latter point as an impediment to Japan's leading role in nonproliferation efforts, see Eiichi Katahara, 'Japan's Plutonium Policy: Consequences for Nonproliferation', *The Nonproliferation Review* 5/1 (Fall 1997).

39. Alagappa (note 21) p.3.

40. Samina Ahmed, 'Pakistan's Nuclear Weapons Program', *International Security* 23/4 (Spring 1999) p.185.

41. Jaswant Singh, 'Against Nuclear Apartheid', *Foreign Affairs* 77/5 (Sept.–Oct. 1998) pp.41–52.

42. Ganguly (note 22) p.158.

43. Hagerty (note 21) p.27–8; and Singh (note 41) p.41.

44. Such concerns prompted Prime Minister Rao to begin preparations for an Indian test at the

end of 1995 on the grounds that it was 'now or never' (see Ganguly, note 22, p.168). The test was never carried out.

45. See Victor Cha, 'Engaging North Korea Credibly', *Survival* 42/2 (Summer 2000) pp.136–55.

46. These quotations come from Yasmeen (note 26) p.54. Similarly, when Pakistan realized that the implicit threat of nuclear action succeeded in deterring India from transversing the Line of Control in the 1990 Kashmir conflict, '... the success of the nuclear bluff reinforced the leadership's belief in the value of nuclear weapons both as a deterrent and as a tool of diplomatic bargaining...this became enshrined as an article of faith'. (Ahmed, note 40, pp.189–90).

47. Yasmeen (note 26) p.44. For example, the IRBM Ghauri test in April 1998 was hailed as enabling Islamabad to negotiate with India from a position of parity and strength (p.48).

48. Sisir Gupta, 'The Indian Dilemma', in Alastair Buchan (ed.) *A World of Nuclear Powers* (Englewood Cliffs, NJ: Prentice-Hall 1966) p.62, cited in Ganguly (note 22) p.152.

49. Bracken (note 33) pp.417–18.

50. Sagan (note 12).

51. Bracken (note 33) p.420.

52. Richard Betts, 'Wealth, Power and Instability: East Asia and the United States after the Cold War', *International Security* 18/3 (Winter 1993–94); Aaron Friedberg, 'Ripe for Rivalry: Prospects for Peace in a Multipolar Asia', *International Security* 18/3 (Winter 1993–94); Calder (note 15); and Paul Bracken, *Fire in the East* (NY: HarperCollins 1999).

53. See discussion in Robert Jervis, *Meaning of the Nuclear Revolution: Statecraft and the Prospect of Armageddon* (Ithaca, NY: Cornell UP 1989) Ch.6. As Jervis notes, when the weapon is so powerful that the two can destroy each other, then necessarily power converts to outcomes not through military clashes but by indirect processes and subjective assessments (p.182).

54. As Sagan notes, 'The belief that nuclear power and nuclear weapons were deeply linked to a state's position in the international system was present as early as 1951 when France's first five-year plan saw the links between nuclear weapons and France as a powerful country' (Sagan, note 12, p.78).

55. Nicholas J. Wheeler, 'The Dual Imperative of Britain's Nuclear Deterrent: the Soviet Threat, Alliance Politics and Arms Control', in Mark Hoffman (ed.) *UK Arms Control in the 1990s* (NY: Manchester UP 1990) p.36; and Stephen Pullinger, 'A Role for UK Nuclear Weapons After the Cold War?' *ISIS Briefing* 41 (Jan. 1994) p.2.

56. As Hagerty observed, 'Indian leaders noted the symbolic bestowal of great-power status on China and the fact that the membership of the Security Council and the nuclear club were now identical' (Hagerty, note 21, p.21); also see for concurring arguments Lawrence Scheinman, 'Challenges in South Asia to Nonproliferation Regimes', CNS Occasional Papers 3 (n.d.), Center for Nonproliferation Studies >http://cns/miss.edu/pubs/opapers/op3/schein.htm<. Or as another expert put it, 'Although New Delhi doubtless has genuine cause for concern about China's nuclear program, ... India's program is also driven by the desire for the prestige and international standing that New Delhi has observed being accorded in the international system to substantial nuclear weapons powers, including China' (Sandy Gordon, 'Capping South Asia's Nuclear Programs', *Asian Survey* 34/7 (July 1994) pp.666–7.

57. Cited in Strobe Talbott, 'Dealing with the Bomb in South Asia', *Foreign Affairs* 88/2 (March–April 1999) p.116.

58. Yasmeen (note 26) pp.43–56, 44; Ahmed (note 40) pp.179, 3; Gordon (note 56) p.667.

59. Goldstein (note 2) pp.271–2.

60. For related discussions, see Itty Abraham, *The Making of the Indian Atomic Bomb: Science, Secrecy and the Postcolonial State* (NY: Zed Books 1998); and Sumit Ganguly, 'Explaining India's Nuclear Policy', *Current History* 98/632 (Dec. 1999) pp.438–40.

61. Gordon (note 56) p.669.

62. Goldstein (note 56) p.254.

63. It is granted that the sanctions against India after the 1974 test were quite severe. The US cut off all nuclear cooperation with India. The 1976 Symington amendment to the annual

foreign aid bill proposed suspending economic and military assistance to countries without IAEA safeguards (Ganguly, note 22, pp.160–1).

64. Tariq Rauf, 'Learning to Live with the Bomb in South Asia: Accommodation Not Confrontation', *The Bulletin of Atomic Scientists* (Jan.–Feb. 1999) pp.14–16.
65. Yasmeen (note 26) p.50; and Ahmed (note 40) p.190. This assessment was informed by previous US one-time waivers of the Pressler amendment to sell $360m in military hardware to Pakistan.
66. Agreed Principles <http://usinfo.state.gov/regional/nea/mena/india1.htm>; and Rauf (note 64) p.2.
67. The implications of these findings for nonproliferation regimes are discussed below.
68. See David Karl, 'Proliferation Pessimism and Emerging Nuclear Powers', *International Security* 21/3 (Winter 1996–97).
69. Karl (note 68) pp.90–3. Also see Lewis Dunn, *Controlling the Bomb: Nuclear Proliferation in the 1980s* (New Haven, CT: Yale UP 1982); Lewis Dunn, *Containing Nuclear Proliferation*, Adelphi Paper No. 263 (London: IISS 1991); Karl Kaiser, 'Non-Proliferation and Nuclear Deterrence', *Survival* 31/2 (March–April 1989); Steven Miller, The Case Against a Ukrainian Nuclear Deterrent', *Foreign Affairs* 72/3 (Summer 1993); and Yair Evron, *Israel's Nuclear Dilemma* (Ithaca, NY: Cornell 1994).
70. Peter Feaver, *Guarding the Guardians: Civilian Control of Nuclear Weapons in the United States* (Ithaca, NY: Cornell 1992); Bruce Blair, *The Logic of Accidental Nuclear War* (Washington DC: Brookings Institution 1993); Scott Sagan, *The Limits of Safety: Organizations, Accidents, and Nuclear Weapons* (Princeton UP 1994); Scott Sagan and Kenneth Waltz, *The Spread of Nuclear Weapons: A Debate* (NY: Norton 1995); and Bracken (note 52).
71. On preemption and nuclear proliferation, see Gordon Chang, *Friends and Enemies: The United States, China and the Soviet Union, 1948–72* (Stanford UP 1990); Gordon Chang, 'JFK, China, and the Bomb', *Journal of American History*, 74/4 (March 1988); Karl (note 68) pp.966–7; Scott Sagan, 'The Perils of Proliferation: Organization Theory, and the Spread of Nuclear Weapons', *International Security* 18/4 (Spring 1994) pp.66–107; and William Burr and Jeffrey Richelson, 'Whether to Strangle the Baby in the Cradle: The United States and the Chinese Nuclear Program, 1960–64', *International Security* 25/3 (Winter 2000–01).
72. Bracken (note 33) p.420.
73. Bracken (note 52) pp.112–13; also see Brookings Institution/Council on Foreign Relations, *After the Tests: US Policy Toward India and Pakistan* (NY: CFR Press 1998) pp.2–3; and Calder (note 15).
74. Again quoting Bracken, '... the sources of instability in Asia are ones that cannot be eliminated through hot lines and high-tech locking devices to prevent the unauthorized launch of weapons. It may be better to have these safety measures in place than not to have them, but they divert attention from the more primitive animosity that lies below the surface and can be inflamed ...' (Bracken, note 33, p.420; also see Friedberg, note 52).
75. David Kang, 'Asian Bandwagons' in John Ikenberry and Michael Mastanduno (eds.) *International Relations Theory and the Asia-Pacific* (Columbia UP 2002).
76. For critiques of ethnocentrism in the proliferation debate, see Waltz's arguments in Sagan and Waltz (note 70); Peter Feaver, 'Optimists, Pessimists, and Theories of Nuclear Proliferation Management', *Security Studies* 4/4 (Summer 1995) pp.754–72; and Ahmed Hashim, 'The State, Society, and the Evolution of Warfare in the Middle East', *Washington Quarterly* 18/4 (Autumn 1995) pp.53–76.
77. Thanks to Avery Goldstein for raising this point.
78. Goldstein (note 2) pp.8–9.
79. Ibid. pp.276–9.
80. See Canberra Commission, *Report of the Canberra Commission on the Elimination of Nuclear Weapons* (Canberra, Australia: Dept. of Foreign Affairs and Trade 1996); and National Academy of Sciences, *The Future of US Nuclear Weapons Policy* (Washington DC: National Academy Press 1997).
81. For the classic statement, see Thomas Schelling, *The Strategy of Conflict* (Cambridge, MA: Harvard UP 1960) Ch.9.

82. Hagerty (note 21) pp.24–6; Devin T. Hagerty, 'Nuclear Deterrence in South Asia: The 1990 Indo-Pakistani Crisis', *International Security* 20/3 (Winter 1995–96) pp.79–114.

83. Marc Trachtenberg, 'The Influence of Nuclear Weapons in the Cuban Missile Crisis', *International Security* 10/1 (1985) pp.137–63, 139; also see McGeorge Bundy, 'Existential Deterrence and its Consequences', in Douglas MacLean (ed.) *The Security Gamble: Deterrence Dilemmas in the Nuclear Age* (NJ: Rowman & Littlefield 1984) pp.3–13; and Devin T. Hagerty, *The Consequences of Nuclear Proliferation* (Cambridge, MA: MIT Press 1998) p.26.

84. Goldstein (note 2) pp.44–6.

85. Hagerty (note 21) pp.23–4; Hagerty, 'Nuclear Deterrence in South Asia' (note 82).

86. Alagappa (note 21) p.6.

87. Sumit Ganguly, 'Explaining Indian Nuclear Policy', *Current History* (Dec. 1999) p.440; and Yasmeen (note 26) p.49. For additional arguments on how crisis stability and strategic stability conditions deriving from first-strike uncertainty are reinforcing for India and Pakistan, see Ganguly (note 22) p.177. For the draft nuclear doctrine, see Embassy of India website >http://www.indianembassy.org/polic.../nuclear_doctrine_aug_17_1999.html<. For reaffirmations of India's minimum credible deterrent arguments, see Clinton-Vajpayee joint vision statement March 2000, 'US-India Relations: A Vision for the 21st Century' at >http://usinfor.state.gov/regional/nea/mena/india1.htm<.

88. On the 1990 crisis, see Sumit Ganguly, 'Political Mobilization and Institutional Decay: Explaining the Crisis in Kashmir', *International Security* 21/2 (Fall 1996) pp.76–107. Nevertheless, two problems sit on the horizon. First, if first-strike uncertainty and the fear of escalation stabilize conflict at the nuclear level, then instability at lower levels of violence may eventually result. On the stability-instability paradox, see Robert Jervis, *The Illogic of American Nuclear Strategy* (Ithaca, NY: Cornell UP 1985) p.31; and Glenn Snyder, 'The Balance of Power and Balance of Terror', in Paul Seabury (ed.) *The Balance of Power* (San Francisco: Chandler 1965). Second, where existential deterrence is the most problematic potentially is with the Sino-Indian dyad. Beijing has the capabilities to inflict a high level of damage on India, although at current levels, it could not be assured of a successful first strike. However with growth in Chinese capabilities (and India's inability to develop ballistic missiles to target Chinese assets with confidence), first-strike uncertainty could be undermined.

89. Bruce Russett, 'The Real Decline in Nuclear Hegemony', in Czempiel and Rosenau (eds.) *Global Changes and Theoretical Challenges* (Lexington, MA: Lexington Books 1989) pp.177–93, 185; T.V. Paul, 'Nuclear Taboo and War Initiation in Regional Conflicts', *Journal of Conflict Resolution* 39/4 (Dec. 1995) pp.696–717.

90. Nina Tannenwald, 'The Nuclear Taboo: The United States and the Normative Basis of Nuclear Non-Use', *International Organization* 53/3 (Summer 1999) pp.433–68; and Amy Sands, 'The Nonproliferation Regimes at Risk', CNS Occasional Paper 3 (n.d.), Center for Nonproliferation Studies, >http://cns.miis.edu/pubs/opapers/op3/sands.htm<.

91. Tannenwald (note 90) p.437.

92. Ganguly (note 87) p.440; and Alagappa (note 21) p.6.

93. Domestic groups who counseled against the May 1998 tests, held little sway prior to the tests (see Yasmeen, note 26).

94. Positing the conditions for nuclear rollback is beyond the scope of this study. As Sagan argues, the likelihood of rollback increases when security threats moderate and/or security guarantees are forthcoming from other interested parties. Thus, South Africa publicly disposed of its program of six disassembled weapons in 1991 after the Soviet threat in Angola and Namibia ended. Argentina and Brazil in 1990 abandoned their programs because they did no longer saw each other as threats. And Ukraine, Kazakhstan and Belarus all gave up the arsenals they inherited from the Soviet Union because of security assurances from the US (Sagan, note 12, pp.60–2). However, as Goldstein argues, such optimistic predictions from the security model for proliferation have to be tempered by the technological considerations, i.e., as long as nuclear weapons remain the dominant technological innovation in military strategy, '[T]he presence of nuclear weapons, regardless of polarity, drives a strategic logic that weakens confidence in security as a collective good supplied through international alliances and encourages the pursuit of an independent deterrent capability as the ultimate guarantee of national security' (Goldstein, note 2, p.222).

95. Alagappa (note 21) pp.2–3.
96. China is a member of the NPT and signed the CTBT but has transferred nuclear and missile technology to Pakistan and Iran. India and Pakistan are not members of NPT, CTBT, or MTCR and actively oppose some of these conventions because they see these as freezing permanent gaps in capabilities between established powers and themselves (Daniel Plesch, 'Anarchy in Action: Western Policy on Weapons of Mass Destruction', *Global Beat* (April 2000) >www.nyu.edu/globalbeat/nuclear/plesch0400.html<).
97. Sands (note 90).
98. Evan Medeiros, 'Northeast Asia in 1999: Current Threats to Nonproliferation Regimes', CNS Occasional Paper 3 (n.d.), Center for Nonproliferation Studies >http://cns.miis.edu/pubs/opapers/op3/medeiros.htm<; Alistair Iain John, 'Prospects for Chinese Nuclear Force Modernization: Limited Deterrence Versus Multilateral Arms Control', *The China Quarterly* (June 1996).
99. France was dropped as a Dialogue partner in 1995 after its tests but was reinstated in 1996. Parties to the Zone are Australia, Cook Islands, Federated States of Micronesia, Fiji, Kiribati, Nauru, New Zealand, Niue, Palau, Papua New Guinea, Republic of Marshall Islands, Solomon Islands, Tonga, Tuvalu, Vanuatu, Western Samoa (Dialogue partners: Canada, China, EU, Japan, ROK, UK, US, and France). In addition, the Southeast Asia Nuclear Weapon Free Zone (SEANWFZ) Treaty is even more stringent than Rarotonga, requiring negative security assurances from the NWS and extending the nuclear-free zone among the seven ASEAN members continental shelves and exclusive economic zones (no NWS have signed yet; the US and France object to the unequivocal nature of treaty's security assurances). In addition, the 1997 Almaty Declaration has called for a Central Asia NWFZ endorsed by Kyrgyzstan, Kazakhstan, Tajikistan, Turkmenistan, and Uzbekistan. See *Inventory of International Nonproliferation Organizations and Regimes 1996–1997* (Center for Nonproliferation Studies, Monterey Inst. of Int. Studies, May 1997) pp.52–60; and Tariq Rauf, 'Successes of the Nuclear Non-Proliferation Regime' (8 Oct. 1999) at Center for Nonproliferation Studies, >cns.miis.edu/cns/projects/ ionp/iaea.htm< pp.5–8.
101. See work by the Center for International Strategy, Technology, and Policy at Georgia Tech's Northeast Asia Cooperative Regional Security Initiative since 1992 at >http://www.cistp.gatech.edu/programs/lnwfz-nea.html<; also see the Funabashi Commission for Disarmament and Arms Control. This development might also garner Chinese support as Beijing has expressed interest in NWFZs and announced in July 1999 that it would sign the SEANWFZ protocols (which would make it the first NWS to do so).
102. Parties agree to refrain from direct or indirect actions aimed at undermining any nuclear installation or facility and agree to provide lists and descriptions of nuclear facilities and locations annually and whenever there is a change to the status quo. Both sides claim the other's lists are not complete. (See *Inventory*, note 99, pp.63–4).
103. Established in 1985 to promote the welfare of South Asia and collective self-reliance. In the past, proposals for South Asian nuclear weapons ban and disarmament have been raised in this venue (Pakistan in 1987).
104. >http://usinfo.state.gov.regional.new/mena/india1.htm<. Past Chinese behavior indicates that they, too, might be positively inclined to a Northeast Asia nuclear-free zone. Beijing more so than the United States (because of extended deterrence commitments) has proposed multilateral NFU and NSA agreements among P-5 countries. It has a bilateral NFU with Russia (Sept. 1994); an NSA with Ukraine (Dec. 1994) and with Kazakhstan (Feb. 1995) (Jozef Goldblat, 'The State of Nuclear Arms Control and Disarmament: Reversing Negative Trends', *Disarmament Diplomacy* No. 44 >www.acronym.org.uk/44neg.htm<).
105. In the former case, all the countries in the region have supported in principle starting Conference on Disarmament (CD) negotiations on the banning of further production of weapons-usable fissile material as barrier to further nuclear proliferation – in conjunction with this agreement might be the development of a comprehensive register of highly enriched uranium and plutonium stockpiles. In the latter case, membership for this new entity would consist of four current groups: the Zangger Committee, Nuclear Suppliers Group, Australia Group, and MTCR. Outstanding countries like the two Koreas, India, and Pakistan have committed in principle to these groups.

TABLE 4
REGIONAL AND BILATERAL INSTITUTIONS

Country	SEANWFZ	KEDO	NEA	SAARC	Rarotonga
US	No	Yes	Yes	n/a	Accepts protocols
Russia	No	No	n/a	n/a	Accepts protocols
China	No	No	n/a	n/a	Accepts protocols
Japan	No	Yes – original board member	Yes	n/a	Dialogue partner
DPRK	No	No	n/a	n/a	No
ROK	No	Yes	Yes	n/a	Dialogue partner
ROC	No	No	n/a	n/a	No
India	No	No	n/a	Yes	No
Pakistan	No	No	n/a	Yes	No
Australia	No	Yes	Yes	n/a	Yes
NZ	No	Yes	No	n/a	Yes

Sources: compiled from *Inventory of International Nonproliferation Organizations and Regimes: 1996–1997* (Monterey, CA: Center for Nonproliferation Studies 1997); 'Northeast Asian Participation in Arms Control/Nonproliferation Regimes', available on the Center for Nonproliferation Studies, website at >http://cns.miis.edu/cns/projects/eanp/fact/nearegms.htm<; 'Japanese Participation and Positions Regarding Various Arms Control and Nonproliferation Agreements, Organizations, and Regimes, July 1999', at >http://cns.miis.edu/cns/projects/eanp/fact/japan.htm<.
Notes:
SEANWFZ: South East Asia Nuclear Weapon Free Zone Treaty (Bangkok treaty) (1995). Precursor was 1971 ASEAN original five declaration of ZOPFAN (Zone of Peace, Freedom and Neutrality). No NWS have signed the protocols.
KEDO: Korea Energy Development Organization (1995). To provide for financing and supply of LWRs to DPRK and heavy fuel oil.
NEA: Nuclear Energy Agency (1958). Semi-autonomous body of OECD (formerly European Nuclear Energy Agency). To promote cooperation between members regarding: safety and regulatory aspects of nuclear power and on development of nuclear energy. No direct nonproliferation responsibilities although opposed to in principle.
SAARC: South Asian Association for Regional Cooperation (1985). To promote welfare of South Asia, collective self-reliance. In past proposals for South Asian nuclear weapons ban have been raised in this venue (Pakistan in 1987).
Rarotonga: South Pacific Nuclear-Free Zone Treaty (Rarotonga treaty) (1986). Not to manufacture, acquire, possess or control any nuclear explosive device anywhere within treaty zone. Protocol I obligates France, UK, US not to manufacture, station or test in the zone (3 states acceded March 1996). Protocol 2 obligates China, France, Russia, US, UK not to use or threaten to use any nuclear explosive device against parties of the Treaty (all acceded March 1996). Protocol 3 obligates China, France, Russia, UK, US not to test any nuclear device in Zone.

PART III

POLITICAL AND DIPLOMATIC DYNAMICS

5

How Size Matters: The United States, China and Asymmetry

BRANTLY WOMACK

Most discussions of the United States and China focus on the relationship between the two. This article takes a different tack. Before addressing the differences between the United States and China, we will consider an underlying similarity of their international situations. In its relationships with most other Asian countries, China is the larger player in terms of demography, economy and security. Similarly, the United States is the larger partner in most of its global relationships and in all of its European and American relationships. Are there then similarities in the basic situation of foreign policy and posture between United States as a global power and China as a regional one? If it makes a difference to be big, then the United States and China have something in common that is worth exploring.

Of course, the question of whether size matters is not an innocent one. From the Athenian response to the Melians during Peloponnesian wars[1] to the neo-realists, Western theorists have generally assumed that the more powerful dominate and the less powerful comply. Asymmetry is viewed essentially as a cat-and-mouse relationship in which marginal advantage allows the stronger to dictate its terms, unless the weaker side can offset its disadvantage by balancing its power through alliances. If the weaker power is growing faster than the stronger, then anticipation of different power relations in the future might change the cat-and-mouse relationship into a relationship between older and younger cats.[2] From the realist perspective, the basic question of international relations is who will dominate whom. Size, in its most general sense, gives the answer.

By contrast, other theorists from the time of Grotius to present-day globalization have argued that interdependence constrains the arbitrariness of the powerful.[3] If all states are constrained by their self-interests to avoid the opportunity costs implicit in exclusive and unilateral behavior, then size does not matter.[4] Not only are all states regardless of size constrained by interdependence, but they are also constrained internally by the logic of the global marketplace. A country can choose to 'go it alone' like contemporary Myanmar, but it is in effect choosing to forego the opportunities of international trade and thus is weakening itself. Jacob Burckhardt writing in the nineteenth century noted such dilemmas even in ancient states, but at present and for the foreseeable future globalization has made interdependence infinitely more intimate.[5] Economic interdependence is increasingly reinforced by the ease of communications and the emergence of global problems such as the environment and nuclear proliferation. Now one country's sports utility vehicles can submerge another country's ports, but only at the risk of submerging its own as well. From this perspective, then, the shared international context is the ultimate reality, and size is merely a question of packaging.

These two perspectives, realism and interdependence, are admirably summed up and applied to China by Michael Swaine and Ashley Tellis.[6] They argue that, until China achieves economic parity with the United States, there is no strategic difference between the perspectives. A realistic China would subordinate military growth to modernization until the economy could support a credible military challenge; likewise, an interdependent China would make economic growth its top priority. The perspectives diverge when China would reach economic parity with the United States, which the authors estimate would be no earlier than 2015–20. At this point realism would predict a shift of priorities from economics to military and China would become assertive *vis-à-vis* the US, while the interdependence perspective would predict that China would stick with the policies that had brought it such success and would remain cooperative in the international arena. Swaine and Tellis argue against the interdependence perspective and fully expect China to shift to an assertive grand strategic policy when the opportunity presents itself. Despite the rather dire prediction (from an American point of view, at any rate), Swaine and Tellis reject the options of preemptive containment and preemptive appeasement in favor of engagement. Clearly, the interdependence perspective would also recommend engagement. Thus, the two contradictory perspectives have the same view of the current era of China's international presence, which should run at least 35 or 40 years from 1980 to 2015–20, and in the meantime they also make the same general policy recommendation to the reigning global superpower.

The practical expectations and the theoretical paradigm of this essay are fundamentally different from both realism and interdependence. Practically speaking, I expect that by the time the United States and China might reach economic parity, the international standing of each and their relations with one another will have already been irrevocably shaped by the competence or incompetence of their leadership in their respective realms, and by the actual course of their interaction with one another. Neither integration nor confrontation can be assumed. If China alienates Asia, or if the United States alienates the world, the grand face-off hypothesized by Swaine and Tellis would happen under quite different terms than they imagine, if at all. If on the other hand the United States and China continue their current, relatively successful management of their existing asymmetric relationships, there is no reason to assume that China would trade a successful and relatively low-risk policy of cooperation for the high-risk glory of being king of the hill. The current era is far from being diplomatic dead space waiting for the accumulation of economic capacity. It poses profound challenges to both the United States and China that are generically similar, because the task for both lies in the proper management of asymmetric relations.

The theoretical problem is *how* size matters rather than whether or not size matters. Both the United States and China are now on the large-country side of numerous asymmetric relations. Contrary to the assumptions of the realists, it is normally either impossible or imprudent for the stronger side to subjugate the weaker. The failed attempts by France, the United States and China over the past half-century to subjugate Vietnam amount to controlled experimental proof of this thesis. Of course normally it is even less possible or prudent for the weaker to attempt to subjugate the stronger. David and Goliath stories aside, this statement may appear to be a tautology. However, even when a much smaller country is stronger militarily and is victorious, a disparity in population or economy can create insuperable problems of control and occupation. An example would be Japan's occupation of China during World War II. Therefore asymmetric relationships are normally characterized not only by a disparity of resources, but also by mutual, if sometimes implicit, acknowledgment of autonomy.[7] They are negotiated relationships, not simply ones of demand and evasion.

However, the disparity in asymmetric relationships does make a difference. The larger side has less risk and less opportunity in the relationship. The smaller side has more at stake, and therefore it can be expected to be more attentive. More attention does not necessarily mean a better understanding, because the smaller side tends to exaggerate its risks and opportunities, while the larger side underplays them. Dependence is a quite different relationship from interdependence, and the insensitivity of the larger power can amplify the paranoia of the smaller and lead to conflict.

This study introduces a new paradigm for understanding asymmetric relations and applies it to the United States and China. We begin on fairly level ground with a rough empirical exploration of types and degrees of asymmetry in China's relations with Asia and in the global relations of the United States. Three dimensions of asymmetry are considered: scale (represented by population), economic capacity (represented by Gross National Product), and military capacity (represented by military expenditures). The data show that China's relationship to the rest of Asia is complex but in general asymmetric. The US relationship to the rest of the world is more completely asymmetric. Therefore if asymmetric relations do require special attention both China in its regional context and the United States in its global context could provide good cases for analysis.

The second section sketches a general theory of asymmetric relations. The basic point is that the disparity that defines asymmetric relations implies that the relationship of the larger to the smaller will be quite different from the relationship of the smaller to the larger. The difference in capacity creates a difference in attention and perspective, and it can lead to structural misperceptions that reinforce one another. While there are mechanisms for controlling asymmetric misperceptions, each side has different expectations even in a stable relationship. The larger side expects deference from the smaller, while the smaller expects acknowledgment of autonomy from the larger. Proper handling of asymmetric relations is especially important in multilateral situations, because a central power may not be larger than all the regional partners as a whole. In such cases, the asymmetry of the central power's relationship to each state in a region is not true of its relationship to a potential combination of states. Hence sustainable regional or global leadership requires the maintenance of a community of interest and the avoidance of alienating other players.

The third section applies asymmetric analysis to China's regional relations and to US global relations, concluding with a discussion of relations between the United States and China. Although China's regional relationships are complicated by the immediate presence of Japan, India and Russia and the looming global presence of the United States, its adjustment to leadership in Asia is eased by its heritage of imperial China, its identification with the Third World, and the non-predatory character of its current economic success. As the world's sole superpower the United States is in a less complicated position globally than China is in regionally, and its role is eased by the magnitude of its asymmetric advantages, the experience of Cold War leadership, and its universal values. On the other hand, these advantages increase the risk of alienating other countries if the United States is not sensitive to the perspectives and concerns of the less powerful.

The fourth section concludes by analyzing US-China relations in terms of asymmetry. Clearly the different postures of each country during incidents such as the 1999 bombing of the Chinese embassy in Belgrade can be related to the insensitivity typical of stronger powers and the paranoia typical of weaker ones. An issue such as Taiwan is further complicated by Taiwan's insecurity *vis-à-vis* China, which encourages it to pursue a balancing stratagem of enmeshing the United States in its defense.

If we look beyond the bilateral relationship of the United States and China and the problem of Taiwan, recent experience has demonstrated that the next 15–20 years will be marked not only by incremental growth, but also by unforeseeable crises and problems that will have multilateral consequences. In the long term the rest of the world – and especially Asia – will not be passive observers of the US-China relationship. If they are alienated by China's regional leadership and reassured by the American global leadership, China will never reach effective parity with the US because the rest of the world will also stand against it. If other states are reassured by China's regional leadership but alienated by American global leadership, then China might be the first among equals of America's potential enemies, but it would not stand alone, and the parity point will depend as much on alignment of forces around a precipitating crisis as it would on China's economic capacity. If China and the United States both sustain their current patterns of credible leadership, then the parity point anticipated by Swaine and Tellis might some day be reached, but by then the track record of at least 35 years of competent diplomatic leadership on both sides might suggest alternatives to hegemonic confrontation. In contrast to realism and interdependence, attention to the management of asymmetric relations suggests that the diplomacy of the current era will be decisive regarding future options.

THE UNITED STATES AND CHINA AND THEIR NEIGHBORS

While there is no doubt that both the United States and China are the larger partners in most of their significant relationships, there are major differences in the parameters of their international situations. China has a total land border of 22,143 km with 14 neighbors, and close sea neighbors as well. The United States has land borders of 12,248 km with two neighbors, and is also the major economic and political power in a global neighborhood.

The purpose here is to sketch briefly and to discuss the dimensions and magnitude of disparity between China and its Asian neighbors and between the United States and its regional and global partners. The three dimensions addressed are demographic scale, economic capacity and military capacity. For the sake of simplicity each of these are reduced to a single indicator. Population is an obvious indicator of demographic scale, but it should be remembered that scale also involves the inertial magnitude of a state. Economic capacity is indicated by gross national product (GNP), though there are certainly other factors, such as degree of self-sufficiency in natural resources, that should be factored in to a more complete comparison of economies. Military capacity is perhaps the most difficult dimension to measure since in order to be comprehensive it should involve questions of equipment and mobilizational capacity. Moreover, military expenditure, our indicator for military capacity, is difficult to estimate in consistent, comparable terms. World Bank's estimates are used here, supplemented where necessary by those of the Stockholm International Peace Research Institute, in the hope that estimate biases will at least run in the same direction. The analysis here concentrates on existing disparities rather than on growth rates and anticipated disparities for two reasons. First, forecasting adds another order of magnitude to the uncertainties of comparison. Second, the focus of this contribution is not future asymmetries, but current ones.

In the three basic categories of population, economy, and military there are significant differences in the relative situations of the United States and China. Both are major world figures in at least one category. China is not only more populous than its neighbors, but also comprises 21 per cent of the world's population (the US is 5 per cent). Similarly, the US GNP comprises 27 per cent of the world total (China is 3 per cent), and its military budget in 1999 was 36 per cent of the world total (China is 3 per cent).[8] Because population does not have the international 'reach' of economic and military capacity, China is only a statistical global presence, while the United States is the central figure in the two more interactive categories. Nevertheless, population creates an inertial mass of societal scale that affects regional relations. The closer the neighbor, the more a difference in demographic scale matters.

Figures 1 and 2 demonstrate generic similarities and important differences between the United States and China as large countries. The disparity[9] between the United States and its continental neighbors is great[9] in every category, and even if we include the major hemispheric neighbors the

FIGURE 1
CHINA AND ITS NEIGHBORS, 1998

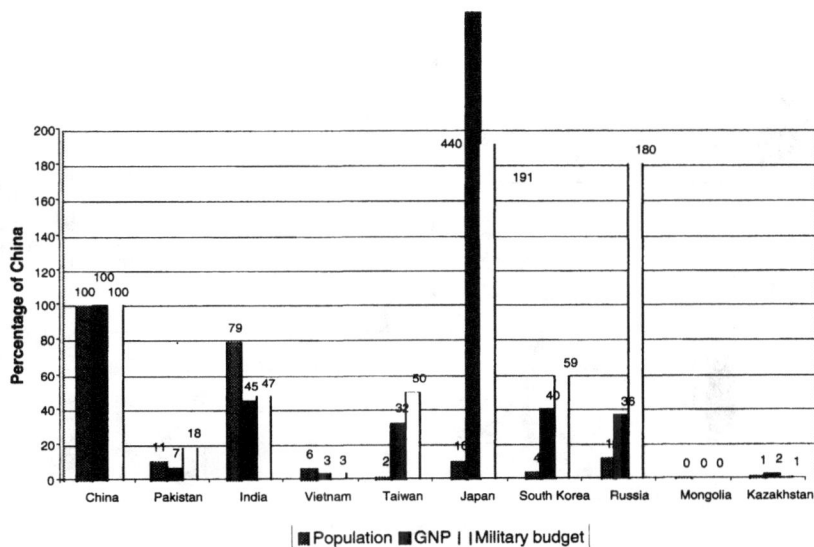

Source: Calculated from World Bank, World Development Report, 1999–2000 (NY: OUP 1999), and Taiwan data from the Stockholm International Peace Research Institute, *SPRI Yearbook 2000*.

population disparity remains clear and the economic and military disparities are overwhelming. If we move to the 'global neighborhood', which is appropriate given the economic and military relations of the United States, the US retains a great disparity in economic capacity and close to an overwhelming disparity in military budget. Since the disparity in military budgets is probably a conservative measure of difference in military capacity,[10] it is obvious that the world's only superpower is indeed in a league by itself in this category. Only in population, and only if one includes China or India in the global comparison, is the United States smaller.

China's situation *vis-à-vis* its neighbors is more complex than that of the US. On the one hand, China certainly has a large population. Except in comparison to India there is an overwhelming demographic disparity. In GNP China enjoys in general a less but still great disparity. The one regional exception is Japan, but it is an exception of such magnitude that it turns the tables. China's GNP is only 22 per cent of Japan's, so the current magnitude of China's economy has the same ratio to Japan as China's population does to the rest of the world.

FIGURE 2
UNITED STATES AND ITS NEIGHBORS, 1998

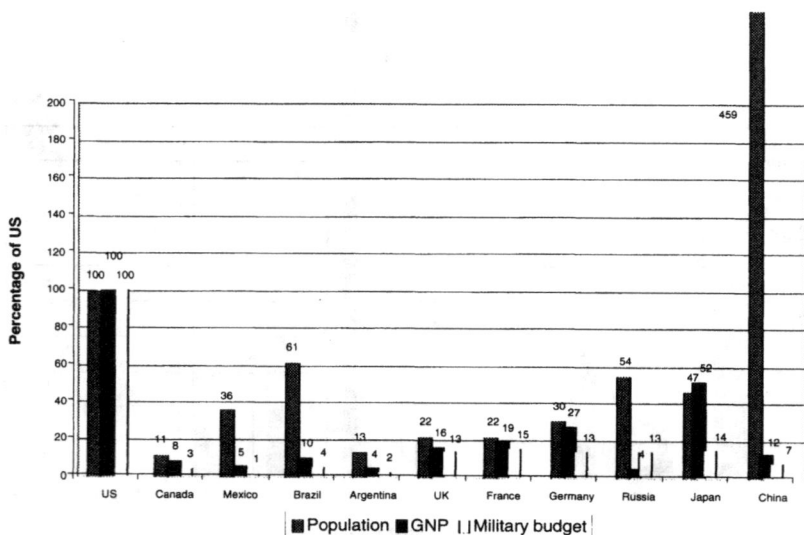

| ■Population ■GNP ⊔Military budget |

Source: Calculated from World Bank, World Development Report, 1999–2000 (NY: OUP 1999), and Taiwan data from the Stockholm International Peace Research Institute, *SPRI Yearbook 2000*.

Looking at military expenditures the situation becomes yet more interesting. Japan spends a smaller percentage of its GNP on the military, and this lowers its disparity in military budget to roughly twice that of China's. However, most of China's neighbors spend a higher percentage of their GNP than China on military, so Russia's military budget is almost double that of China, while India, Taiwan and South Korea are each in the 50 per cent range. Although that remains a significant disparity, it is interesting to consider that China's disparity in military budget *vis-à-vis* Taiwan is roughly comparable to Japan's military advantage *vis-à-vis* China.[11]

By these three simple measures, then, China's regional neighborhood is considerably more complicated than even the global neighborhood of the United States. In global terms, China has the seventh-largest GNP and thus is a significant but by no means a leading player. Militarily China's budget puts it in a fourth-tier group at 3 per cent of the world's military expenditures, along with Italy and Russia, and significantly behind the second tier of Japan and France (7 per cent each), and the third tier of the

United Kingdom (5 per cent) and Germany (4 per cent).[12] China's military budget is only 7 per cent of that of the world's only superpower.

China's global shortfalls in economic and military capacity are more impressive than its regional advantages, and therefore China can perhaps best be described as a regional presence on the way to becoming a regional power. Given China's relative prospects for economic growth one can expect that global economic and military gaps will be lessened, but they will not be overcome in the foreseeable future. One can also anticipate that China's current regional advantages will increase, though because of the linkage between its economy and the region its growth will be less remarkable relative to the region than to the developed world in general.

The general implication is that the management of regional relations will be far more important and problematic for China than the comparable regional questions are for the United States. China is in no position to declare or enforce a Monroe Doctrine. China has quite significant local partners in every quadrant of its regional relations, the most obvious being Japan, Russia and India, and in turn these partners have relations with others beyond. Where it does have a preponderance of economic and military weight in bilateral relations, the complexities of third-party and multilateral relations act as countervailing considerations. The case of Taiwan is only the most obvious example, since it directly involves the United States. Therefore regional foreign policy strategy for China based on domination rather than on perceived mutual interest would be self-isolating and self-defeating.

The American situation seems quite different. Individually and collectively the rest of the hemisphere is no match, and the United States continues to intervene unilaterally in the affairs of neighbors. The 1989 invasion of Panama in order to capture General Noriega is a post-Cold War example. Unlike interventions elsewhere in the world, the question of group support – NATO or the UN, for example – does not arise. Even at the global level, the United States is much more clearly the big power than is the case for China in Asia.

Paradoxically, the American preponderance does not make US foreign relations less problematic. Rather, the disparity creates a set of relationships in which the US position is profoundly different from that of its partners. America's global and hemispheric partners are acutely aware of both the opportunities and the risks presented by the United States. Their attention to the United States does not necessarily lead to compliance, nor does it necessarily yield an accurate understanding of American policy. Cuba has withstood the unrelenting hostility of the United States for more than 40 years. To be sure, its fate is as much a teacher by negative example as it is proof that resistance is possible, but in fact Castro has demonstrated that opposition to domination by the United States can create domestically a sense of threatened community and national cohesion. The case of Cuba – and of Vietnam, Iraq, Iran and many others – demonstrate that the foreign policy challenge that the United States faces in the post-Cold War era is not how to dominate asymmetric relations, but how to negotiate them.

By the same token, though smaller in scale, the challenge that China faces with most of Asia is how to provide opportunities to less powerful neighbors and allay their fears. The tension over the Spratly Islands is symbolic of a sense of insecurity that China's growing economic and military presence creates in its smaller neighbors. As the next section explains, the difficult problem of asymmetric relations for the larger side – whether the United States in its global role or China in its regional role – is how to sustain the relations by reinforcing mutual interests and diminishing the partners' sense of vulnerability.

HOW SIZE MATTERS

In order to analyze the effect of asymmetry on the international relations of the United States and China we must first sketch a general theory of asymmetry that can be applied to these cases. Although the sketch will be presented with the cases in mind, its claim to plausibility rests on its generality and on its logic.[13] What we eventually apply to relations between China and Vietnam or between the United States and Mexico, for example, should apply in turn to relations between Vietnam and Cambodia and between Mexico and Guatemala. Therefore, at the risk of becoming uncomfortably abstract for the moment, this section will present the paradigm of asymmetric analysis while the next applies the paradigm to the United States and China.

We begin with an analysis of bilateral asymmetry, since the relationship between two states is the basic dyad from which more complex situations are built. Disparity in capacities leads to different patterns of attention in the relationship. In turn, the fact that the relationship look different depending on whether one is at the large or the small end leads to a characteristic structural pathology of misperception in which the insensitivity of the larger and the paranoia of the smaller can amplify one another. Fortunately mechanisms exist that control structural misperceptions, but even in stable relationships there are differences in the basic expectations of each side. Having sketched dyadic relations, the section moves on to multilateral situations of asymmetry. Although multilateral situations are constructed from dyadic relations, the relationship of the central power to the whole is different from its relation to each part. In the best of worlds, an order is structured by the central power that each participant feels is beneficial or at least less risky than imagined alternatives. In the worst of worlds, each participant feels that its vital interests are threatened by the erratic and self-serving behavior of the central power, and thus they may see no alternative to fighting desperate battles or to combining forces against the center.

It may appear that asymmetry is a solution rather than a problem in international relations. The more imbalanced the relationship, the more natural it might seem that the stronger side dominates. In fact, however, disparity is not the same as vulnerability. It is rarely the case that the stronger side is free to exercise its full power against the weaker, and even in such struggles the weaker side's more urgent motivation of survival often eventually prevails against attempted domination. But even in a situation of coexistence, strong and weak are in profoundly different positions in the relationship.

Asymmetry is defined by disparity. An asymmetric relationship is one in which the disparity is great enough so that it shapes the structure of the relationship. Of course, all of the terms of this definition are problematic: what is 'disparity', what is 'great', what is 'enough?' However, for the purposes of clarifying the analytical model we will avoid these sticky empirical questions for the moment, returning to them when we apply the model to the United States and China. And it should be noted that there are many cases that are so obviously asymmetric that these empirical boundary questions do not arise.[14] For example, in the US-Canada relationship or the Sino-Vietnamese relationship, one does not have to pick apart the dimensions of asymmetry, stipulate a metric, and define a threshold in order to perceive an asymmetric structure.

Disparity implies that the larger side (A) has less to gain or lose in the relationship than does the smaller side (B). Not only does B occupy a smaller share of A's international horizon, but A's greater domestic capacity tends to raise the general salience of domestic concerns relative to international concerns. In normal times, A's attention to B will tend to be sporadic and partial, because the leadership of A will have more important matters to attend to. A's misperceptions of B are likely to be errors of inattention. A is likely to respond slowly to moves by B, or to respond with blunt instruments that it intends to be limited sanctions but are perceived by B as mortal threats.

By contrast, the opportunities present in the relationship are more important and more vivid to B, because they represent a larger percentage of B's international outlook and of its total activities. Risks are even more vivid to B than opportunities. Regardless of A's intentions, disparity creates a situation in which B is exposed to A's preponderance, whether it be demographic, economic or military.[15] From A's point of view, B will seem hypersensitive to encroachments and to threatening behavior. From B's point of view, any incident not only raises the question of 'why did this happen?' but also 'where will it end?' B's errors are those of over-attention. It assumes that A is as interested in the relationship as it is.

Unfortunately, the errors of inattention by the larger side and over-attention by the smaller side reinforce one another in crisis situations. From B's side, mounting paranoia precludes attempts to mollify A, and as the crisis mounts those in the leadership who are perceived as friendly to A are sidelined. From A's side, the failure of a minor sanction leads easily to a more severe one, and as the leadership unwillingly turns its attention to 'the B problem' they do not want to hear from their experts about B and its troubles, but about how to prevail in punishing B. A typical train of events might be the following. Sanctions that A intends as a limited gesture of displeasure are interpreted by B as a mortal threat. B then allies with another large power, an action that A interprets as an offensive alliance. The downward spiral of the relationship proves the hawks on both sides correct, and a conflict that was unnecessary becomes inevitable.

A good example of the negative complementarity of misperceptions is the conflict between China and Vietnam in the 1970s.[16] Because both sides had illusions of victory and there was no history of a 'normal' bilateral relationship, Vietnam flouted China's expectations of gratitude and deference and China responded with sanctions. Vietnam felt threatened and reluctantly agreed to an alliance with the Soviet Union, which from China's perspective made Vietnam a threat. China saw even the invasion of Vietnam in February 1979 as teaching Vietnam a 'lesson', although it is hardly surprising that Vietnam saw the destruction of its northern five provinces as a mortal threat. On the more positive side, the normalization of Sino-Vietnamese relations since 1991 is firmly founded on the mutual experience of a costly and unproductive hostility. Many frictions remain in the relationship, but both sides strive to maintain stability and to contain disagreements.

The major tasks in managing asymmetric relations are those of preventing and containing vicious circles of misperception. Prevention is accomplished by neutralizing issue areas, whether through inclusive rhetoric or through routinization. If one side's public posture on an issue is perceived to exclude the interests of the other side, then it is likely to become politically charged and to general a counter-posture. Inclusive rhetoric on an issue, especially inclusive rhetoric that both sides officially endorse, can create a sheltered space in the relationship where cooperation rather than conflict is expected. Likewise, the routinization of an issue area can convert an arena of potentially incendiary high politics into one of low politics. Border commissions are an example. Routinization does not require that a problem be solved by the experts, but that frictions in an issue area be handled first in a non-confrontational arena in which continuity with the relevant policy history will be a prime desideratum. Together, inclusive rhetoric and issue routinization permit the creation and expansion of a neutralized core in an asymmetric relationship. A neutral core stabilizes the relationship not only by removing fuel from the fire, but also by creating an inertial interest in a smoothly running relationship that can buffer the nervousness of B and the inattention of A.

Not all issues can be neutralized, and those issues that are neutralized at one time might picked up and politicized under different circumstances. If a confrontation cannot be prevented, what measures can contain the cycle of misperceptions? If the fire is started, what can control the flames? The most basic constraint on misperception is the history of the relationship, because that sets the common sense expectations in interpreting the present. Of course, examples from distant history can also be used to demonstrate the aggressiveness or perfidy of the other side, but the existing inertia of the relationship should create horizons of plausibility that make extreme interpretations less likely. Sometimes the continuity of expectations is so disrupted that anything seems possible, and this is a particularly dangerous time for asymmetric relations. Recent examples of novel contexts would include the Balkans in the 1990s and Indochina in the 1970s. In these cases instead of providing a well-trodden path of common sense expectations, history fired the ambitions and fears of participants.

States can strengthen expectations of mutual benefit by using diplomatic ritual. The exchange of official visits and common pronouncements of mutual respect contribute to a bilateral political atmosphere in which alarmist interpretations of the other's behavior appear less plausible. The most important aspect of visits of state is not the specific problems solved and contracts won through summit negotiation – the 'deliverables' – but the general affirmation of the importance and stability of the relationship. For example, the exchange of visits between Jiang Zemin and Bill Clinton in 1997–98 was not very productive in terms of 'deliverables', but it did move the relationship beyond the situation in which a minor event like the arrest of Harry Wu could appear to endanger the whole relationship. The function of diplomatic ritual should also be distinguished from the opportunity visits provide for personal friendship among individual leaders. The temporary advantage of a personal friendship among leaders is offset on the one hand by the risk of them not liking each other and on the other by the inevitable change of personnel. Precisely because it does not stress concrete accomplishments or personal friendships, diplomatic ritual confirms the stabilizing effect of historical continuity by involving both leaderships in an explicit, though general, commitment to stability.

It might appear that security would be a one-sided question in an asymmetric relationship. But A does have security concerns relative to B. What A needs from B is deference, that is, the implicit commitment by that it will act in awareness and acceptance of the bilateral power disparity. Deference implies that B will not endanger A's security by foolhardy actions or by alliances hostile to A. Perhaps the most elaborate manifestations of deference were the tribute missions of the Chinese empire, but in modern times deference is usually more evident in the restraint shown by smaller countries in their pursuit of activities that they know would be sensitive to their larger partners. Deference does not require submission. A magnificent example of armed deference was the Vietnamese gesture after defeating the Ming occupation army of sending the Chinese generals and 100,000 men unharmed back to Beijing in 1427.[17] Had the Vietnamese celebrated their triumph by slaughtering the army that had occupied their territory for 20 years, the Chinese would certainly have launched reprisals. The Vietnamese gesture showed China that it had nothing to fear from Vietnam, but also nothing to gain by further invasions.

For the weaker side, bilateral security is of course a larger concern, and it requires that A clearly acknowledge the boundaries and autonomy of B. Since A does not need protection from B, it might look on territorial and economic boundaries as irrational limits. But to the extent that A pushes against B's space, the disparity of capacity becomes a threat to B. Therefore B can be expected to be hypersensitive to gestures by A that imply a subversion of the barriers between them, and conversely it will appreciate gestures that acknowledge sovereign autonomy.

The relationship between A's expectation of deference and B's expectation of acknowledgment is delicate, but not in itself contradictory. It is certainly possible for B to be autonomous and yet act in awareness of its asymmetry with A, and it is possible for A to acknowledge and abide by limits in its influence on B and still expect that it will be treated with all due respect. Most asymmetric relationships manage to join the two most of the time. However, the more emphatically A demands deference, the more contradictory deference and autonomy appear to B. Conversely, the more assertive B is concerning autonomy, the more it appears to A that B might become dangerous. At the extreme end, an attempt by A to force deference by military means is a denial of autonomy, and a decision by B to do whatever it takes to preserve autonomy from A is likely to deny deference.

If we look beyond individual asymmetric relationships to clusters of relations, to what extent can we speak of asymmetric systems? It should be noted first that bilateral relations are not derivative from systems. Each state looks out over its own walls. This point requires emphasis because large, distant states are tempted to view smaller ones only in terms of their alliances or their regional clusters.[18] That being said, it is true that the world beyond the walls of the individual state is a matrix of interacting states rather than a collection of unrelated bilateral relationships. In terms of asymmetries, the matrix that any state confronts is not rigid, but it is also not easily changed. Except for the occasional Genghis Khan, one's neighbors are not optional. And it is rare for states to leap ahead suddenly in their capacities, though the experience of the last 50 years is proof that situations can be transformed over time. From the vantage point of any particular state at any particular time, therefore, there is an international order[19] in which it confronts an array of familiar actors of different potencies and at different distances. The largest power plays a particularly important and central role in the matrix, but each state from its particular location confronts its own situation.

The strongest state in a region – and *a fortiori* a world superpower – confronts a situation in which each state in its system or subsystem will be especially attentive to its behavior. It is in a leadership position not because it can simply command compliance within the system, but because all within the system, friends, foes and in between, will be watching closely and will behave in response to a central initiative. Not only will the bilateral relations of the strongest with each state be among the most important relations for each partner, but even its actions addressed to other states will be scrutinized by all the rest for its implications. Clearly all sides have an interest in controlling their own misperceptions, but it is the responsibility of the stronger power to take the lead in providing structure to new relationships. Especially in multilateral situations, the fact that the strongest power occupies center stage makes it very difficult for others to take the lead. Perhaps in some cases of routinizing issue areas other states could take the initiative, but in diplomatic ritual and inclusive diplomacy the strongest power must play the major role. However, being at center stage means that the strongest state does not have a dominant external referent for its own foreign policy, so its external relations are likely to be driven by domestic considerations.

Credibility becomes a primary value for the effectiveness of the strongest state. In a multilateral asymmetric situation the difference between disparity of capacity and actual vulnerability is even greater than in a bilateral relationship. Imagine a situation in which nine equally weaker states are in a system in which the strongest is three times the capacity of any of them. Each of them individually would be in a relation of great disparity with the central power, but collectively the smaller states would exceed the strongest by the same ratio. Moreover, if the strongest state began to commit its capacity in two or three relations, it would greatly change the ratio of its deployable resources to the remaining states. To rephrase Machiavelli's famous saying that the appearance of virtue is more important than virtue itself, we could say that the appearance of power is more important than power itself. On the other hand, if the strongest power is not responsive to challenges then its will to deploy its capacity might be doubted. The credibility dilemma, then, is that both capacity and responsiveness must be believable. The acme of diplomatic skill for the strongest power is to limit the situations in which its will to commit might be tested.

A final characteristic of an asymmetric system is the degree to which compliance is the result of a community of interests rather than the result of prudence in the face of a preponderance of power. To the extent that a given matrix of international relations stabilizes expectations and allows the pursuit of ones own ends, then the order serves the interests of the weaker state even if the order is originated and shaped by the strongest. It might seem that the strongest would be indifferent to the motive for compliance, but in fact a community of interests would be more favorable for cooperation and reduce the likelihood of defection. The strongest power will certainly be tempted to pursue exclusive rather than inclusive aims and to attempt to maximize its power advantages in individual transactions. Not to drive a hard bargain from a position of strength means to forego the most favorable result. But if the central state acts only for its own interests then weaker states will feel entrapped and vulnerable, and while they might comply under duress, they will scheme to limit their exposure to domination.

In sum, the position of the strongest power in a region may be an enviable one, but it is not easy to sustain. As a state becomes habituated to center stage it may tend to project its domestic politics as foreign policy, which would erode international confidence in the quality of its leadership. The credibility of capacity must be preserved without lessening it through unnecessary engagements. A community of interests must be sustained by providing leadership that includes common goals and that in bilateral transactions is sensitive to the concerns of weaker states. These challenges are especially difficult because they are not embodied in a powerful and threatening opponent, but rather are the admonishments of prudence in a unipolar situation. It is easier for a strong state to deal with an alien evil empire than to run its own empire well. A strong state can make up in brawn what it lacks in brain, but by doing so it is lessening its advantage of disparity, decreasing the potential for cooperation, and increasing the possibility of defection and collusion.

BEING BIG AFTER THE COLD WAR

Both the United States and China are in novel asymmetric situations in post-Cold War world. As the previous analysis suggests, novelty is a dangerous situation in asymmetric relationships because the routines and habits that controlled misperceptions in the past become out of date. It is easy for the strong to be unaware of the threat to the weak posed by their actions, and for the weak to lose a sense of proportion in judging their actual vulnerability. The negative complementarity of such misperceptions is difficult to control in a new context.

Rather than narrate China's Asian diplomacy and American world diplomacy, this section will concentrate on some broad features of each that are especially relevant to asymmetric leadership.

China

In general, China is well positioned to handle a leadership role in Asia gracefully. First, the traditional Chinese empire was arguably the world's most successful case of sustained unipolar leadership. Its patriarchal structure was avowedly hierarchical and placed China at the center, but its relations with other states were based more on legitimation and mediation rather than on conquest. China considered itself culturally and morally superior, but the principles of rule were construed as universal human principles rather than as national or racial prerogative.[20] Traditional China was content to receive deference from kings rather than to rule directly over alien peoples.[21] Commercial relations were based on mutual advantage, and government involvement in trade was more concerned with controlling domestic disruption by restricting channels and levels of trade rather than forcing China's advantage in transactions.

Second, from the Opium War in 1840 until China 'stood up' in 1949, China had its own traumatic experience of being a weak state at the mercy of the strong. Two strands of foreign policy resulted from this experience. The first was revolutionary activism, which strengthened its relations with liberation movements but by the same token threatened non-communist governments. The second is best symbolized by the Five Principles of Peaceful Coexistence: mutual respect for sovereignty and territorial integrity; mutual non-aggression; non-interference in each other's internal affairs; equality and mutual benefit; and peaceful coexistence. These principles were first proposed in 1954 in joint statements with Zhou Enlai and Nehru in New Delhi and then with U Nu in Burma shortly thereafter. They were incorporated into the declaration of the First Afro-Asian Conference (the Bandung Conference) in 1955. After taking a back seat to revolution in the 1960s and (anti-Soviet) anti-hegemonism in the 1970s, they were incorporated into the Constitution of the People's Republic of China in 1982. These principles provide an excellent ideological underpinning for inclusive rhetoric, and along with other policy principles (such as the unilateral declaration of no first use of nuclear weapons) they show a fraternity with the Third World and sensitivity to their concerns.

Third, China's current era of reform has combined rapid economic progress with major improvements in its relations with neighbors. In 1980 relations were tense on most of China's borders and it did not have economic relations with South Korea or Taiwan. Twenty years later, the Spratly Islands are the most significant remaining sovereignty dispute and open economic relations are well established. Although China certainly raises concerns among its neighbors as a competitor in trade, aid and foreign investment, these concerns are balanced by opportunities that it presents for trade and investment. In any case, it is clear that China's economic growth has not been based on the domination of its neighbors or of colonies, in contrast to both Western and Japanese imperialism.

China's behavior during the Asian financial crisis is an example of China's regional responsibility at its best. China's decision not to devalue its currency was widely viewed as an important measure in preventing a currency devaluation war in Asia. In contrast to the US and Japan, who were seen as more self-interested in their reactions, China's currency peg and its assistance to the Hong Kong currency peg were seen as actions that demonstrated a regional consciousness and an ability to take and hold strategic policies despite short-term losses.[22]

Despite such gestures, it is hardly surprising that China's neighbors are concerned about China's rapid growth. As China's economic and military capacity expand to fill its demographic scale, other states in the region are looking at a disparity of capacity that tends to put the initiative in the relationship in China's hands. Even if China's national aims do not involve an encroachment on other regional interests, China's interests are different from its partners. A good example of different sensitivities was an aborted Chinese proposal in 1994 to build and staff a major construction site in Cambodia.[23] From the Chinese perspective the proposal was part of an active aid and investment program in Cambodia. From the perspective of some Cambodians, however, it amounted to creating a Chinese city in their country, and reminded them of how attractive their land might be to immigrants. Even in relationships that are apparently close and friendly, for instance, current relations with Myanmar, the bilateral disparity leads to underlying anxieties. Burmese reservations are indicated by the joke that if all Chinese urinated at the same time Burma would be flooded.

The Spratly Islands are the most prominent point of controversy between China and Southeast Asia. Not only do they involve China, Vietnam, Malaysia, Philippines, Taiwan and Brunei in a sovereignty dispute, but they also raise more general concerns about China's relationship to Southeast Asia and about China's behavior in situations of major disagreement. Claims of sovereignty are by their nature contradictory, and island claims are more difficult to compromise than land borders. At present all states are working to maximize their specific holdings and this has led to minor confrontations. Since the islands are extremely small and inhospitable and there is wide variation in estimates of mineral resources, it is unlikely that the controversy would become serious. Nevertheless, the persisting conflict brings the image of China's military might deep into Southeast Asia, providing a cause for concern in the region and for encouraging a continued American presence in the region.

China exists in a complex ecology of foreign relations, and it is less successful in relations with Japan and the United States than it has been with smaller powers. Relations with Russia are the exception that prove the rule, in part because of Russia's rapid decline and a mutual interest in stabilizing Central Asia, and in part because the primary problem for both countries is the United States. To quote from the most recent Joint Communiqué:

> China and Russia support forces of peace, stability, development and co-operation in the international arena, while defying hegemonism, power politics and group politics, and oppose attempts to amend the

basic principles of international law, to threaten others by force or to interfere in other countries' internal affairs.[24]

Meanwhile the Central Asian cooperation of China, Russia, Kazakhstan, Tajikistan and Kyrgyzstan that began in Shanghai in 1996 with discussions of border relations has grown into annual meetings of presidents and foreign ministers and has expanded beyond issues of border security to include economics and the environment.[25]

While the US presence simplifies China's relations with Russia by giving both countries a common problem, China's relations with Japan are complicated by the US-Japan alliance. In any case, however, Sino-Japanese relations would be ambiguous. China and Japan are in a situation of countervailing asymmetries. China is strong in demographics and growth rate; Japan is far greater in economic capacity. Of course, Japan compensates for the economic disparity by being the largest contributor of official development assistance (ODA) to China.[26] The economic structures are quite different as well. The Japanese economy is radically dependent on external resources and markets, while the Chinese economy is one of the most self-sufficient in the world. The military situation is mixed because Japan's budgetary and naval superiority is at least made more problematic by China's nuclear arsenal. The Japanese history of militarism until 1945 and yet pacifism for the past 55 years contrasts with China's century of victimization followed by 30 years of ideological aggressiveness.

These countervailing asymmetries mean that each side is sensitive to different aspects of the relationship and correspondingly less sensitive to issues that the other side is most aware of. On the other hand, each looms large in the regional view of the other, and it is unlikely that either side would sacrifice the entire relationship to a partial misunderstanding. There is no bottom line to the relationship. The extremes of either hostility or intimate friendship are the least likely resting points on the spectrum of general possibilities.

China's relation with Taiwan is perhaps the best example of asymmetry. China's One China policy can easily be seen as a demand for deference, while Taiwan's reluctance can be construed as a suspicion that a meaningful acknowledgement of autonomy requires recognition of separate sovereignty. Meanwhile Beijing's treatment of Taiwan as a domestic issue excites Taiwan's fears, and Taiwan's pragmatic diplomacy affronts China's dignity. The 1996 confrontation over Lee Tenghui's visit to Cornell University and the ensuing saber rattling in the Taiwan Strait is the best of many possible illustrations of the asymmetric character of the standoff.

China should be credited with a masterstroke, however. The change in China's Taiwan policy from 'liberation' to 'peaceful reunification' in 1979 had two profound effects on the relationship. First, the unilateral opening to Taiwan attracted Taiwanese business and undermined governmental resistance. Secondly, while the idea of 'liberation' denied any autonomy to Taiwan and defined the relationship as a mortal struggle, the policy of 'peaceful reunification' implied acknowledgment of the existing realities and a process of convergence based on inducement rather than on force. While 'peaceful reunification' has not eliminated the possibility of hostility, it has created a possibility for peaceful convergence that otherwise would not have existed.

In general, then, China's diplomacy has dealt rather well so far with a complicated regional environment. Of course, it is possible that China will become arrogant as its power increases and it becomes accustomed to regional prominence. It is also possible that future confrontations with Taiwan, Japan or the United States could force China's regional relations into rigid alignments, derail its economic development, or worse. But while asymmetry makes these scenarios possible, it does not make them inevitable.

United States

The United States is in less familiar territory as the world's only superpower than China is as a (returning) regional power. It is very familiar with world leadership in the bipolar situation of the Cold War, and it has been the world's largest economic and military power for even longer, but the US has never in its history faced the task of unipolar world leadership. It does, of course, bring some major advantages to the task, but each of these advantages has a negative side as well.

The first American advantage is the size of the disparity with its regional neighbors and with the rest of the world. In contrast to China's position in Asia, the United States has clearly asymmetric relations with every state in its region and in the world. It is therefore foolhardy and self-isolating for other states not to be deferential. The negative side of such complete asymmetry is that it allows a large margin for error. The problem of being a 'hyperpower' is that it can become convenient to maximize one's own interest and to dismiss the growing alienation of other countries as mere peripheral noise.[27] There are an increasing number of cases – US withdrawal from the Kyoto treaty on global warming and US policies toward Cuba, for instance – where world opinion is unanimously critical of the United States.

The danger is that of alienation producing evasion and collusion in the medium and long term. Even in the short term a vicious circle of sanctions and paranoia could drive individual countries to desperate confrontations. While one might take the continued success of the US in hemispheric relations as proof that effective resistance is not possible, it should be recalled that the world is a much bigger and more complicated place, and even in military matters the American advantage could be much reduced by multiple simultaneous engagements.

The second American advantage is that of established Cold War leadership. Since the United States was already the leader of the non-communist world before 1989, post-Cold War leadership merely means the expansion of its existing domain to include former communist countries, and they are in general quite receptive and deferential. For instance, there is little need for change in the American presence in Asia or in Western Europe. The negative side of Cold War continuity is that the habit of bipolarity dies hard. Cold War leadership was an alliance against communism. It could justify harsh measures against particular states because of the threat to the alliance as a whole. In the post-Cold War world, harsh policies such as continuing sanctions against Iraq appear to be unilateral exercises of American power against weaker states, and since all other states are weaker states, world sympathies can lie with the victim. For this reason it is even more important in the post-Cold War era for sanctions to be multilateral, such as in the 1991 Gulf War and in the Balkans.

The third American advantage is the habit of conducting foreign policy according to universal principles. Since the time of Jefferson the United States has thought of itself in universal terms, and as a result it is not difficult ideologically to adjust to unipolar leadership. Although during the Cold War American foreign policy was often formed in response to Soviet actions, American ideology was always formulated in terms of such values as freedom and democracy, and these transcend their Cold War framework. These values have general support from the developed world and from elements within developing countries as well. However, to many countries the American effort to instill the values of freedom, the free market and democracy appear to be impositions of American values. Especially in Asia, the counter-concept of 'Asian values' has been used to highlight the greater sense of community in Asian cultures, but more importantly to object to the domination of American values. From the other side of the spectrum, many developed countries consider the United States behind the times morally in issues regarding foreign aid, the death penalty, and the environment.

In general, the American advantages over its partners create a situation in which the disparity is great, the habit of multilateral leadership is well established, and there is self-confidence in leadership direction. On the other hand, these factors contribute to a material, political and ideological distance between the United States and its partners that could result in alienation. Erratic or exclusively self-serving behavior could unsettle the exchange of deference and autonomy. Partners could become paranoiac, the United States could react with sanctions that would only increase the paranoia, and confrontations could occur. An American victory in such confrontations might be Pyrrhic to the extent that there were broad sympathies with the loser and the American preponderance were reduced by the struggle. The possible problem can become vivid if one recalls the alienation of many European states from the US involvement in Vietnam, and then transposes this situation into one where there is no overarching alliance against a common global opponent. One might adapt Nietzsche's terms and ask if the US in the post-Cold War era might have become asymmetric, all too asymmetric.

CHINA VIS-À-VIS THE UNITED STATES

Having discussed the situation of both the United States and China as strong powers in asymmetric situations, we can conclude with an analysis of the prospects of relations between the two. The US-China relationship is especially interesting because it is itself asymmetric but the smaller side is a regional leader in its own right. China cannot afford to ignore the US because its regional role and more generally its foreign policy as a whole are profoundly affected by its relations with the United States. On the other side, China's demographic scale and rapid economic growth make it unusually important to American policy and especially to long-term prospects.

An optimist might conclude that the implicit interdependence would create a center of gravity for the relationship that would self-correct minor crises and keep the relationship within the bounds of normalcy. This has been the case with the relationship thus far, and 20 years of robust normalcy is strong evidence for continuation. From the passage of the Taiwan Relations Act in March 1979 to the spy plane incident of April 2001 – and undoubtedly beyond, by the time this analysis is being read – normal relations between the United States and China have been buffeted by numerous high-profile crises which appeared serious at the time and have bent but not broken the continuity of the relationship. While the relationship has been robust, it has never appeared to either side to be unproblematic. It is therefore worthwhile to consider the asymmetry of the US-China relationship and what the effects of asymmetry might be.

The danger in an asymmetric relationship is that each side perceives and reacts to the other in a manner that in turn heightens the concerns of the other side. If the United States views China as another, smaller US, then it will project its global expectations into China's behavior, and perceive a risk of challenge that does not in fact exist. Alarmist concerns about China fit into this category, and they are most easily explained by the need for a new Cold War enemy than by China's capacities or behavior.[28] There is nothing China could do to allay these fears because it is not the origin of them. To be sure, actions by China such as establishing closer relations with Russia can be interpreted as part of a grand design aimed at the United States, and it is true that common concerns about the United States play a part in Sino-Russian relations. But sufficient explanations exist for this behavior that involve defensive and hedging motives rather than grand malevolent schemes, and these are more appropriate to the situation of a smaller power.

On the other side, if China perceives the United States as China writ large it would view the United States as far more coordinated and China-oriented than it actually is. China is likely to perceive (or misperceive) an intentional pattern of containment in scattered American actions, and then extrapolate the pattern into a mortal threat. The Chinese reaction to the bombing of its embassy in Belgrade in 1999 shows the potential for paranoia. It is clear to a disengaged observer that the bombing was infinitely more likely to be an accident rather than a signal of American hostility, but the weaker side in an asymmetric relationship is not a disengaged observer. The bombing was an existential experience of the disparity of power between the United States and China and the possibility that that power could be used against China. The initial American insensitivity to China's perspective on the bombing helped turn shock into anger, but the root of China's reaction was the fact of its vulnerability.

While it is to the interest of both sides to maintain a friendly relationship, mutually reinforcing misperceptions may preclude that option. Although the notions of 'engagement' and 'international openness' are intended to promote mutually beneficial relations, they cannot guarantee them. If deference to the real power of the United States appears to China to compromise its autonomy, then China will be more confrontational. If China's demands for autonomy appear to the United States to be denying American global leadership, or if China appears to be creating or organizing a counter-force to the United States, then the United States will be more assertive. Foreseeable trends do not mitigate the possibility of serious misunderstanding. As China becomes stronger it may worry less about the US advantage, but the United States is likely to worry more about Chinese deference. If public opinion becomes more influential in Chinese foreign policy, it is likely to amplify rather than reduce Chinese sensitivity to autonomy. The concrete diplomatic challenges will remain those of making structural misperceptions less likely and minimizing crises that can occasion vicious circles of misperception.

The mechanisms discussed earlier for controlling structural misperceptions can be applied to the case of the United States and China. An excellent instance of issue neutralization is the granting in 2000 of Permanent Normal Trade Relations (PNTR) to China, replacing the annual Congressional review of Most Favored Nation (MFN) status. More generally, China's entry into the World Trade Organization should help move many trade issues to multilateral frameworks. Another, less successful, example is the annual review of China's human rights record at Geneva. While it is undoubtedly frustrating for the United States not to have its views prevail in a multilateral context, the UN forum provides some triangulation on issues of fundamental disagreement. Perhaps a bilateral commission could provide more satisfying results.

The importance of diplomatic ritual was recognized by the first Bush administration in sending Secretary of Commerce Barbara Franklin to Beijing and Hong Kong in December 1992. This visit broke the ban on official Cabinet-level contact with China imposed after Tiananmen. It was very important for controlling Chinese concerns about the sale of 150 F-16 fighter jets to Taiwan that had been announced in October 1992, and it provided the incoming Clinton administration with a diplomatic platform which otherwise would have been considerably more ambiguous.[29] More prominently, President Reagan's visit to China in 1984 and the exchange of visits between President Jiang Zemin and President Clinton were of fundamental importance in officially confirming a framework of normalcy for the relationship. Thanks in part to such efforts, the relationship now has a 22-year track record of self-stabilizing survival that makes its own contribution to the common sense and common expectation of normalcy.

While many possible triggers of misperception might be imagined (and the embassy bombing in Belgrade as well as the spy plane incident off Hainan demonstrate that occasionally the unimaginable happens), at the present time and for the foreseeable future Taiwan is the most likely vortex for confrontation. Despite its diplomatic recognition that Taiwan is a part of China, the United States tends to perceive China's interest in Taiwan as part of a general aggressiveness. For its part, China sees continued and increasing US involvement in Taiwan's defense not only as unwarranted interference in internal affairs, but also as evidence of a larger American containment policy. Meanwhile, to the extent that Taiwan is itself paranoiac concerning China's intent to reunify, it has reason to encourage American and Chinese misperceptions in order to confirm that Taiwan would be the trigger to a larger confrontation. If Taiwan can achieve this identification, then it is no longer a small power confronting a large one, but instead the front line of an even larger power. Of course, to the extent that Taiwan strives for such an alliance with the United States it is heightening its bilateral tension with China, and it might well discover, as many small states have in the past, that promises made by large powers in peacetime are rethought in crisis. Thus Taiwan's risk-avoiding strategy of seeking to nail down American guarantees might be a serious danger to its security.

In more general terms, the fate of relations between the United States and China rests on the general context of regional and global relations. If China is the only exception to generally healthy relations of the US with the rest of the world, it is less likely to be an exception. If American global leadership remains well accepted then the risk to China of individual confrontational behavior is increased, and there would be no peer support for its position. If, on the other hand, there would be a general perception that the US is dangerously erratic and high-handed in its behavior, then it would be more likely that China would feel paranoiac and would engage in confrontational behavior, and that there could be a community of support for a Chinese confrontation. If China is seen as aggressive by its Asian neighbors and disrespectful of their autonomy, then it would undercut the possibility of support in confrontations with the United States.

The difference between these expectations does not rest on a profound change in the balance of power between the United States and China, but rather on different scenarios of how each country manages its asymmetric relations.

NOTES

1. The Athenian answer to the plea for mercy from the defeated island of Melos in 416 BC was, to translate freely, 'Of men we know, and of the gods we believe, that the strong rule when they can and the weak serve when they must.'
2. See Dale Copeland, 'Economic interdependence and war: A theory of trade expectations', *International Security* 20/4 (Spring 1996).

3. As Grotius puts it, 'There is no state so powerful that it may not at some time need the help of others outside itself, either for purposes of trade, or even to ward off the forces of many foreign nations united against it.' Hugo Grotius, *Prolegomena to the Law of War and Peace* (Indianapolis, IN: Bobbs Merrill Library of Liberal Arts 1957; original 1625) p.16.

4. Jeffry Frieden and Ronald Rogowski, 'The impact of the international economy on national policies', in Robert Keohane and Helen Milner (eds.) *Internationalization and Domestic Politics* (Cambridge: CUP 1996) pp.25–47.

5. Jacob Burckhardt, *Weltgeschichtliche Betractungen* (Berlin: Ullstein Bücher 1966 (first published posthumously in 1905 from materials dating from 1864 to 1893) p.79.

6. Michael Swaine and Ashley Tellis, *Interpreting China's Grand Strategy: Past Present and Future* (Santa Monica, CA: RAND 2000) esp. pp.182–230.

7. This thesis is similar in result to Alexander Wendt's Lockean model of anarchy in *Social Theory of International Politics* (Cambridge: CUP 1999) pp.279–97. The difference is that Wendt makes a cultural argument for the modern respect for sovereignty, while I am merely asserting that a marginal advantage in capacity does not necessarily mean that domination is possible or convenient. I would expect that a Lockean culture would develop from such experiences, and along with Wendt I would think that a Kantian culture would ultimately be the most rational adjustment to long term coexistence.

8. Stockholm International Peace Research Institute (SIPRI), 'Recent Trends in Military Expenditure', at >http://projects.sipri.se/milex/mex_trends.html<, p.1.

9. Let me suggest a standardization of disparity adjectives. Disparity is 'clear' when the larger exceeds the smaller by half (smaller is less than 67 per cent), it is 'great' when the larger is double (smaller is less than 50 per cent), and it is 'overwhelming' when the larger is ten times the smaller (smaller is less than 10 per cent).

10. The marginal utility of a better weapon can exceed its marginal cost.

11. If one takes into account the dispersion of military expenses necessary in a large country, then China has a smaller percentage of possibly deployable resources vis-à-vis either Japan or Taiwan and therefore its relative position is weaker than the aggregate numbers would suggest.

12. SIPRI (note 8) p.1.

13. Part of the theory is presented in more detail in my unpublished MS, 'Asymmetry and Misperception: The Cases of China, Vietnam, and Cambodia'.

14. These questions are infinitely more important in defining parity than in defining disparity, because parity requires the drawing of a thin line of equality, while disparity points to the vast spaces on either side.

15. Demographic risk here refers to problems affected by the demographic scale of the countries involved. For instance, forest fires in Indonesia might seriously threaten air quality in Singapore, but forest fires in Singapore would be merely a curiosity to Indonesia, since Singapore has only three million people and far fewer trees.

16. The best general narrative of the period is Nayan Chanda, *Brother Enemy* (NY: Macmillan 1986). The best account of the Chinese side is Qiang Zhai, *China and the Vietnam Wars, 1950–1975* (Chapel Hill: Univ. of North Carolina Press 2000).

17. See Nguyen Khac Vien, *Vietnam: A Long History* (Hanoi: Gioi Publishers 1993) p.76.

18. An example would be the American interpretation of the Vietnamese occupation of Cambodia in the 1980s as a 'proxy war' between the Soviet Union and China. The reality was not simply more detailed than this stereotype, it was far more complex.

19. 'Order' not in the strong sense of an enforced world rule of law, but in the sense of what Max Weber calls a system of 'sozialen Chancen' (social likelihoods).

20. The most eloquent presentation of this is Wang Gungwu, 'Early Ming Relations with Southeast Asia', in John K Fairbank (ed.) *The Chinese World Order* (Cambridge, MA: Harvard UP 1968) pp.34–62.

21. The Qing mentality of empire is well described in James Hevia, *Cherishing Men from Afar* (Durham, NC: Duke UP 1995) esp. pp.30–56.

22. For a detailed description of Southeast Asia's opinion of the behavior of the United States, Japan and China during the Asian financial crisis, see Wimonkan Komumas, 'Half a Hegemon: Japan's Leadership in Southeast Asia' (Charlottesville: Foreign Affairs PhD dissertation, 2000).

23. See Nathaniel Thayer, 'Chinese City of Dreams', *Phnom Penh Post*, 12–25 Aug. 1994, pp.1, 8.
24. *China Daily*, 19 July 2000.
25. *China Daily*, 6 July 2000.
25. See Quansheng Zhao, *Interpreting Chinese Foreign Policy* (NY: OUP 1996) pp.148–82.
27. The term 'hyperpower' was coined by French Foreign Minister Hubert Védrine (with Dominique Moisi) in *Les Cartes de la France a l'heure de la Mondialisation* [The assets of France in the era of globalization] (Paris: Fayard 2000).
28. The best-known statement of the alarmist position is Richard Bernstein and Ross Munro, *The Coming Conflict with China* (NY: Knopf 1997). An analysis of the alarmist faction in Washington is provided by Robert G. Kaiser and Steven Mufson, '"Blue team" draws a hard line on Beijing; Action on Hill reflects informal group's clout', *Washington Post*, 2 Feb. 2000, p.1.
29. At the time, this visit was unfairly lampooned in the press as a post-election boondoggle.

6

Taiwan in Japan's Foreign Relations: Informal Politics and Virtual Diplomacy

PHIL DEANS

This contribution examines the informal institutions which exist to maintain one of East Asia's most important, but least studied, bilateral relationships: that between Japan and the Republic of China on Taiwan (ROCT). It addresses and engages the growing body of literature on the significance of informal politics in East Asia, and attempts to develop it by showing how the assumptions about the functioning of informal politics are affected by operating across state boundaries.[1] The literature on informal politics has focused on the state or sub-state level, and this study of the activities of pro-Taiwan politicians in Japan confirms some ideas already advanced on the operation of informal politics in the region, but the fact that the informal politics in this case are centred in a deeply politicized international arena creates particular problems for the operation of informality. The 'one-China policy' of the People's Republic of China (PRC) means that the Japanese state is unable to maintain formal diplomatic links with Taiwan, and instead relies on semi-formal and informal channels to maintain its contacts. In the place of diplomatic ties Japan and Taiwan have established formal institutions to cover routine issues, but substantive issues are often dealt with through informal networks.

Japan is of greater significance to Taiwan and the relationship across the Taiwan Straits than any outside country other than the United States of America. Geographical proximity, historical legacy, economic complementarity and interdependence and growing security issues mean that the Japanese government is deeply concerned by all developments between Beijing and Taipei.[2] This contribution examines the evolution and changing role and function of Taiwan's political supporters in the Japanese Diet since 1952 with particular focus of the post-1972 period. A combination of shared anti-communist ideology, historical links, and financial reward have been the central motivations of pro-Taiwan groups in Japan. The principle function of the pro-Taiwan politicians has not been directed at changing Japanese government policy, rather it has acted as an informal channel of contact between the ROCT and Japan, thereby facilitating good relations and high-level contact in the absence of formal diplomatic ties. Since the mid-1990s there has been a shift in the role and function of these groups, caused by significant changes in Japanese domestic politics, the re-emergence of security concerns in the Taiwan Strait and changes in international politics which have put the pressure on the effectiveness of informal channels.

There are few studies on relations between states without diplomatic ties, and the anomalous situation of states communicating without the usual legal channels has only received slight attention.[3] Informal channels are effective in this case for a range of historical and socio-cultural reasons. In particular the overlap between the public and private spheres in Japan creates a space in which informal ties can work for state ends. However, the growing conformity of international practice that accompanies the processes of globalization make it increasingly difficult for Japan and Taiwan to maintain the codified ambiguity that has made informal links work. Instead, the increasing regularization and legalization of links in East Asia, as seen by the growing adherence to internal rules and norms embodied in institutions as diverse as diplomatic practice or the World Trade Organization, mean that the space in which informality has been conducted is being narrowed.

INFORMAL POLITICS AND 'VIRTUAL DIPLOMACY'

The stated policy of the Japanese government toward Taiwan is based on the principle of *seikei bunri*, the separation of politics and economics.[4] The central implication of this policy is that the economic sphere is private, outside the realm of the state and formal diplomacy, whereas politics is in the public sphere and is the concern of government, not business. Private (mainly economic) contacts are therefore regarded by the PRC as not extending political recognition and are not in violation of the 'one-China' principle. Of central importance to the maintenance of 'informal' ties is the way in which the public/private distinction, central to much Western political analysis, is contested in East Asia. Within the social sphere as well as in the realm of political economy public and private are instituted differently in Japan. The different meanings of these terms (compared with their use in the West) was reinforced and exacerbated by the way in which the modern state emerged in Japan and how the different institutionalization of public and private was utilized by the Japanese administrative state for developmental ends.[5] It has resulted in an ambiguity over the limits of the state in practical and normative senses. The public/private dichotomy underlies the dominant Western understandings of diplomacy, but the manner in which public and private are instituted in Japan has facilitated the Japanese administrative state's ability to operate a principle of separating politics and economics.

Because in Japan the state/public and society/private boundaries are indistinct, demarcating an issue to the public (state) or private (market/civil society) sphere can be so problematic that some processes can exist in both realms simultaneously. As Dittmer remarks, 'The "state", as in the 'state-society' paradigm, is a category that is far too homogeneous and monolithic, too static and rigid to capture the infinite variety of cross-cutting relationships that we find to be characteristic of informal politics.'[6]

In all modern economies it is difficult to disaggregate political from economic concerns; in the post-1945 Japanese developmental state this task is especially difficult. The fact that many of the Japanese state leadership's key political objectives have been of an economic type has made it easier for Japan to disguise political concerns as economic ones in the case of Taiwan. The overlap of public and private in the developmental state has furthermore enabled the creation of a space where entities can exist that perform functions that are in some ambiguous way both public and private.

In one sense, all the mechanisms for handling relations between Japan and Taiwan since 1972 have been 'informal': direct, official, inter-governmental contact has been impossible, and any moves in this direction has come under immediate and virulent criticism from the government of the PRC. Nevertheless, the governments of Japan and the ROC devised institutions with varying degrees of governmental support to replace the official channels. These institutions are the Japanese 'Interchange Association' (IA, J: *Koryu Kyokai*, C: *Jiaoliu Xiehui*) and the ROCT 'Association of East Asian Relations' (AEAR, C: *Yadong Guanxi Xiehui*, J: *Yato Kankei Kyokai*), renamed in 1991 the Taipei Economic and Cultural Representative Office in Japan. (TECRO, C: *Taiwan zhu Riben Jingji/Wenhua Daibiaochu*, J: *Taiwan chu Nihon Keizai/Bunka Daihyosho*). These institutions are staffed by full-time government officials, although in the Japanese case they are technically seconded from their ministries and not public employees.[7]

The IA and the AEAR belong to Berridge's category of 'representative offices', '...a useful device where non-recognition makes an interests section impossible but where relations with the "pariah" are sufficiently important – and perhaps providing evidence of sufficient improvement – to risk the possibility of giving some degree of offence to its more acceptable rival.[8]

These institutions are regarded as 'formal' institutions, because they have defined roles and responsibilities, receive funding and staff directly from central government (among other sources) and report directly to their respective governments. Many of the activities of the IA, and more explicitly the AEAR/TECRO, involve reporting directly to government, and are therefore by the definition used here 'formal', whereas the work of the pro-ROC/Taiwan groups, being the expression of 'private' interests and not arms of the administrative state, does not. As such they should be understood as formal branches of their respective governments that downplay the link (especially in the Japanese case) for the sake of political expediency.

An important factor that differentiates this arrangement from the standard cases outlined by Berridge is the good will and shared sense of purpose held by both the ROCT and Japanese governments concerning their relations. Both sides strive to maintain an amicable working relationship, and although there are difficulties and sensitive issues, the situation is not comparable to the hostile breaks in relations that are characteristic of the cases Berridge considers. T. K. Chang stated shortly after derecognition, 'The main thing to be stressed is that the breaking up of diplomatic relations was not resulting from war, but rather as a political expedience bought about by politicians not entirely shared by the ruling party itself, still less by the Japanese people at large.'[9]

Given the absence of formal diplomatic ties, Japan and Taiwan can be understood to enjoy a 'virtual diplomatic relationship'.[10] 'Virtual' here is understood to mean, 'that is such for practical purposes though not in name or according to strict definition'.[11] 'Virtual' then is used to explain the difference between the de facto diplomatic exchanges that take place, and the *de jure* situation that regards these as 'private' exchanges.[12]

In Japanese the distinction between *honne* and *tatemae* is useful in explaining the social context of this situation. *Honne* refers to the substantive reality of a situation, the core values or meaning of a set of social relations. *Tatemae* refers to the formal appearance of a set of social relations. It is important to note though that while *tatemae* is of great importance, it is not simply an expedient falsity for covering up a difficult situation.[13] Cheng and Womack contend, 'The binary epistemology of *tatemae* and *honne*, that is, appearance and reality, is a face-saving device, not a Manichean view of good politics versus bad politics.'[14] The *tatemae* (formal reality) of the unofficial Japan-Taiwan relationship is that Japan has no direct contacts with Taiwan and adheres to the 'one-China' principle. The *honne* (substantive reality) is that Japan and Taiwan enjoy a range of semi-formal and informal contacts. Dittmer suggests,

> informal politics consist of *the use of nonlegitimate means* (albeit not necessarily illegal) *to pursue public ends*. Thus it is sandwiched between 'formal politics' at on the one hand and 'corruption' on the other ... *Informal politics*, like corruption, may involve the sue of illegitimate means, but only to pursue *legitimate public ends* – power, 'pork', or policy.[15]

The case of the informal politics of links between Japan and Taiwan can be clearly located within this definition. The aims of Taiwan supporters in Japan can easily be regarded as being the pursuit of public ends promoting ties with a neighboring country but, as is shown below, the motives of Taiwan supporters in Japan may be related to financial advantage as much as to the interests of the Japanese (or ROCT) state. However, Dittmer's definition can be questioned over the issue of legitimacy. It is not illegal for Japanese politicians to maintain close links with Taiwan, and it is not necessarily illegitimate either. The legitimacy of these links can only be defined based on a specific assessment of the normative claims that the ROC on Taiwan may have to maintain contacts with the outside world. Therefore, from the perspective of the Chinese Communist Party (CCP) these links would be regarded as illegitimate, but for advocates of Taiwan's right to have an 'independent' voice, these contacts would be legitimate.

Informality is often regarded as being fundamental to the practice of politics in East Asia, but the literature on informal politics tends to focus on domestic politics, not international relations. It is suggested here that the informal mechanisms used to conduct and promote relations between Japan and Taiwan demonstrate that informal diplomacy can and does play a significant role. Informal channels are of considerable importance in Japanese politics, in particular where relations with China are concerned, and these channels have received some attention from scholars.[16]

Besshi has examined informal contact makers in post-war Sino-Japanese relations, and suggests they are more effective when they are both more official (i.e. have the support of senior political figures) and more secretive.[17] Zhao has written a sophisticated study of various informal mechanisms involved in the normalization of Japan-PRC relations. He states, '... informal practice refers to a set of informal political activities that take place outside the formal state structures (such as legislative, executive and judiciary branches). Therefore it may also be called extragovernmental activities'.[18] 'Informal' channels here mean the less institutionalized and unofficial groups that work in Japan and Taiwan to promote the relationship. Clearly the range of unofficial channels is vast and can consist of academic, business, cultural and tourist exchanges, as well as more obviously political and economic links.

Formal and informal ties each have their strengths and weaknesses. Pressure from the PRC on Japan means that the Japanese must rely more on informal channels in this particular case that they might do otherwise. This case shows how important and effective informal links can be, but also how vulnerable they are. The formal channels, centred on the IA and TECRO, are very good at managing routine contacts and exchanges. However they have severe limitations with regard to dealing with non-routine issues or crises. Informal channels may be better at dealing with unexpected events, but their lack of institutionalization means that they are subject to the vagaries of the specific individuals engaged in supporting Taiwan in Japan. As such the informal channels are fragile and vulnerable and dependent on the interests and motivations of the politicians who profess support for the ROC.

INTEREST GROUPS, INFORMAL POLITICS AND THE ISSUE OF TAIWAN IN JAPAN

The key informal institution in Japan-Taiwan relations has been the Japan-ROC Dietmembers' Consultative Council (*Nikka Kankei Giin Kondankai*, hereinafter *Nikkakon*[19]), which has dominated the Liberal Democratic Party (LDP) pro-ROC interest groups since 1972. Pro-ROC groups have been prominent in the Japanese Diet throughout the post-war era, and have played an important role in politics and policy-making. The first significant pro-ROC association formed in the Diet was the Japan-ROC Co-operation Committee (*Nikka Kyoruoku Iinkai* [JRCC]) which was founded in 1957 under Prime Minister Kishi Nobusuke.[20] Before the switch in recognition the JRCC was the most prominent pro-ROC group in the Diet and it played an important role as an informal channel helping to settle the disputes over Import-Export Bank credits to the PRC and the case of Zhou Hongqing.[21] The JRCC also contained representatives of major Japanese business interests, and it is significant that some of these

Japanese business groups withdrew their support from the JRCC following the announcement of Zhou's 'Four Principles' barring companies with links to Taiwan from trading with the PRC.[22] Increased bitterness over the China question eventually led to the collapse of the JRCC and it disbanded in 1973 partly as a consequence of it being untenable if any contact was wanted with the PRC.[23] However its remnants formed the core of the subsequent *Nikkakon*.

Nikkakon was founded in March 1973 by 27 LDP members who were also members of A-Ken and the JRCC.[24] The first Chairman was Nadao Hirokichi, with Fujio Masanari and Tamaki Kazuo as coordinators.[25] From this time it became the principal organization for expressing pro-ROC opinion in the Diet and sending delegations to visit Taiwan.[26]

Another organization of short-term significance that emerged at this time was the *Seirankai* (Young Storm Association) which consisted of 31 young and strongly anti-communist LDP members who were bitterly opposed to the PRC. They described the derecognition of the PRC as an act of 'unforgivable betrayal' by the 'acts of shameful ingrates' and 'diplomatic Quislings'.[27] This group played a significant role in the civil aviation crisis and contained several up-and-coming Japanese politicians who were to play an important role in Japan-Taiwan relations over the next 20 years, such as Ishihara Shintaro and Kanemaru Shin. *Nikkakon* quickly took over the functions of the defunct JRCC and began campaigning for the ROC in the Diet, complaining vigorously when the ROC's diplomatic property was transferred to the PRC.[28] *Nikkakon*'s role changed, however, after the serious infighting in the LDP that surrounded the change in recognition and the signing of the Treaty of Peace and Friendship with the PRC in 1978. From the mid-1970s *Nikkakon*'s importance switched from promoting the ROC and calling for its re-recognition to its function as an informal mechanism for contacts between political figures from Japan and Taiwan. In much the same way as opposition politicians and pro-PRC LDP members had proved vital in maintaining ties with Beijing before 1972, pro-ROC politicians have been a vital channel[29] of contact between the two sides.

A conscious effort has been made to avoid the term 'lobby' to describe these groups as it does not adequately convey their function and operation. Lobbying is typically defined as 'attempts to influence elected representatives during the passage of legislation'.[30] This definition is inadequate as it is not the representatives who are being lobbied, rather it is the representatives themselves who are supporting Taiwan. Furthermore, since the late 1970s, these groups have been more concerned with maintaining links with Taiwan and promoting Taiwan's interest in the broader context of Japan's relations with the PRC, rather than directly influencing legislation. The broader definition of lobbying as referring to, 'the practices of interest groups, directed not only at seeking support from elected members but also from political parties, public bureaucracies and other public bodies'[31] also fails to capture the role, function and significance of the pro-Taiwan/pro-ROC groups in the Japanese Diet as channels for informal contact between the governments rather than groups pushing the promotion of a single cause.

The importance of the pro-Taiwan groups is their role as a channel for communication between the two sides and as a substitute for regular diplomatic channels, rather than as a type of pressure group. Membership in these groups is primarily pragmatic or expedient rather than ideological. Also, while there have been cases where these groups have tried to directly influence the passage of legislation this has been the exception rather than the rule in the post-1972 period.

THE ROLE OF *NIKKAKON* IN JAPAN-TAIWAN RELATIONS

Nikkakon has provided three main avenues of contact to help the relationship: providing direct links between political and business figures from Taiwan and Japan; forming delegations to attend important ceremonies in the ROC, such as presidential inaugurations, the Double 10 National Day celebration in October and sending delegations to the funerals of dignitaries; and, since 1982, the organization and despatch of the LDP International Economic Countermeasures Investigation Council (*Jiminto Kokusai Keizai Taisaku Chosakai*) to Taiwan to discuss business and commercial matters. Takemi suggests that *Nikkakon* works as a 'pipe' to compensate for the inability of the IA or TECRO to handle highly political issues,[32] and this assessment is borne out when the occasional crises in the relationship are examined: the Diaoyutai/Senkaku dispute, the civil aviation crisis of the early 1970s, and the court battle over the ownership of the Kokaryo dormitories. As an unnamed member of Taiwan's representative office remarked, 'The Interchange Association is the last place we go when we have some kind of problem to solve.'[33]

The ROC's annual 'Double 10' National Day celebration is always attended by a delegation of *Nikkakon* members, and provides a useful opportunity for the Taiwanese and Japanese to discuss issues of mutual concern.[34] *Nikkakon* has also been prominent in sending delegations to the funerals of senior ROC figures, fulfilling one of the functions highlighted by Berridge.[35]

This role was particularly significant after the death of Chiang Kai-shek in April 1975 when a delegation including Sato Eisaku, Kishi Nobusuke, Nadao Horikichi, and Ishii Mitsujiro attended the funeral, as these *Nikkakon* members were able to use the opportunity to express to Chiang Ching-kuo their continuing commitment to the ROC/Taiwan in the wake of Japan's recognition of the PRC three years earlier.[36] This action took place during the bitter dispute over civil aviation links between Japan and Taiwan and was instrumental in the resolution of the dispute, demonstrating both the improvement in the relationship and the major role that *Nikkakon* was going to play in the relationship.[37]

Similarly, *Nikkakon* represented Japan at the funeral of Chiang Ching-kuo in 1988,[38] and was also the key representative institution for Japanese political dignitaries to a ceremony to mark the 100th anniversary of the birth of Chiang Kai-shek in Taipei in September 1986. A delegation of 130 Japanese politicians, led by Kishi Nobusuke, Nadao Horikichi and Sato Shinji and including several serving Japanese Cabinet ministers visited Taiwan for the occasion. However the serving ministers did not attend the full ceremony on the advice of the Ministry of Foreign Affairs (*Gaimusho*) in order not to offend the PRC.[39] This role has come in for criticism, however, with the PRC claiming, 'Some Diet members have tried to create "Two China's" by paying tribute to the "virtues" of Chiang Kai-shek.'[40]

The government of the PRC has been persistently critical of the role of *Nikkakon* in promoting links between Japan and Taiwan, although its informal, private nature makes it a difficult target. Nonetheless, it is difficult for a Japanese politician to hold a senior Cabinet position at the same time as being a senior *Nikkakon* figure – Sato Shinji stood down as chair of *Nikkakon* in 1998 when he took up the position of Minister for International Trade and Industry.

A recent example of *Nikkakon's* concrete influence and ability to achieve results was the change of visa-status for Taiwanese wanting to visit Japan The visa question rose to prominence in May 1990, when the Japanese Ministry of Justice (*Homusho*) announced it was to suspend the right of ROC passport holders to receive a 72-hour visa on arrival in Japan, apparently as part of government policy to crackdown on illegal workers who were taking advantage of the visa-free privilege.[41]

This move was greeted with anger in Taiwan and strong protests from Chiang Hsiao-wu, Director of the AEAR at the time, who threatened to resign over the issue. The Japanese move was apparently the result of an oversight by the Ministry of Justice which was not aware of Taiwan's 'special' status or of the diplomatic implications of such a move.[42] This visa issue was particularly important for Taiwan as many Taiwanese businessmen depended on these short-stay visas to conduct vital business in Japan, and they were also the typical visas used by Taiwanese bureaucrats and other figures making visits to Japan.[43]

The problem was dealt with by the intervention of Kanemaru Shin, at this time one of the most powerful LDP members and Taiwan's leading backer in the Japanese Diet. Following a series of telephone calls between President Lee Teng-hui and Kanemaru, the Ministry of Justice relented and suspended ending the visa privileges until the end of July 1990, when it would introduce a one-year, multiple-entry visa for ROC visitors not engaging in salaried work. This compromise has worked well, but in 1991 the Taiwanese side attempted to persuade the Japanese to return to the old system by offering Japanese tourists multiple-entry 72-hour visas on the condition of reciprocal treatment.[44]

Occasionally reports of the activities of *Nikkakon* members do appear in the Taiwanese press, such as in an interview with Hsu Shui-teh in 1992 where he stated that former Prime Minster Takeshita had played a vital role in obtaining the land for the new site of the Taiwan representative office while he was finance minister.[45] Given its informal nature and the sensitivity of its role, specific details are hard to find. One thing is clear, the ability of *Nikkakon* to influence policy in Japan depended on the domestic political strength of the individual member of *Nikkakon*.

This dynamic is particularly true of Kanemaru Shin. A telephone call to Kanemaru could often arrange an important meeting for the Taiwanese side, as was the case in arranging a meeting between former Japanese Finance Minister Hashimoto Ryutaro and Guo Wanshi in Australia in 1990.[46] Kanemaru's influence was to be the prime force in a major incident in Japan-Taiwan relations: the emergence of the *Shinbokukai*[47] as a rival to *Nikkakon* and the 1991 invitation to President Lee Teng-hui to visit Japan. *Nikkakon* fulfils the functions expected of informal political channels as outlined by Dittmer,

> By the 'filling the cracks' informal politics reveals and bridges shortcomings in the formal system; by basing itself on prepolitical ties and sentiments and the allocation of apolitical incentives, it broadens and deepens the political realm. At the heart of informal politics is power, and legitimacy is its Achilles heel, but it can provide a sort of non-ideological substitute for legitimacy based purely on getting things done, 'black or white cat'[48]

There are limits to the ability of pro-Taiwan figures to influence the relationship. Japan's Ministry of Foreign Affairs is typically reluctant to support any gesture that may harm relations between Tokyo and Beijing. This in part accounts for the initial failure of former President Lee Teng-hui to take up a range of invitations that have been made to him since he stood down as President in March 2000. In April 2001, for example, outgoing Japanese Prime Minster Mori attempted to allow Lee to visit Japan for an operation and encouraged Lee to apply for a visa to visit Japan. However this had not been cleared with the Foreign Ministry and considerable confusion over Lee's application ensued.[49]

Since the mid-1990s a shift can be discerned in the stance of the pro-Taiwan groups in the Japanese Diet. Dramatic political changes occurred in both Japan and Taiwan in the 1990s. In Japan these changes centred on splits and fractures within the LDP and its weakened power, while in Taiwan there was a rapid transition to increasingly democratic forms of government. The mid-1990s saw a marked increase in tension in the relationship between Beijing and Taipei that saw separate incidences of military posturing in the Taiwan Straits in 1995 and 1996. These tensions led to a major reappraisal of the significance of Taiwan to Japan, which had, in the words of a senior LDP politician, 'dropped from our consciousness'.[50]

The changing political climate on Taiwan saw moves away from the rhetoric of reunification and the emergence of politically significant Taiwanese consciousness and Taiwanese nationalism. The ROC supporters in Japan followed these changes and some developed links with the main opposition party, the Democratic Progressive Party (DPP),[51] and it can be argued that in Japan there has been a transformation within *Nikkakon* from being a pro-ROC to a pro-Taiwan group, much more attuned to the new political realities of Taiwan. The distinction between these two positions is that pro-ROC implies support for the reunification strategies of the KMT before the 1990s, whereas pro-Taiwan implies support for the more pragmatic and ambivalent approach to reunification that emerged under Lee.

The impact of the victory of the DPP's Chen Shui-bian in the March 2000 presidential election in Taiwan on these informal links is hard to quantify. Most LDP politicians had developed informal links with key individuals within the KMT and so informal connections between the DPP and Japan will be weaker. Political uncertainties within Japanese politics have also tested the informal links – the scandal that engulfed Kanemaru in the early 1990s, for example, removed one of Taiwan's most powerful and active supporters, as did the fall from grace of former leader of the House of Councillors, Murakami Masatake.

FACTIONS IN JAPANESE POLITICS AND THE CHINA GROUPS:
MEMBERSHIP AND MOTIVATION

Where the case of informal politics in Japan-Taiwan relations differs from most cases of informal politics in Asia is that it is not principally expressed through factional politics. There is a general consensus in the scholarly literature that, within the LDP at least, factions have been centred primarily around individuals and functioned as mechanisms for career advancement, the election of the LDP president and the raising of campaign funds rather than as groups for contesting different policy opinions.[52] A general tendency of some factions to be more 'right-wing' or 'left-wing' on certain issues can be identified, but policy issues are not usually significant in factional affiliation or behavior. Changes in Japanese politics since 1993, especially the fracturing of the ruling LDP may mean that the pattern of factional politics is undergoing a significant shift.

China policy, however, was an area which saw serious policy conflict within the LDP.[53] Significant splits developed in the LDP in the early 1970s centred around attitudes towards the PRC and Taiwan, but it should be noted that the differences over the China question cut across factional affiliations.[54] Opinion on China policy was expressed instead through the pro-PRC and pro-ROC groups that existed in the Diet, what Mendl has called 'supra-partisan' organizations.[55]

However the posture toward China was one issue where there were serious divisions among LDP members, and so the Diet was involved much more extensively than is the case with other areas of Japanese foreign affairs which were typically dealt with in a routine way by the *Gaimusho*.[56] LDP members with links with China had long been a key channel for Tokyo and Beijing to interact. Indeed, as the case of the second Yoshida Letter demonstrates, these informal links could actually define official policy.[57]

The rival China groups were most active at the time of normalization and the years immediately after, up to the signing of the Treaty of Peace and Friendship with the PRC in 1978.[58] While there is interest in Taiwan among non-LDP members, they have not, to date, played a significant role in maintaining the relationship.

Tanaka Akihiko has examined LDP factions and affiliation to either the pro-PRC (*Nihon-Chugoku Yuko Giin Renmei*) or pro-ROC (*Nikkakon*) group. Tanaka shows that before the joint elections for both houses of the

Diet in 1986, 60 LDP members belonged to both groups, while 39 belonged to neither. Tanaka demonstrates that within the LDP although there is a slight tendency for certain factions to contain more members who are in the pro-ROC or pro-PRC groups, there is not a significant relationship.[59] In part, the absence of the relationship between factional affiliation and membership of the different China factions can be put down to the fact that the issue has become much less contentious in Japanese domestic politics since the late 1970s. Langdon has suggested that in the late 1960s and early 1970s it was perhaps the key policy problem within the LDP and factions did bear a greater relationship to China policy.[60]

Hashimoto Yasuo, the Director-General (*Jimukyokucho*) of *Nikkakon*, stated in an interview that although at the time of normalization there were fewer members of the Tanaka faction in *Nikkakon*, this division disappeared in the 1980s and that factions no longer had any relevance to *Nikkakon* membership and that Taiwan therefore had support throughout the LDP.[61]

Nevertheless, continuities can be identified. The Sato faction split following the China recognition crisis in 1972, most of its members joining the Tanaka faction. It is significant though that many of the leading figures of the next generations of pro-Taiwan members (Nikaido Susumu, Kanemaru Shin, Ozawa Ichiro) were important figures within the Tanaka faction. Tanaka's support for opening relations with China was pragmatic, and many of his key supporters maintained their ties with Taiwan. This link has been overlooked because the conflict between Tanaka and the more overtly pro-ROC Fukuda Takeo has polarized debate and pigeonholed Tanaka as 'pro-PRC', rather than as a pragmatist working broadly within Yoshida Shigeru's understanding of Japan's role in East Asia and the world. The pragmatism evident in Japanese politics and the Taiwan issue can be seen in the fact that Sato Eisaku's son, a key figure in *Nikkakon*, was a member of the Takeshita faction, the direct successor of the Tanaka faction. This faction later came under the control of Kanemaru Shin, and then formed the dominant power base of Ozawa Ichiro.

Since the fracturing of the LDP in 1993 it has become much harder to trace and identify pro-Taiwan politicians on the basis on membership of *Nikkakon*. Many of the new (and often short-lived) parties that emerged from the LDP established their own pro-Taiwan groups (invariably also called *Nikkakon*) and some members continued to work closely with their former LDP colleagues with regard to promoting Taiwan after they had left the LDP.[62] The complexity of Japanese party and factional politics makes analysis of the kind conducted by Tanaka in the late 1980s almost impossible. However one thing is clear – many senior members of the LDP and Cabinet ministers in the Obuchi and Mori governments had backgrounds in *Nikkakon*.[63] There were probably more pro-Taiwan figures in the Japanese government 1998–2000 than at anytime since Japan established relations with Beijing in 1972.

However, Taiwanese officials state that is not numbers that matter, but attitude and influence: many *Nikkakon* members only offer tokenistic support to Taiwan, but when a major influential figure offers support, this can be critical to Taiwan 'diplomatic' presence in Japan. One of the most important figures in this regard in the late 1990s was Leader of the Upper House, Murakami Masatake. Murakami and Prime Minister Obuchi were both active supporters of Taiwan, and it is their role that was instrumental in the Japanese government 'no' following the Clinton administration's 'Three Noes' policy with regard to Taiwan in 1999. While in Shanghai, President Clinton announced that the US government would not support Taiwanese independence, would not support a one-China, one-Taiwan policy, and would not support Taiwan's membership of international organizations for which sovereignty was a prerequisite. In an unprecedented case of Japanese policy being closer to Taiwan than that of the United States, the Obuchi government did not make a similar statement at the time of Zhu Rongji visit to Japan in 1999. It has been suggested that Murakami was instrumental in Japanese firms being awarded the contract to build Taiwan first high-speed railway, and in sponsoring a House of Councillors' resolution to maintain the 72-hour visa free status for ROC passport holders.[64]

Given that factional affiliation and stance on the China issue do not have a clear direct correlation with membership of *Nikkakon*, and that pragmatism is clearly discernible amongst pro-Taiwan politicians, it is important to consider what does motivate LDP Diet members to join the pro-Taiwan group. The following section considers three possibilities: ideology, historical connections, and financial reward.

Ideology

Formal ideology has not been a major factor in conservative politics in Japan since 1945. Ideological commitment was certainly a major factor for the Japan Socialist Party (JSP) and the Japan Communist Party (JCP), moreover splits both within and between these parties over pro-PRC or pro-USSR stances were particularly marked in the 1960s and 1970s. Within the LDP, however, positive attachment is much harder to locate. Fukui states, 'None of the LDP Dietmembers identified as pro-Beijing has ever supported communism or Marxism as such, but have argued that the basic force in contemporary China has been nationalism rather than communism.'[65]

Langdon further argues that pro-Beijing groups are motivated by a, '... conviction that friendly relations [with the PRC] are essential'.[66] As a conservative party, an identification with *anti*-communism is plausible, and is cited as key factor by the leadership of *Nikkakon*, and it was certainly stated as a principal reason for the support of Taiwan by senior *Nikkakon* figures in the early 1990s.[67]

It is also worth pointing out that many senior LDP members who belonged to pro-ROC groups were also members of ROC-based organizations such as the World Anti-Communist League. However, even Prime Minister Sato Eisaku, who was forced from office over the normalization issue because of his supposed pro-ROC sympathies, is not a clear-cut 'anti-communist' in this sense.[68]

Furthermore, even before normalization in 1972 many members of pro-ROC groups were not opposed to expanding trade with the PRC, and after 1972 members of *Nikkakon* did not oppose relations with the PRC,[69] rather they wanted, 'to ensure there was no discrimination against Taiwan'.[70]

This trend continues to the present day. Sato Shinji, a former *Nikkakon* spokesman, when asked about the fact that LDP members belonged to both pro-PRC and pro-ROC replied that he did not see this as contradictory as the groups were both 'trying to promote the best interests of Japan'.[71] However, by the end of the 1990s, a resurgent and more powerful *Nikkakon* was again promoting Taiwanese interests, even to the detriment of relations between Beijing and Tokyo.

Another important issue is that anti-communism does not necessarily indicate that the members were privately supportive of the goals of Chiang Kai-shek and ROC. Interviews conducted by Douglas H. Mendel Jr in the 1960s demonstrate that many of the leading 'pro-ROC' figures in Japan had little sympathy with Chiang Kai-shek's stance on the future of Taiwan, and many favored independence for the island. Mendel cites interviews with Kishi Nobusuke and Sato Eisaku from this time that show they were sympathetic to the cause of Taiwanese independence, at least in private, and did not take Chiang's claims about reclaiming the mainland seriously.[72]

This perspective appears to be of growing significance in pro-Taiwan Japanese politicians, as more clearly evidenced in the speeches and actions of the nationalist Mayor of Tokyo, Ishihara Shintaro. Furthermore, senior *Nikkakon* figures in the early 1990s stated that they no longer accepted the then prevailing ROC position that the ROC was the sole, legitimate government of China and that *Nikkakon* broadly supported Japan's relations with the PRC. This change represents a considerable shift within *Nikkakon*, and a redefinition of its role as promoting the interests of Taiwan in-and-of itself, rather than just in competition with the PRC.

The end of the Cold War has also downgraded the significance of anti-communism, regardless of its continuing formal presence in the PRC. It could be argued that the motives of politicians such as Ishihara in supporting Taiwan have shifted from being rooted in anti-communism to increasingly being based on fear or concern about China or even on anti-Chinese sentiment – Ishihara's record of vehemently anti-Chinese statements and attempts to downgrade Japan's history of aggression in China would appear to support this claim.

Historical/Personal Links

Another factor that may contribute to membership of *Nikkakon* is historical or personal links with Taiwan. These can be rooted in either the colonial period, as was the case with Shiina Etsusaburo who was the nephew of Goto Shimpei (the first Chief of Civil Administration of colonial Taiwan), or it can be because of connections with the KMT and the Chiang regime. Kishi and Sato Eisaku were associated with the Choshu elite that had historic ties to Taiwan dating back prior to and throughout the colonial era: they were both returned as members of parliament from the Yamaguchi district, as was Sato's son, Sato Shinji, a later leader of *Nikkakon*.

The JRCC was founded by Ishii Mitsujiro, a faction leader and former private secretary to Ando Sadami while he was governor-general of Taiwan.[73] Ishii led the first major delegation of Japanese politicians to visit Taiwan in August 1956 shortly after the formation of the LDP.[74] However, having a relationship with colonial Taiwan does not mean that an LDP figure would necessarily be a supporter of the ROC. Fujiyama Aiichiro had extensive business concerns in Taiwan during the colonial period but was a consistent advocate within the LDP of developing a closer relationship with the PRC.[75]

A key factor that was stressed by many members of *Nikkakon* and one that is apparent in much of the literature on *Nikkakon*, is the importance of the legacy of Chiang Kai-shek's 'generosity' towards Japan at the end of World War II.[76] Kaya Okinori, one of the key figures in the pro-ROC groups in the post-war era, stated six reasons why Japan should not 'abandon' Taiwan: (i) the long period of friendly relations since 1945; (ii) the ROC's membership of the 'free-world'; (iii) the injustice of derecognizing a free country to normalize relations with a communist one;

(iv) the immorality of abandoning a country that had done no wrong to Japan; (v) Japan's four-fold indebtedness to Taiwan; and (vi) the absence of a crisis that would make derecognition unavoidable.[77]

Central to Kaya's position was the idea of Japan's indebtedness to Chiang Kai-shek for his policy of 'returning malice with virtue' (*yi de bao yuan*). Kaya stated that Japan owed a special debt because:

(1) Chiang Kai-shek had opposed the abolition of the Imperial Household after the war;

(2) Chiang had been 'strict but generous' toward Japanese soldiers and civilians in China after Japan's surrender greatly assisting their repatriation;

(3) Chiang had vigorously opposed the division of Japan into zones of occupation; and

(4) Chiang had given up the right to reparations from Japan.[78]

Iguchi Sadao, a Japanese ambassador to the ROC, cited Chiang's policy of 'returning malice with virtue' as contributing the most to the closeness felt between Japan and the ROC.[79]

Both Sato Shinji and Hashimoto Yasuo also stated that Chiang's speedy repatriation of Japanese from China after 1945 and his opposition to any Soviet involvement in the occupation were also sources of Japanese 'gratitude' toward Chiang and the ROC.[80]

The reason for Chiang's position on this issue is under-explored but it is likely that Chiang was motivated by anti-communism and a desire to establish cordial relations in the post-war era. It was the legacy of this 'generosity' and the associated good feeling toward the Chiang family that generated such good will towards Chiang Hsiao-wu during his time as Director of the AEAR. These factors continue to be relevant, and were frequently cited in interviews by *Nikkakon* members, but were of declining significance, as Kaya's generation has passed from political influence.

The issue of returning malice with virtue has become the central myth in relations between Japan and the ROC. It is a myth not because it may or may not be factually true, but because it has become the central story around which pro-ROC support has been mobilized. The 'actions' of Chiang Kai-shek are less significant than the way in which Taiwan's supporters in Japan have attempted to mobilize them to promote relations between Japan and Taiwan.

However, the 'returning good for evil' myth is of much less significance for younger supporters of Taiwan in Japan, as evidenced by the controversial book *Taiwanron* (*On Taiwan*) by the right-wing cartoonist Kobayashi Yoshinori.[81] Kobayashi is bitterly critical of Chiang Kai-shek and the KMT as a principal cause of Taiwanese suffering, and links his support for Taiwan to Japan's colonial presence and Taiwanese sympathy for the Japanese.

Finance and Money

A further important factor in motivating pro-ROC sympathies of LDP members is the controversial and contentious issue of financial provision for Japanese politicians. The importance of huge campaign funds in the Japanese electoral system is well known and well documented. Cheng and Womack summarize the scholarly consensus on informal politics in Japan as follows,

> As Curtis, Fukui and Fukai underscore, informal politics in Japan is perennially riveted to two major activities, pork barrel and power politics, or put another way, resource transfers to one's own constituency and queuing for one's turn for a Cabinet position in the overall context of re-election battles.[82]

This sub-section addresses the pork barrel question, placing it in the context of the political competition within the LDP.

What, though, is the financial incentive in backing a specific foreign policy issue, such as supporting Taiwan? Because this issue is such a contentious and politically sensitive one, concrete details are hard to find: a Japanese politician is hardly likely to admit to receiving these kinds of funds in writing or in an interview. However, it is possible to speculate with regard to these ties without straining the imagination, and off-the-record suggestions and opinions were gathered through interviews in 1991–93 and 1995. It is clear that business interests were very important in backing the JRCC in trying to find ways around Zhou Enlai's 'Four Principles' in 1970 and it is not unreasonable to assume that these companies remunerated the politicians involved. Furthermore financial links between the right-wing oil tycoon Sasakawa Ryoichi and the pro-Taiwan, strongly anti-communist *Seirankai* have been the subject of considerable debate.[83]

In the 1970s and early 1980s the financial incentive was the least important of the three factors considered here. However, this situation was to change for a number of reasons. One has been that the generation with strong ties to the Chiang family or with personal memories of Chiang's generosity after World War II has died off and been of less importance to Japanese politics. Although these historical factors are still cited by *Nikkakon* members, their actual relevance can increasingly be questioned.

Another important issue has been the remarkable changes in both Taiwan and the PRC since 1972. The growing distance between President Lee Teng-hui and the legacy of both Chiang Kai-shek and Chiang Ching-kuo, was considerable, and the traditional ROC claims are being downplayed or even abandoned. These trends are likely to continue with the new DPP administration of Chen Shui-bian. The dramatic changes in the PRC as a result of Deng Xiaoping's 'Open Door Policy' and the introduction of market socialism mean that an anti-communist posture looks dated. The vicious internal LDP battles over the PRC *or* the ROC have died down since the signing of the Treaty of Peace and Friendship between Japan and the PRC in 1978.

The issue of finance was one of increasing significance in the 1990s. The late 1980s and early 1990s saw an intensification of factional conflict within the LDP, that resulted in the splitting of the LDP into several parties in 1993, with a core retaining the title of LDP. The competition within the LDP at this time required increasing amounts of money to finance campaign expenses and to secure the support of important sections of the party, and so led to an increased demand for finances. At the same time, an ever-richer Taiwan was prepared to spend money in the pursuit of a higher international profile under the remit of President Lee Teng-hui's 'pragmatic diplomacy'.

The fragility of informal ties, especially where money is concerned, was clearly demonstrated by the formation of the *Shinbokukai* and the near-fiasco of Kanemaru Shin's invitation to President Lee. In May 1991, a delegation from *Nikkakon* made its annual visit to Taiwan. During the visit a group of *Nikkakon* members, led by Kanemaru Shin, held a separate, smaller meeting attended by Chiang Hsiao-wu and senior ROC political and business figures, and announced the formation of the *Kokusai Seisaku Kenkyu Shinbokukai* with the express intent of 'promoting exchange between Japan and Taiwan'.[84] Significantly, one of the key figures on the Japanese side was Hattori Reiijiro, Chairman of the Seiko Company and a board member of the Interchange Association.[85] The *Shinbokukai* was a rival to Nikkakon that was much closer to the emerging generation of Taiwanese politicians (such as Lee Teng-hui). Its inauguration threatened to reduce the significance of *Nikkakon*, and the funding that the Taiwanese may have channelled through this link to individual Japanese politicians. Along with the formation of the *Shinbokukai* in 1991 Kanemaru made an invitation to President Lee to make a 'private' visit to Japan. When this move was discovered by Kanemaru's rivals in the LDP, the news was leaked to the Japanese press, resulting in protests from the PRC which prevented the visit from taking place.[86]

Kanemaru's fall from grace in 1993 and subsequent death have left the Taiwanese with a major gap in their informal ties with Japan. This situation made worse by the animosity the *Shinbokukai* incident generated in the traditional pro-ROC figures, Sato Shinji and Fujio Masanari.

The remarkable political changes in Taiwan in the 1990s have changed its profile in Japan. One consequence of this shift has been that the non-LDP parties, which had previously taken a rather distant approach to Taiwan, are developing stronger links.[87]

Also, sympathy and support for Chiang Kai-shek and the Kuomintang became increasingly anachronistic as the KMT transformed itself under Lee Teng-hui – with the election of Chen Shui-bian, the significance of the KMT link and the legacy of Chiang must be questioned even further. Support for Taiwan is now often couched in terms of respect for Taiwanese democracy (in contrast to the PRC's authoritarianism) rather on issues of historical legacy.

The emergence of security issues in the mid-1990s further invigorated the anti-PRC/pro-Taiwan element within Japanese politics, and the issue of Taiwan gained prominence in debates over the renegotiation of the Guidelines of the US-Japan security Treaty. The new Guidelines stated that Japan could support the US in the 'areas surrounding' Japan and the Chief Cabinet Secretary Kajiyama Seiroku – a long-time Taiwan supporter – said that the 'areas surrounding' Japan 'naturally include the Taiwan Strait'.[88] This statement was subsequently 'finessed' by *Gaimusho* which insisted that the 'areas surrounding' are situational' rather than 'geographical' but this comment has been contradicted by other parts of the Ministry of Foreign Affairs (MOFA).[89]

The motives of Taiwan supporters in Japan and are mixed and complex, and the categories of ideology, historical and personal ties, and financial reward should not be regarded as mutually exclusive but as complimentary. What is telling about all the incentives for Taiwan's supporters is their fragility. Conservative parties, such as Japan's LDP, rarely have a positive ideological basis, and opposition to 'communism' is of only limited use given the rapid transformation of the PRC's economy in the 1980s and the 1990s. Increasingly, support for Taiwan has become a vehicle for Japanese nationalism and the expression of anti-Chinese sentiment, as the case of Ishihara Shintaro demonstrates. Personal and historical ties have a limited timeframe, and as the Japanese-speaking generation in Taiwan passes from influence over time it is unclear how this particular relationship will be sustained. It is not yet clear how changes in the Japanese electoral system will change the money-based nature of Japanese politics, although the reforms were designed in part to reduce graft and corruption. One thing is clear – financial incentive is a precarious position on which to base such a vital channel of diplomatic communication.

CONCLUSIONS

Informal politics has been central to the operation of relations between Japan and Taiwan since 1972. The various pro-ROC groups in Japan have been of vital significance in managing and maintaining the post-recognition Japan-Taiwan relationship. The informal, personal level of contact and influence offered by *Nikkakon* has been a key channel of direct contact for problem solving and the discussion of high-level issues of mutual concern. It has shown that the pro-Taiwan lobbies within Japan perform a vital role as an avenue for contact between the two, being able to mediate difficult circumstances and deal with issues that the formal institutions of the IA and TECRO cannot handle.

Furthermore, these ties are supported by a range of popular perceptions and images that support the relationship. However, because this link is dependent on personal contact, when the personal connections are threatened – by old age, political intrigue or other factors – then this channel comes under severe threat.

The domestic political turmoil in Japan since 1992 has severely hampered the use of this channel, and has left the Taiwanese side without its most useful means to contact Japan. Taiwan's democratization and the positive view of Japan held by many Taiwanese however has increased sympathy in Japan: in April 2001, four of the major Japanese newspapers published editorials calling for former President Lee Teng-hui to be granted a visa to visit Japan for medical treatment.[90]

The informal ties provided by *Nikkakon* are very fragile. The turmoil within Japanese politics in the mid-1990s has also meant that Japanese politicians are both more occupied with domestic concerns and more cautious about where their money comes from. Informal ties are fragile because they tend to be personality-based and therefore not institutionalized. They are also limited in their ability to deal with issues of high politics, in particular issues of military security, such as those that have emerged since 1995. With regard to domestic politics, Dittmer suggests that informal politics in East Asia has not disappeared in the processes of political development. Instead it has become more codified, and the two key threats to informal politics are suppression and marketization.[91] In this case marketization is difficult: diplomacy cannot be privatized in this way. Suppression, in the form of growing opposition from the PRC to Japan's informal links wi:h Taiwan, is a constant threat.

Furthermore, informal ties cannot survive well in the increasingly formalized and legal framework that manages diplomacy – the increased involvement of international law in international relations in East Asia (mainly through institutions such as the WTO and APEC) mean that the blurring of public and private realms is harder to perpetuate. As diplomatic changes and the processes of globalization put increasing pressure on Japan and Taiwan to accept international (western) norms with regard to public and private the space for informal politics is being narrowed, and this is change presents the key challenge for Japanese diplomacy with regard to Taiwan in the future.

NOTES

The author gratefully acknowledges the support of the Japan Foundation Endowment Committee (JFEC Grant No. 108) in preparing this study.

1. For recent studies see Lowell Dittmer, Haruhiro Fukui and Peter N.S. Lee, *Informal Politics in East Asia* (Cambridge: CUP 2000); the special issue of *Asian Survey* 36/3 (March 1996); and John Quansheng Zhao, *Japanese Policymaking: The Politics Behind Politics; Informal Mechanisms and the Making of China Policy* (Westport, CT, and London: Praeger 1993).
2. For background to Taiwan in Sino-Japanese relations see Phil Deans, 'The Taiwan Question in Sino-Japanese Relations: Reconciling the Irreconcilable', in Marie Söderberg (ed.) *China and Japan* (London: Routledge 2001).
3. The two principal works on this issue are Deon Geldenhuys, *Isolated States: A Comparative Analysis* (Cambridge: CUP 1990); and G.R. Berridge, *Talking to the Enemy: How States without 'Diplomatic Relations' Communicate* (London: Macmillan 1994).
4. *Seikei bunri* is the abbreviated form of *seiji keizai bunri* (C: *zhengzhi jingji fenli*). The characters are mutually intelligible to readers of Japanese and Chinese. Interestingly it has been claimed that the phrase was first used by the PRC Premier Zhou Enlai as a way of encouraging the Japanese to develop contacts with China. Ikeda Masanosuke states that it was Zhou Enlai who initiated the notion of separating political and economic concerns, Ikeda Masanosuke, *Nitchu boeki kosho hiroku* (Tokyo: Naigaijijo kenkyusho 1968) p.9, cited in Chae-jin Lee, *Japan Faces China: Political and Economic Relations in the Postwar Era* (Baltimore and London: Johns Hopkins UP 1976) p.231, n.24.
5. See Phil Deans 'The Capitalist Developmental State in East Asia' in Ronen Palan, Jason Abbott with Phil Deans, *State Strategies in the Global Political Economy* (London and NY: Pinter 1999) pp.78–102.
6. Lowell Dittmer, 'East Asian Informal Politics in Comparative Perspectives', in Dettmer *et al.* (note 1) p.290.
7. For background on the creation of the IA and the AEAR, see David Nelson Rowe *Informal*

'Diplomatic Relations': The Case of Japan and the Republic of China, 1972–74 (Hamden, CT: Shoe String Press 1975),

8. Berridge (note 3) p.52.

9. T.K. Chang, 'The Private Agreement Between Associations of the ROC and Japan Respecting Continuation of Economic Ties', *Asian Outlook* (Feb. 1973) p.28.

10. This discussion is based on Phil Deans, *Virtual Diplomacy: Japan-Taiwan Relations since 1972* (forthcoming).

11. *Concise Oxford Dictionary* (1982). This understanding of virtual then is its traditional one, not the William Gibson-inspired technological 'cyberspace' understanding of 'virtual'.

12. The Japanese use the term *minkan* (C: *minjian*) to denote 'private' in this context, with *minkanjin* meaning 'a private citizen', and it can also be translated as 'civil'. In Chinese this expression implies 'among the people', and is often translated into English as 'popular' or 'folk' as in folk tales (*minjian gushi*) or folk music (*minjian yinyue*).

13. Chalmers Johnson, '*Omote* (Explicit) and *Ura* (Implicit): Translating Japanese Political Terms' in Chalmers Johnson *Japan: Who Governs? The Rise of the Developmental State* (NY and London: Norton 1995) pp.157–82; Takeo Doi, *The Anatomy of Self: The Individual Versus Society* (Tokyo: Kodansha International 1985).

14. Ten-jen Cheng and Brantly Womack, 'General reflections on Informal Politics in Asia', *Asian Survey* 36/3 (March 1996) pp.321–2.

15. See Dittmer (note 6) p.292.

16. See the special issue of *Kokusai Seiji* which directly addressed informal contact makers and Japan's international relations, *Kokusai Seiji (International Relations* [sic]) 'Nihon Gaiko no Hiseishiki Channeru', 75 (Oct. 1983), especially Yukio Besshi, 'Sengo Nit-Chu Kankei to Hiseishiki Sesshokusha', pp.98–113. Accounts of informal groups and Japan's relations with the PRC can be found in Zhao (note 1); Chae-jin Lee, *Japan Faces China* (note 4) and also in Chalmers Johnson, 'The Patterns of Japanese Relations with China, 1952–1982', in *Japan: Who Governs?* (note 13) pp.235–64.

17. Besshi (note 16) pp.112–13.

18. Zhao (note 1) p.4; See also his article '"Informal Pluralism" and Japanese Politics: Sino-Japanese Rapprochement Revisited', *Journal of Northeast Asia Studies* 8/2 (Summer 1989) pp.65–83.

19. There is no elegant translation of *kondankai* into English, but the phrase implies a social and amiable discussion group, and is often used in the context of parent-teacher associations or after-school social groups. I have chosen to translate '*Ka*' (the Chinese *Hua*) as ROC, rather than 'Taiwan' or 'China' as this captures the pro-KMT intent of the Japanese.

20. This section is based on Kurata Nobuyasu, 'Nikka Kyoryoku Iinkai no Rekishiteki Yakuwari' in Uno Seichi, *Kobun kara Ritokei e: Nikka 80-nen no Kiseki* (Tokyo: Waseda UP 1992) pp.333–49; and Ikei Masaru, 'Nikka Kyoryoku Iinkai: Sengo Nichi-Tai Kankei no Kosatsu' *Hogaku Kenkyu* [Law Studies] 53/2 (1980) pp.1–28.

21. A move by the Japanese to allow the use of government credits in 1963 and then a controversy over the return of a 'defector' to the PRC led to threats from the ROC side to terminate relations. See Rin Kinkei [Lin Ch'in-ching] *Ume to Sakura: sengo no Nikka kankei* (Tokyo: Sankei Shuppan 1984) pp.202–13.

22. John Welfield, *Empire in Eclipse Japan in the Postwar American Alliance System* (London: Athlone Press 1988) p.292; and Sadako Ogata, 'The Business Community and Japanese Foreign Policy: Normalization of Relations with the PRC', in Robert A. Scalapino (ed.) *The Foreign Policy of Modern Japan* (Berkeley and London: Univ. of California Press 1977) pp.185–91.

23. Welfield (note 22) pp.300, 308.

24. The Asian Problems Study Group (*Ajiya Mondai Kenkyukai* or A-Ken) was established in Dec. 1964 and comprised 98 right-wing LDP members such as Ishii Mitsujiro and Funada Naka. For background on A-Ken see Sadako Ogata, 'Japanese Attitudes Toward China' *Asian Survey* 5 (Aug. 1965) pp.389–98; and Lee (note 4) pp.49–50.

25. Takemi Keizo, 'Nichi-Tai Kankei', in Wakabayashi Masahiro, Ryu Shinkei [Liu Jinkai] and Mastunaga Masayoshi (eds.) *Taiwan Hyakka* (Tokyo: Taishukan Shoten 1990) p.101. Takemi

argues that Nadao represents the 'first generation' of pro-Taiwan members while Fujio and Tamaki represent the second, but he does not elaborate on why he makes this distinction.

26. One such delegation in Sept. 1973 'apologised' publicly for Prime Minister Tanaka Kakuei's recognition of the PRC 'Treading Air', *FEER* (7 Jan. 1974) p.12.

27. See 'Forming the Battle Lines', *FEER* (25 Feb. 1974) pp.23–4, and 'Seiran-kai: The young 'Turks' flex their muscles' *FEER* (13 May 1974) pp.21–2.

28. Lin (note 21) pp.368–9.

29. In Japanese the term *paipu* (pipe) is more common than *channeru* (channel).

30. Vernon Bogdanov (ed.) *Blackwell Encyclopaedia of Political Science* (Oxford: Blackwell 1991) p.337.

31. Ibid.

32. Takemi (note 25) p.102.

33. Unnamed official, working for Taiwan's Association of East Asian Relations (AEAR) in Tokyo, cited in 'Ties that Bind: Chiang Memorial Meeting Underlines Tokyo-Taipei Links', *FEER* (25 Sept. 1986) p.18.

34. Takemi (note 25) pp.101–2.

35. Berridge (note 3).

36. 'Severing a link with the past', *FEER* (18 April 1975) p.20.

37. For the airlinks dispute see Ssu-ma Sang-tun, *Zhong-Ri Guanxi 25 Nian*, 3rd ed. (Taipei: Lien-he Pao 1988) pp.365–77; and Lin Ch'in-ching, *Sengo no Nikka Kankei to Kokusaiho* (Tokyo: Yuhikaku 1987) pp.145–54.

38. Takemi (note 25) p.102.

39. 'Ties that Bind' (note 33) pp.16–18.

40. 'Japan's Court Ruling Creates "Two China's"', *Beijing Review* 30/22 (1 June 1987) p.10.

41. *Lien-he Pao* (1 June 1990). This move was not directed at Taiwan specifically, but at other Asian countries. However 'unofficial sources' estimated that up to 10,000 ROC citizens were overstaying in Japan, *China Post* (1 June 1990) p.1.

42. Unattributable interview with senior IA, March 1993.

43. Miki Chang, *Taiwan no Senryaku: Gyakususuru no Doragon* [Taiwan's Strategy: The Counter-attacking Dragon] (Tokyo: Chuo 1995) pp.193–4.

44. *China Post* (29 March 1991) p.6.

45. *Hsin Hsin-wen* (28 Nov.–5 Dec. 1992) p.85. In the same interview Hsu reported Takeshita as stating that he helped Taiwan because Fujio Masanari had asked him to.

46. *Hsin Hsin-wen* (21–27 Nov. 1992) p.107.

47. The *Shinbokukai*, or 'New Harmony Association' was founded as a rival to *Nikkakon* in 1991. Details below.

48. Dittmer *et al.* (note 1) p.306.

49. Unattributable interviews in Taiwan and Japan, March and April 2001. See also *Lienhe-pao* (11 April 2001).

50. Unattributable interview with a senior LDP politician, Aug. 1999.

51. An interesting example is Prime Minister Mori, who developed a personal relationship with the DPP leader (and ROC President since March 2000) Chen Shui-bian.

52. The following discussion of LDP factions is derived from Haruhiro Fukui, *Party in Power: the Japanese Liberal Democrats and Policy-Making* (Canberra: Australian National UP 1970) pp.57–80; Nathaniel B. Thayer, *How the Conservatives Rule Japan* (: Princeton UP 1969) pp.15–57; and J.A.A. Stockwin, *Japan: Divided Politics in a Growth Economy* (London: Weidenfeld 1982) pp.125–33.

53. Tanaka Akihiko, *Nit-Chu Kankei, 1945–1990* (Tokyo UP 1991) p.198. See also Frank C. Langdon, 'Japanese Liberal Democratic Factional Discord on China Policy', *Pacific Affairs* 41 (Fall 1968) pp.403–15.

54. For an overview at the time of normalization, see Fukui (note 52) p.256.

55. Wolf Mendl, *Issues in Japan's China Policy* (London: Macmillan for RIIA 1978) p.47.

56. Tanaka (note 53) p.198.

57. In 1964 former Prime Minster Yoshida Shigeru wrote a letter to clarify the status of Japanese governmental credits that were extended to the PRC through the Import-Export Bank. This

document became the basis of a new *modus operandi* for Japan-ROC relations. See Zhao (note 1) pp.139–40.

58. The two best English language accounts of this period are Lee (note 4) and Welfield (note 22).
59. Tanaka (note 53) p.200. Tanaka shows that the correlation between membership of the groups and factional affiliation is less than 0.1 per cent.
60. Langdon (note 53).
61. Interview with Hashimoto Yasuo, *Nikkakon* Secretary-General (25 Feb. 1993). See also Honzawa Jiro, *Taiwan Robii* (Tokyo: Datahouse 1998).
62. Unattributable interviews with Japanese politicians in Tokyo, Dec. 1998.
63. Press reports suggested that 11 out of 18 members of the Dec. 2000 cabinet were *Nikkakon* members, while a further three were very friendly. See BBC *Summary of World Broadcasts* FE/4030 F/2 (22 Dec. 2000). Only Kato Koichi could be unambiguously described as ro-PRC.
64. Unattributable interview, Tokyo, March 2001; and *Free China Journal* (18 April 1998).
65. Fukui (note 52) p.247.
66. Langdon (note 53) p.410.
67. Unattributable interviews, March 1993.
68. See Douglas H. Mendel Jr, 'Japanese Policy and Views Toward Formosa', *Journal of Asian Studies* 28 (1969) pp.513–34.
69. Fukui (note 52) p.251.
70. Interview with Hashimoto Yasuo, 25 Feb. 1993.
71. Interview with Sato Shinji, March 1993. This statement is quite telling. Taiwanese officials interviewed in Sept. 1996 complained that *Nikkakon* was not helping Taiwan as it used to, and that Sato Shinji had become little more the mouthpieces for *Gaimusho*.
72. Douglas H. Mendel Jr, 'Japan's Taiwan Tangle', *Asian Survey* 4 (1964) pp.1073–84. Mendel also identifies similar attitudes in the Japanese bureaucracies: *The Politics of Formosan Nationalism* (Berkeley: Univ. of California Press 1970) pp.201–6. See also Mendel's article 'Japanese Policy and Views Toward Formosa', *Journal of Asian Studies* 28 (1969) pp.513–34.
73. Welfield (note 22) p.116.
74. Kurata (note 20) p.335.
75. See Fujiyama Aiichiro, *Seiji Wagamichi* [My Way in Politics] (Tokyo: Asahi Shimbunsha 1976) esp. pp.166–71.
76. This was cited by all members of *Nikkakon* interviewed through the 1990s. See also Wakamiya Yoshibumi, *The Postwar Conservative View of Asia: How the Political Right Has Delayed Japan's Coming to Terms with its History of Aggression in Asia* (Tokyo: LTCB International Library Foundation 1999) pp.125–38; and Ikei (note 20). This section has benefited from discussions with Kijima Joji.
77. Kaya Okinori, 'Taiwan kirisute no bokyo o omashimeru', in *Senzen sengo hachijunen* (Tokyo: Keizai Ourai Sha 1976) pp.337–54.
78. Ibid.
79. Iguchi Sadao, 'The Taiwan Problem and US-China relations', in Kajima Morinosuke (ed.) *Japan in Current World Affairs* (Tokyo: Japan Times 1971) pp.109–25.
80. Interviews with Sato Shinji, 7 March 1993, and Hashimoto Yasuo, 25 Feb. 1993.
81. Kobayashi Yoshinori, *Taiwanron* (Tokyo: Shogakukan 2000). Kobayashi's book generated a major debate in Taiwan, with Taiwanese of recent mainland origin bitterly criticizing his portrayal of Taiwanese history, while pro-independence figures in Taiwan offered him support.
82. Ten-jen Cheng and Brantly Womack, 'General Reflections on Informal Politics in East Asia', *Asian Survey* 36/3 (March 1996) p.323.
83. 'Seirankai: the young "Turks" flex their muscles', *FEER* (13 May 1974) p.13.
84. *Hsin Hsin-wen* (20–26 May 1991) p.74. The Association is usually abbreviated to Xinmuhui or Shinbokukai in press reports.
85. *Taiwan Soran 1992*, p.39

86. For details see Deans (note 10) Ch.4.
87. For example, the Minseito had its own *Nikka Kankei Giin Kondankai* headed by Nakamura Masao, *Taiwan Soran*, p.1147.
88. BBC *Summary of World Broadcasts* [*SWB*] FE/3002 F/1 (1997); *Japan Times Weekly International Edition* (3–9 Nov. 1997) p.6.
89. See the statement by Akiyama Masahiro, the Administrative Vice-minister of the Japan Defence Agency, *SWB* FE 3274 E/1 (9 July 1998).
90. See the issues for 12 April 2001 of *Asahi Shimbun, Mainichi Shimbun, Sankei Shimbun*, and *Yomiuri Shimbun*. See also *Taipei Times* (13 April 2001).
91. Dittmer *et al.* (note 1) p.306.

PART IV

ECONOMIC AND ENVIRONMENTAL DYNAMICS

7

A Regional Economic Order in East and Southeast Asia?

DANNY UNGER

The focus of this discussion will be on Southeast Asia. However, even for analytic purposes it is difficult to isolate Southeast Asia from the rest of East Asia or the Asia-Pacific. In economic or security terms, Southeast Asia does not constitute a region.

My task in this essay is to try to abstract from the dynamism and confusion of today's East Asia to say something about the nature of the key actors and their interactions in the medium-term future. Ideally, an essay of this kind would identify the principal guideposts in an admittedly murky terrain to help us apprehend the current situation. Such a discussion would identify the principal axes of debate and position the main actors along those axes. This essay will indeed try to identify the dominant actors in East Asia and Southeast Asia. Furthermore it will note the principal ideas and processes that seem to be shaping the region today. However, because several trends are of such tremendous significance and their ultimate outcomes so uncertain, the task of providing even a series of clear probabilistic predictions of the directions in which events may unfold is daunting.

Instead of hazarding guesses as to how several simultaneous and fundamental regional and global trends will interact to produce change in and around Southeast Asia, the bulk of my discussion will organize the various ongoing changes using an analytic framework suggested by Dani Rodrik.[1] Rodrik's framework draws on Mundell-Fleming's formulation of the constraints that limit national economic policy makers. A macro-economic policy maker can at best hope to achieve two of three widely pursued goals: a fixed exchange rate, monetary policy-making autonomy, and an open capital account. (As was observed in the wake of the Asian currency collapses beginning in 1997, policy makers in several Asian countries nonetheless attempted to pursue all three goals at once.) In a discussion of global economic integration, Rodrik offered a twist on Mundell-Fleming, arguing that at best we can aim to achieve two of the following three potential aims: enhanced economic integration; participatory and accountable politics; and maintenance of the nation-state as the principle locus of economic regulation. To the extent that we hold all three of these possible goals as desirable, Rodrik warns that not all (these) good things go together. In brief we will have to at least give lesser priority to one of these three objectives.

In the context of ever-closer harmonization of economic regulatory policies within the European Union, Rodrik's argument may not appear particularly disturbing. In the European context, the nation-state's dominant role in economic regulation has been eroded significantly. Admittedly, even in Europe the further loss of national regulatory autonomy faces fierce resistance. In East Asia, however, it is not clear that any identifiable and potentially powerful coalitions favor the significant diminution of national economic policy-making autonomy through deeper regulatory integration at either regional or global levels. Neither is it clear that powerful groups in the region are ready to jettison either of the other two elements of Rodrik's trinity. Hence, I propose to use Rodrik's framework as a means of probing the tensions and trade-offs confronting Southeast Asian policy makers. Implicit in the use of this framework to organize this discussion is my conviction that the extent and nature of economic integration in the region is of enormous importance in understanding likely regional political and security developments.

In the section immediately below, I outline what I believe to be the most profound trends confronting policy makers attempting to manage change and observers trying to understand it. I briefly discuss the problematic roles of the East Asia/Asia-Pacific region's principal states, noting the flux in the region's political structure (as defined by relative state powers). In the course of this discussion I attempt to cover some of the principal political and security developments that might be expected to constitute the focus of an essay of this kind. I also describe the diversity and influence of a variety of other actors in the region. Thus, reflecting an assumption that domestic politics matter in explaining states' international behavior, I summarize broad trends in some of the region's key states' domestic political arrangements. Having identified the critical actors and influences, I then explore the ways in which they may interact to affect regional economic integration, participatory and accountable politics, and the dominant roles of states as regulators of economic activity. In these latter sections I focus my attention more closely on the Southeast Asian region, for the most part the four largest capitalist economies, Indonesia, Malaysia, the Philippines and Thailand.

REGIONAL ACTORS AND INFLUENCES

Even starting with the most simplifying (realist) assumptions, trends in East Asia's emerging structure of power are not easy to discern. The region's four historic powers all pose us with questions about their future capabilities and goals. Most dramatically, of course, Russian influence in the region remains near its nadir, despite more active diplomacy and sharper differences until late 2001 with the United States under President Putin. Growing cooperation with China has not significantly enhanced Russian regional influence.

Japanese political influence in the region also has failed to wax over the last decade and even its economic power has waned. Growth in Japanese imports from Asian developing countries, and aid and investment flows to those countries all have decreased over the same period. The timing of a Japanese economic recovery, of a restoration of a stable domestic political ruling coalition, or of the assertion of a more confident regional posture also are unclear. Then Prime Minister Ryutaro Hashimoto did float a proposal in 1997 (the Hashimoto Principle) for regular Japanese consultations with Southeast Asian states on security issues. The proposal, however, garnered little audible response on the part of Southeast Asian states afraid of antagonizing China.[2] Yet, in November 1999 Japan proposed to send its Maritime Safety Agency ships to help patrol Southeast Asian seas disturbed by rising piracy. The latter proposal gained at least some support in the region.[3] Japan also continues to promote regional cooperation and institution building, on monetary and other issues. Japan now supports the ASEAN Plus Three (ASEAN plus China, Japan, and South Korea) formula, despite its exclusion of the United States.

In contrast with Russia and Japan's diminished regional profiles, China and the United States both have increased sharply their influence in the region over the past decade. Nonetheless, predicting the future regional policies of either country poses challenges, particularly in the case of China. Chinese policies, of course, will be shaped in large part by domestic economic and political developments that are themselves uncertain. Even if we rule out the exceedingly unlikely – but nonetheless often entertained – possibility of the collapse of a centralized Chinese state, a wide range of plausible domestic developments remain. Divergent domestic economic and political changes over the next two decades could predispose a considerable range of security policies and a wide variation in the means to pursue those effectively.

China's strong economic growth has made it possible for it to sustain rapid rises in military spending, albeit from a low base and with still limited force projection capabilities. China continues to boost its capacity to threaten Taiwan militarily. China also has been busy in Southeast Asia, asserting its claims in the South China Sea, boosting its influence in Cambodia and Laos and, in particular, Burma. China lends assistance to the Burmese navy and may ultimately, as a result, gain increased access to the Indian Ocean. Indian security officials haven taken note of this development.

China used the 1997 economic crisis to its advantage. The Chinese leadership gained credit in the region for not intensifying economic pressures by devaluing its own currency. High-ranking Chinese visitors to Southeast Asian countries in the aftermath of the crisis apparently encouraged leaders in the region to resist US pressures for economic reform and warned (as did, in fact, many French officials, to say nothing of Americans) of US hegemonic ambitions. These Chinese diplomatic overtures may have reaped benefits.[4]

China's policies in the Spratlys have been the focus of much concern in the region and have helped to spark increased spending on air and naval forces and new initiatives to boost regional military cooperation. The ASEAN states hope to be able to develop the capacity to patrol regional waters without depending on the US Seventh Fleet. Reduced naval procurements in the wake of the crisis, however, and very limited interoperability among ASEAN forces limit their capabilities.[5] While Chinese naval forces might not today be able to overwhelm those of even Malaysia or Singapore in the South China Sea, Chinese forces are expanding rapidly. Meanwhile, as one observer suggests, on the issue of the Spratlys the Chinese are using salami tactics (taking a series of incremental steps, any one of which appears too minor to warrant stiff opposition) successfully.[6]

The principal short-term questions about US commitments in the region revolve around the performance of the US economy, sinking savings and the associated large foreign international debt. Slow US economic growth might again focus Congressional attention on large bilateral trade deficits with countries in the region and generate a new round of trade tensions. Exports to the United States are particularly important to those countries attempting to recover from the economic crisis. If the United States fails to advance trade liberalization talks in the World Trade Organization and US protectionism increases, the result could be renewed local interest in regional trade arrangements. Despite ongoing interest in, for example, the ASEAN Plus Three formula (China, Japan, South Korea and ASEAN), any major move toward a less open form of East Asian regionalism might depend on the Japanese economy managing a robust recovery. The sense that export competition among Southeast Asian producers was giving way to trade complementarity, evident in the early 1990s, has diminished. Today, Southeast Asian exporters are facing stiff challenges, particularly from China.

Longer-term uncertainties about US policies center on whether the United States will continue to maintain US forces in Korea and Japan and whether the Bush administration plans to deploy a missile defense system in the region. In the United States itself, the key question concerns the sustainability of domestic commitments to finance US regional security dominance. The US Seventh Fleet has been able in part to compensate for the loss in 1992 of access to the Subic Bay naval base in the Philippines. Access to Singapore's huge new base at Changi since 2000 has been particularly important in this regard.[7] Furthermore, the United States continues a variety of military exercises, most of them bilateral, in the region. Nonetheless, before 11 September political and fiscal pressures had the potential to force onto the domestic political agenda questions about the extent to which US policies in the region served broad US interests.

It also is unclear the extent to which the United States will continue energetically to champion in the region 'revolutionary' values (democracy, human rights, market liberalism). American promotion of these values in the past challenged both entrenched elites and deeply rooted international norms supporting national sovereignty. Today, deepening of democratic regimes in the region means that US exhortations reach more sympathetic ears, even if resistance to unilateral US pressures is apt to remain strong. The focus on terrorism will have to diminish the US concern for democracy. In brief, trends in neither China nor the United States are easy to discern. Turning to relations between the region's dominant political actors, China and the United States, does not clarify the region's security picture a great deal. The region's two dominant political powers are not likely to enjoy close, cooperative and tension-free relations. Beyond this assertion, however, no scenario for relations between the two can be ruled out easily. The new Bush administration initially appeared to be intent on bolstering relations with Japan, even if at the cost of greater tensions with China. Leaders of the less powerful states of Southeast Asia will follow bilateral developments between China and the United States closely, hoping that relations do not deteriorate to a point requiring them to align themselves with one power against the other on issues of major importance to either.

Capturing the region's political structure becomes still more difficult when we acknowledge that the four powers that have for so long dominated the region increasingly have to contend with middle-level regional powers (such as Taiwan, Vietnam, Malaysia, Australia, Singapore, Indonesia, Thailand, and both Koreas). The security policies of these states are not easy to predict over the medium term. The Korean peninsula may or may not remain divided and how unification plays out will affect profoundly future Korean security perceptions, as well as those of its immediate neighbors. Furthermore, it is possible that neither Indonesia nor Taiwan will remain independent political actors. Taiwan faces possible absorption by China while Indonesia ultimately may lose control over more than East Timor.

Around Southeast Asia, considerable uncertainty further clouds security issues. The directions of economic and political change in Burma and Vietnam, for example, offer multiple possibilities. Thailand's recent emphasis on maritime capabilities is not easy to interpret.[8] Several ASEAN states have fairly impressive air and naval capabilities and increasingly are bolstering those forces.

For insular Southeast Asian states an emphasis on air and naval capabilities is to be expected. The Indonesian navy, for example, must maintain security against piracy, smuggling and illegal immigration, to name only some non-traditional threats, among thousands of islands over a vast area. The shift toward a maritime strategy for Thailand is more novel.[9] The Thai navy expects to develop a two-ocean capability to protect its marine resources and, with a base at Krabi, its Southern Seaboard Development projects. Until little over a decade ago, Thai military forces were largely concerned with counterinsurgency operations. The shift to conventional and then maritime emphases has been quite rapid. Border clashes between Thai and Burmese forces early in 2001 will not reverse this move toward a maritime strategy. Sheldon Simon suggests that with rising democracy military forces tend to shift from a focus on armies toward air forces and navies.[10] This observation reverses the causal ordering advanced by Otto Hintze, who argued that England's limited army, dictated by its geopolitical position, facilitated the establishment of limits on monarchical power and, ultimately, the rise of parliament and democracy.[11]

Major uprisings in Southeast Asia aimed at overthrowing governments occurred in 1986 in the Philippines, 1988 in Burma, 1992 in Thailand, and 1998 in Indonesia. The economic crisis resulted in leadership or regime changes in several countries in the region.[12] A Congressional Report Service report was gloomy on the impact the crisis could have on the region, noting that 'a prolonged economic decline could fuel nationalism, undermine regional co-operation, and foster confrontation over long-standing territorial and other disputes'.[13] The crisis aggravated tensions over labor migration as large numbers of Indonesians were returned from Malaysia and Burmese from Thailand. As a result, the crisis placed new strains on the norms of cooperation within ASEAN.

ASEAN promotes transparency and avoidance of provocation in defense doctrines among its members.[14] In many respects, the organization has been very successful, with some scholars describing ASEAN as a security community.[15] The creation of the ASEAN Regional Forum and ASEAN's expansion to ten members were in part efforts to guard against any loss of regional influence when China's power was expanding and new regional groupings such as the Asia Pacific Economic Cooperation group (APEC) emerged. From its inception, however, ASEAN's success was rooted in the nurturing of a normative community. Its members' principal concerns, rather like those of the Concert of Europe, were to sustain regional stability and the rule of conservative regimes. ASEAN is now facing new challenges given the far greater diversity in regime types among its members. Since 1967, the regime made up of five semi-democratic or soft authoritarian states has evolved into a grouping including communist, military authoritarian, semi-democratic and democratic ones. In the latter states, political participation has increased, making it more difficult for leaders to make binding decisions in ASEAN's traditionally informal settings in which officials negotiated with their regional counterparts. Elite domination of foreign policy making in the region no longer can be taken for granted.[16] Greater participation makes inevitable increasingly complex two-level games in these discussions. As a result, discussions within ASEAN will tend to evolve from collegial efforts at fostering consensus in the direction of more formal negotiations, perhaps spelling the end of the 'ASEAN Way' of informal, consensus decision making.

Characterizing the regional structure of power requires us to define the region and the resources most critical in evaluating relative power. Expanding trade flows and East Asia's enhanced energy dependence underline the critical roles of naval power in the area. The importance of sea-lane security suggests that any account of the region's security structure needs to accommodate powers such as India and Australia. Australia is a central player in the Five-Power Defense Agreement (Australia, Indonesia, Malaysia, Singapore, and the United Kingdom) and, at least until tensions over East Timor strained relations between them, in the 1995 Agreement to Maintain Security between Indonesia and Australia. Moreover, if we grant to nuclear weapons pride of place, the region's structure of power not only changed dramatically in 1998, but can be expected to continue to change as Indian (and, perhaps, Pakistani) nuclear capabilities expand. For their part, in 1995 the Southeast Asian states endorsed the creation of a Southeast Asian Nuclear Weapons-Free Zone, obliging the regional states to refrain from testing, obtaining, or exercising control over nuclear weapons.

It is increasingly untenable to discuss the East Asian security context solely in terms of states. Non-state actors have proliferated in the region and exercise major influence on several issue areas linked to security. Important non-state actors include new or newly configured regional associations such as APEC and ASEAN. ASEAN now encompasses all ten states of Southeast Asia and provides the auspices for the region's only forum for recurrent and multilateral discussion of security issues (the ASEAN Regional Forum, since 1994).[17]

While multinational firms are hardly new to the region, their significance in China and across Southeast Asia is vastly greater today than it was in the late 1980s. This increasing importance is particularly marked in the cases of multinational banks and investment and securities firms. Non-governmental organizations also are far more influential in the region than they were in the recent past. These groups may be based outside the region but also include important homegrown groups. Non-governmental organization concerns encompass issues with at least indirect security significance, such as labor migration and environmental issues. Many environmental issues challenge the region, ranging from the depletion of common resources (fishing) to air pollution caused by uncontrolled burning of forests. Within several Southeast Asian countries environmental issues increasingly have become livelihood concerns for marginalized groups pressed onto ever less productive land. This issue is acute in Thailand where millions living in forest preserves are faced with eviction from the forests when the government awards logging contracts.[18] The rising impact of non-governmental organizations around the region complements the expanding importance of non-traditional, transboundary security issues. Among these issues are piracy, labor migrations,[19] and drug trades. The profits from drug trading help support sub-national military movements and foster corruption among government officials.

Perhaps the most profound local influences are not specific to the region. In particular, the information revolution has the potential to restructure the most fundamental social and political institutions. While it is difficult to hazard even general predictions, it is clear that the dramatic falls in the costs of information and in the capacity of states to quarantine information are having profound effects on the relative advantages of different kinds of economic and political organizations. Protest movements in the region, such as those against former President Estrada in the Philippines beginning late in 2000, reflected the impact of new communications technologies. As has been noted frequently, access to abundant and nearly cost-free information challenges us to rethink even the significance of propinquity as a fundamental factor shaping economic and political organization. The point of this observation is to acknowledge a profound force that complicates efforts further to apprehend the region and its likely evolution.

If the region's structural character is difficult to assess, it also is true that important domestic political changes make predictions difficult. We can expect most of the region's polities to undergo significant changes in the next few years ranging from fundamental regime shifts to the entrenchment of existing democratic regimes. Democracy in the region, particularly in Indonesia, clearly is susceptible to regime change also. With or without democratization, rapid but unsteady economic growth, massive population shifts to urban areas and from farms to factories, and a relative dearth of social insurance mechanisms in the region have the potential to comprise in combination a precarious underlying social base for states' behaviors in the region. After all, many historians have argued that rapid urbanization and industrialization are associated with aggressive foreign policies. Furthermore, the argument that democratic states do not war with one another does not apply to transitional and unstable democracies.

This discussion has aimed to make the argument that the region, however defined, poses us with a bewildering array of fundamental trends that complicate our efforts to predict future events. In the sections that follow, this discussion is made more concrete and tractable by limiting our focus for the most part to the states of Southeast Asia. The discussion examines, in turn, each of the elements of Rodrik's policy trilemma.

ONGOING ECONOMIC INTEGRATION

By whatever measures, most of the economies of Southeast Asia are becoming increasingly closely tied to the global and the Asia-Pacific regional economies. The economic crisis that began in 1997 has not diminished dependence on trade, even if it has meant a reduction in capital inflows to the Southeast Asian economies. What has been surprising has been the limited extent to which the countries in the region have turned away from global economic integration. Rather, for the most part they have reaffirmed their commitments to openness.

In the wake of collapsing currencies, financial systems, and economies in the region, many dismayed observers perceived a harbinger of the end of the latest surge of liberal capitalism.[20] Many of these observers also anticipated, whether with glee or concern, that a nationalist backlash in the region would take root in opposition to liberal economic measures. These liberal policies were in part products of pressures coming from the International Monetary Fund and the US Treasury Department. It certainly is true that in the crisis' aftermath, US government officials grew less zealous in championing full and rapid lifting of all capital controls in developing countries. Nonetheless, on the whole liberal 'triumphalism' seems still much in evidence. President Clinton's rhetoric during his November 2000 speech at Vietnam's National University in Hanoi, for example, offered little hint that American official confidence in the virtues of open markets was spent. The president argued that economic openness produced growth and described globalization as 'the economic equivalent of a force of nature, like wind or water'.[21] Indeed, well after the impact of the economic crisis in the region was evident, China entered the World Trade Organization.

Four factors help to account for the relatively muted backlash against economic openness in Southeast Asia. First, the countries in the region remain heavily dependent on external financing and export markets. Indeed, the tentative economic recoveries already evident by 1999 depended heavily on exports. This dependence on the part of Southeast Asian economies is even greater than evident in data on trade and investment. Foreign firms in these countries account for the bulk of manufactured exports.

To gain an appreciation of the dependence of the Southeast Asian economies, we can contrast them with the East Asian Newly Industrialized Economies (NIEs). A principal difference between the two groups of countries lies in their respective human capital endowments, with the latter having far more technically skilled workers. This reservoir of skilled workers meant that the NIEs managed more smoothly the transitions from lower- to higher-skilled manufacturing industries as abundant skilled labor kept wage cost rises moderate during most periods, rarely rising more rapidly than productivity increases. Perhaps not coincidentally, South Korea and Taiwan were less dependent than the Southeast Asian economies on foreign-owned manufacturing production.

This problem of export dependence among the Southeast Asian economies has other facets as well. Southeast Asian economies, unlike the NIEs at a comparable stage of development, face overwhelming manufacturing export competition from China. In addition, the characteristics of global manufacturing production during the 1970s, when the NIE economies rapidly changed economic structures, differed from those today. Gary Hamilton argues that earlier 'producer driven' production patterns granted successful producers some economic leverage. Today, however, production increasingly is 'demand responsive' and dominated by price-sensitive commodity chains.[22] This change means that huge foreign buyers with procurement, distribution and marketing networks exercise greater leverage at the expense of manufacturers. The result is likely to be a shift in terms of trade against manufacturers, particularly of labor intensive-goods, like that faced by producers of agricultural and natural resource commodities. For the Southeast Asian economies, their roles in the shifting global division of labor have enhanced their dependence.

A second element helping to explain ongoing commitment to economic integration is the short duration of the economic collapse combined with its relatively mild impact. Strong growth in the United States economy and imports helped to soften the crisis' impact. For all the suffering experienced in the region on the part of the most vulnerable population groups and the overnight loss of large fortunes, by many measures misery was less extensive than the falling figures suggested. Increases in the incidence of poverty fell short of the many dire predictions generated early in 1998. Even in Indonesia, the hardest hit economy, government statistics on poverty recorded an increase initially of only about 50 per cent. While this change meant increased misery for millions of Indonesians, the rise in poverty was slighter than a fall in production of 14 per cent led many to expect. Nonetheless, the economic recoveries in Southeast Asia generally have been uncertain and, by the end of 2000, increases in poverty for Indonesia, the Philippines and Thailand combined had reached 50 per cent.[23]

A third factor helping to account for the mild and limited forms of backlash against liberal economic policies and their champions in Southeast Asia is rooted in the nature of political oppositions in the region. In contexts where economic opportunities often are linked to political connections, it is perhaps not surprising that newly active opposition political movements in these countries often themselves assumed liberal guises.[24] As a result, the same forces pushing for greater political democracy also, in many cases, call for the state to shift toward a neutral and regulatory economic role. To some degree, these groups' calls for transparent market operations are in the classical liberal tradition. These new political actors may not so much favor the market for its efficiency as for the liberties it affords against capricious political power and the awarding of scarce economic privileges. In the

Southeast Asian context, many liberals resist what they believe to be an unduly intimate marriage between market and political power. In this sense, the political opposition in the Philippines to President Marcos' crony capitalism can be seen as a regional vanguard.

A fourth factor may also have crucial effects in the longer run in limiting any backlash against economic openness in the region. In response to the crises, governments opened up previously sheltered sectors of their economies to foreign ownership. The sudden lifting of barriers and the precipitous drops in asset prices, particularly in foreign currency terms, drew in buyers. As these foreign firms establish themselves and expand, they will have a major impact on corporate governance patterns in these economies in the longer run. To the extent that these trends lead to some degree of convergence between Southeast Asian and rich industrialized economies, we can expect closer economic integration between them.

In the shorter term, however, foreign firms exploiting situations of economic distress by snapping up bargain-priced local assets have helped to generate economic nationalist sentiments. In Thailand, the victorious party in the January 2001 election proposed a moratorium on farmers' debt along with some curbs on foreign penetration of the economy. A new party called for halting the sale of state enterprises or financial institutions to foreigners. During the elections, candidates criticized the then governing Democrat party for handing over Thai assets to foreigners. In Thailand, foreign firms were not being welcomed without reservations. Nevertheless, once foreign firms are in place, they will not easily be dislodged. Indeed, their presence will reinforce dependence on an open market strategy and probably will discourage a deeper backlash against liberal economic policies. Even in Malaysia, despite Prime Minister Mahathir's often heated rhetoric and the absence of constraining International Monetary Fund conditions, foreign firms' access to the Malaysian economy has not been curtailed directly.

In sum, then, it does not appear likely that the crisis will have significantly dented the long-standing open orientation of the region's larger (non-socialist) economies toward the global economy. Plausibly, the economies are moving in the opposite direction. Any retreat from openness that does occur is likely to result at least as much from increasing political participation as from the crisis itself. Enormous pressures are increasing for changes in the direction of more transparent accounting and corporate governance, more effective prudential regulation of financial institutions, and increasing dependence on equity rather than bank financing of firms. These changes will tend to undermine any backlash. Furthermore, they suggest a weakening of arguments for closer and institutionally rooted East

Asian integration in favor of movement toward global integration based on International Monetary Fund and World Trade Organization norms. Such a shift was symbolized by the aborted nature of Japan's proposed Asian Monetary Fund in September 1997 and the central governance role played by the US-dominated International Monetary Fund. Despite a variety of initiatives aimed at strengthening regional cooperation (discussed below) the broad trends feature ongoing commitments to global multilateralism and openness.

Economic integration continues to be a principal goal for dominant coalitions in the region. Following Rodrik, participatory and accountable politics, together with continuing national dominance of economic regulation, cannot also comprehend ongoing economic integration. The discussion above suggests that change will have to come either in the nature of politics (addressed in the next section) or in the extent to which national states create their own economic regulatory regimes independently. Some observers would argue that, in the Southeast Asian context, politics have been neither participatory nor accountable, so that, at least in theory, it is possible to sustain the other two goals of closer economic integration and national regulatory autonomy. The discussion above suggests that at least to some degree the larger Southeast Asian economies (even Malaysia) lost their relative regulatory autonomy in the wake of the 1997 crisis. The likely future locus of economic regulation in Southeast Asia is the subject of the following section.

PARTICIPATORY AND ACCOUNTABLE POLITICS

Most students of Southeast and East Asia concur that the crisis cramped the style of some 'Asian' or 'developmental' capitalist variant. For many observers, including Southeast Asians, as noted above, this move toward market reforms was a welcome shift that would boost economic and political competition, leading to greater economic efficiency, more equal opportunity, and enhanced accountability in politics. Other analysts saw the economic straits as evidence of either ruthless US pursuit of commercial advantage or, in more structural terms, of a mismatch between a local mercantilist economic model and a globalized financial system.

Many commentaries on the crisis recognized in it a fundamental disjuncture in the international economy. Exactly such fundamental disjunctures often have been linked to critical political and policy turning points in the past. The most prominent example of this kind of argument links postwar global economic regulation to the experiences of depression and war from the 1930s and the 1940s. According to this argument, the

Bretton Woods institutions were predicated on capital controls that would grant to national economic policy makers the leeway necessary to pursue full employment policies. For mid-century elites in rich democracies, war avoidance required moderate politics, which in turn necessitated full employment. The goal of full employment, in its turn, rested on Keynesian economic management, which would be impossible in the absence of capital controls. In brief, Germany, Japan and Italy, as the authors of global war, also were the ghost writers of the Bretton Woods documents.

In the wake of the Asian crisis, many analyses extended this argument about 'embedded liberalism'[25] to the developmental state. If the global and regional conditions that once sustained developmental states have changed, then we may expect shifts in domestic political and economic arrangements to ensue. The 1997 crisis, according to this view, reflected the eclipse of the political conditions necessary to sustain developmental states. These conditions included a US preoccupation with bipolar strategic competition and, therefore, a tolerance for predatory trade practices among security allies in East Asia (or, in an alternative formulation, a refusal by American leaders to allow US commercial policies to be dictated by narrow vested interests.) More important, the developmental state was rooted in global economic conditions characterized by capital controls and, at home, at least some degree of directed credit. The allocation of scarce capital was the industrial policy tool of choice in the developmental states of East Asia.

The Asian developmental state, argued Khoo Boo Teik, was a nationalist project that eventually incurred the displeasure of the United States.[26] Richard Higgott maintained that 'at the core of the recent economic crisis in East Asia is an incompatibility between the developmental statist and the Anglo-American model of capitalist economic development'.[27] Robert Wade and Frank Veneroso suggested that liquidity crises of limited severity in East Asia were turned into large economic disasters as a result of International Monetary Fund misdiagnosis of the crises as solvency crises and failure to recognize the impact of their prescriptions on heavily leveraged firms in debt-based economies.[28] For Bruce Cumings, the larger significance of the crisis lay in the US 'attempt to bring down the curtain on "late" development'.[29]

Ruggie's argument about embedded liberalism was, essentially, that the political incorporation of labor had required a retreat from the nineteenth century's more full-blooded version of capitalism with its periodic wage drops and unemployment surges. While Asian developmental states, by contrast, often featured labor exclusion and repression, the two models of capitalism both were nourished by a particular configuration of economic and political conditions. These conditions made it possible for both embedded liberal and developmental states to grant primacy to politics, in alleged contrast with the tenor of today's or the nineteenth century's liberalism. It is in the refusal openly to grant primacy to (a particular) politics, that contemporary liberalism offends many Southeast Asian sensibilities. As Kanishka Jayasuriya argues, neo-liberalism requires limits on political participation in order to allow the implementation of market policies with a minimum of political interference.[30]

The magnitude of the political stakes at risk during the economic crisis emerged particularly clearly in Malaysia. On the one hand, it is true that Malaysia was less vulnerable in 1997 than were Indonesia and Thailand and was not, therefore, driven to seek International Monetary Fund assistance. It also is true, however, that in 1998 Prime Minister Mahathir found himself facing the strongest challenge yet to his two-decade tenure as premier. The struggle to define the appropriate policy response to the crisis played itself out as a political contest for leadership of the United Malays National Organization, and hence of Malaysia. It is possible, then, to explain Malaysia's less orthodox response to the crisis in terms of its lower level of dependence on external finance and the nature of domestic political conflict. On the other hand, as Teik notes, Malaysia has long pursued an economic strategy rooted in a political logic designed to contain communal and political violence. The strategy has been remarkably successful and helps to explain the depth of Mahathir's resistance to pressures to abandon this national development project. As Teik put it, at stake in Malaysia was 'an entire social compact, constructed and accepted over almost thirty years, that made possible a peculiar configuration of political stability, interethnic acceptance, and social progress'.[31]

If developmental states were challenged by changes in the global economic order, they also faced domestic pressures for broader political participation and efforts to curb the links between political power and favored business clients. What are the prospects today for participatory and accountable politics in Southeast Asia? On the one hand, democratic regimes that could be characterized in those terms can be found, if at all, only in the Philippines and Thailand. On the other hand, in those countries as well as Indonesia and Malaysia, pressures for fewer restrictions on mass political participation and for more accountable political institutions are strong. Hence, it does not seem adequate to note as an easy solution to Rodrik's dilemma that existing regimes are not characterized by participatory and accountable politics. Considerable evidence suggests that domestic political arrangements are changing in this direction.

This contribution is not focused upon detailed examinations of domestic political changes in the different Southeast Asian countries. Two arguments about the potential feedback effects of policies on politics, however, are worth introducing because they suggest that participatory and accountable politics may indeed be imminent in the region and because they apply to several of the region's political economies. The first argument concerns the impact of increasingly detailed and transparent rules regulating financial institutions and corporate governance. A second argument hinges on the potential impact that social welfare programs in Southeast Asia may some day have on local political dynamics.

Reforms adopted in the wake of the economic crises in Southeast Asia established not only new or modified procedures, for example bankruptcy and foreclosure mechanisms, but also a variety of elaborations of business codes to enhance transparency and guard against business owners abusing economic power. Some of these new legal codes take the form of administrative rulings, but most of them require fairly detailed legislation. With legislatures shaping fundamental issues of grave concern to powerful economic interests, the ability to influence legislation is apt to grow more important. As a result, investments in political parties and efforts to achieve political dominance in the legislature may also rise. This reasoning would suggest a deepening of commitments to democratic norms of policy competition.

Competition to shape detailed legislation departs from a situation in which legislatures adopt only broad legal codes and state officials exercise wide discretion in implementing the law. The latter pattern, of course, is evident everywhere to varying degrees. However, if state officials rather than legislators make most crucial policy decisions, influence over the former is likely to be the principal goal of political power. State officials in the Southeast Asian countries worst hit by the crisis are losing some of the regulatory powers they formerly enjoyed in both writing and implementing legislation. This loss of officials' control, in turn, may foster the channeling of political competition toward struggles between parties for dominance in the legislature.

Of potentially greater significance, however, is the way that a shift from wide official latitude in implementing policies to more narrowly targeted legislation might be expected to affect popular groups such as consumers, tax payers, labor unions, or the elderly. These groups generally seek policies that have an impact across society and their targets of influence are more likely to be the legislature. To the extent that the political process limits the roles of legislation and enhances discretion for bureaucrats, few incentives exist either for these groups to organize or for political entrepreneurs to mobilize them. In contrast, a shift toward a greater legislative function suggests more incentives for groups to mobilize and for politicians to cast appeals in response to, and aimed at generating, such mobilization. In short, instead of participation being limited for the most part to vertically organized, contending clientage networks, enhanced political participation and political competition, and more policy competition might emerge in the wake of the crisis.

Greater social welfare spending in the region may have a similar result. The countries of Southeast Asia as a group have limited social welfare expenditures. With aging populations and more wealth, several countries by the late 1990s were initiating or expanding existing but modest programs. When the crisis hit, concern for the impact on the most vulnerable led to substantial external assistance, primarily from the Asian Development Bank, the Japanese government, and the World Bank. This assistance was funneled into existing programs, in order to expand their coverage, or helped fund new initiatives. Although still unclear, these new or expanded projects could take root and lead to permanent increases in social spending. Factors like population aging, affluence, and growing vulnerability to externally generated economic shocks suggest that social programs are likely to expand in the future.

If social spending does grow, it too could shape politics and the respective roles of legislators and bureaucrats. Social welfare programs, like wage policies, or indeed macroeconomic policies, tend to generate broad social coalitions favoring or opposing them. Policy conflict over such issues runs horizontally, pitting broad socioeconomic interests against one another. Conflicts between such broad coalitions can be resolved in participatory political systems through legislatures. In Southeast Asia, however, the technocratic policy making that once governed most macroeconomic decisions worked against generating such broad political coalitions. Legislatures made policy, if at all, only on issues that divided groups on the basis of more selective interests. Social welfare spending may depart from this pattern. Conflict over increased spending for unemployment benefits, for example, is apt to divide interests broadly along class lines. Social welfare programs not only are more likely to divide interests into broad political coalitions, but typically are more comprehensible and visible to voters than are exchange rate or monetary policies. And while economic pressures are likely to continue to require that to a significant degree macroeconomic policy decisions are delegated to state agencies governed by narrow economic rather than political concerns, social welfare spending could encourage the emergence of broader political coalitions not rooted in ethnic identities. The impact of such a development could be profound for ethnic politics, the strengthening of political parties, and the incentives facing politicians in the region.

The potential significance of these developments for Southeast Asian politics can be illustrated by analogy. In the United Kingdom, political parties grew in importance and assumed the familiar role of articulating comprehensive policy platforms only in the nineteenth century after the size of the electorate passed some minimal threshold. By analogy, in several Southeast Asian polities, elections, parties, and legislatures may become the true locus of politics only when legislators make decisions that visibly affect, positively or negatively, large political coalitions. Increasing the roles of legislatures in economic regulation and possible significant expansion in social programs may have such an impact. In short, new forces, most of them products of the economic crisis, are simultaneously pushing for and against participatory politics in Southeast Asia.

Having argued that we cannot assume that nonparticipatory and nonaccountable politics will remain the norm in Southeast Asia, we turn now to consider the locus of economic regulation. If the states of the region still seek economic integration while their politics grow more participatory and accountable, Rodrik's argument suggests that either regional or global institutions will have to usurp the state's traditionally dominant roles in regulating national economies.

THE SITE OF ECONOMIC REGULATION

A world economy made up of nation-states with active, participatory democracies cannot accommodate, suggests Rodrik, both close economic integration and full national autonomy in economic decision making. If still more economic integration is the goal, then the nation-state must surrender some of its autonomy to multilateral institutions, whether regional or global in character. The embedded liberal or developmental state bargain underlying the postwar political economy must be still more fully surrendered.

The economic crisis provided considerable support for this conclusion. In return for International Monetary Fund support, Indonesia and Thailand accepted extensive Fund involvement in economic and institutional reform (the level of intrusion shifted less abruptly in the Philippines). Because the crisis was not, for the most part, rooted in macroeconomic imbalances, the reform agenda focused on deeply intrusive institutional changes. This interference with institutions having deep political and social roots, aimed at policy harmonization, is akin to the process through which the European

Union negotiates entry agreements with aspiring member states. This comparison suggests a potentially tidy solution to the Rodrik challenge: If domestic economic regulatory power in Southeast Asia is moving from states to the International Monetary Fund, this shift would provide a means to overcome Rodrik's trilemma.

It is premature, however, to conclude that the 'deep integration' agenda has been accepted widely in Southeast Asia. Many observers predicted a backlash to the agenda in Southeast Asia and we see some evidence to support the expectation. Given political volatility in several countries in the region (extreme in Indonesia) and the precarious nature of economic recoveries, it surely is too early to arrive at definitive judgements. It therefore seems appropriate to consider the possibility that areas of economic regulation might shift from the nation-state to regional, rather than global, multilateral institutions. Much of the literature on the Asian developmental states has encouraged the belief that regional institutional solutions would be more appropriate than global ones. Robert Wade and Frank Veneroso made this argument forcefully in the wake of the crisis. They suggested that a Japanese initiative like the Asian Monetary Fund was better suited to address the nature of the crisis than were International Monetary Fund prescriptions rooted in misdiagnoses and a failure to understand core features (high levels of savings and debt leverage) of the region's economies. Moreover, within prominent regional institutions such as ASEAN, some voices argued for cultivating a distinctly Asian approach to multilateral challenges.

The economic crisis, however, did little to boost confidence in the region's multilateral institutions. As Amitav Acharya notes, the crisis tended to undermine the arguments of liberal institutionalists. ASEAN was rooted in a constructivist's understanding of international cooperation with its emphases on socialization and the development of collective identities. The 'ASEAN Way' was explicitly aimed at the development of common norms.[32] When the crisis hit, however, regional dependence on external powers was underlined and existing multilateral institutions were unable to prevent rising tensions among the stricken Asian countries. Furthermore, those regional institutions themselves contributed little to the stabilization or resolution of the crisis.

The institutions, however, were not passive. Among the proposals advanced from within the region to address the crisis was the Manila Framework announced in November 1997 for enhanced regional monitoring of banking, macroeconomic indicators, and capital flows; a scheme floated at the ASEAN ministerial meetings in December 1997 in Kuala Lumpur to use local currencies in intraregional trade; a February 1998 proposal for mutual surveillance of various key economic indicators among the countries in the region; and a July 1998 plan to create an ASEAN Investment Area. The Asian Development Bank, for its part, boosted its lending sharply between 1996 and 1997. Meanwhile, an ASEAN-Post Ministerial Conference was devoted to discussion of safety nets in the area.[33] Furthermore, as Etel Solingen notes, even at the height of the crisis the countries not only sustained their economic openness, but were able to keep to their expansion agenda, admitting three new members (Burma, Cambodia, Laos).

The rationale for regional institutions typically is not so much the smaller numbers involved, but that in some respects countries within a region are more fully integrated than is the universe of countries represented in global multilateral arrangements. In the case of Southeast Asia, the argument for regionalism cannot rest on economic or security arguments. In fact, even if we include all of East Asia, the security argument remains untenable. The key player in the East Asian security picture is not in the region. This point was exactly the one emphasized by US officials opposed to Malaysian Prime Minister Mahathir's 1990 initiative to create an East Asian Economic Group. The Americans did not want to see a 'line drawn down the center of the Pacific' that would define an East Asian region economically and, as a consequence, might imperil US security commitments in the region.

Any argument for regionalism in Southeast Asia in particular must be rooted in common problems and perspectives and the development of a normative community. The idea of an 'ASEAN Way' expressed this view. ASEAN was, in part, a product of converging domestic political arrangements. In all the member countries, internationalist coalitions, in both economic and identity terms, dominated local politics.[34] ASEAN enlargement, however, has increased the diversity among its members. Democratization and neo-liberal reforms in some member states have narrowed the gap between them and the dominant states in global multilateral institutions.

These changes suggest that the incentives for regional organizations may be diminishing. One of the clear indicators of these new tensions has been the tendency for Thai and Philippine ministers to depart from the norm of noninterference in domestic affairs in favor of a policy of 'flexible engagement' (or 'constructive intervention' or 'enhanced interaction'). Thai officials argue that contagion in the financial crises and the impact of Sumatran fires on neighboring countries belie the notion that domestic issues are solely the concern of those countries. These Thai officials also note that one result of Burmese entry into ASEAN is greater difficulty in the

ASEAN-European Union meetings (the Bangkok meeting of ASEM in 1997 was cancelled due to Burma's invitation as an observer). Thailand also must cope with Burmese refugees produced by domestic political turmoil. Finally, the need for the Thai and Philippine governments to dispatch peacekeeping forces to East Timor (Malaysia also sent a small contingent) carried the same message.

Nonetheless, despite these challenges stemming from different conceptions of regional cooperation, evidence late in 2000 indicated that interest in new regional arrangements was still strong. At the ASEAN+3 summit, for example, China proposed a free trade agreement with ASEAN.[35] Several governments have mooted proposals for bilateral free trade agreements as well as for an ASEAN+3-wide free trade area.

As it now operates, ASEAN may not be able to manage the tasks it confronts. In the wake of the crisis, tensions among some of the members became particularly acute. Indonesia's neighbors had to contend with smoke from Sumatran fires. Labor migration induced tensions between Indonesia and Malaysia, and between Burma and Thailand. Singapore's relations with both Malaysia and Indonesia came under greater stress. Both Prime Minister Mahathir and then President Wahid launched attacks on Singapore for 'taking advantage' of its neighbors.[36] Amitav Acharya suggests that changing domestic politics may make cooperation with Western powers more likely. He also suggests the possibility that the poor performance of regional institutions may motivate efforts to strengthen them and to accept forms of 'intrusive regionalism'.[37]

CONCLUSION

Political leaders in Southeast Asia confront a wide variety of complex challenges that have the potential to undermine the relative stability among most of the region's states that was evident since about 1980. The divisions between communist and non-communist states have eased, but new strains have emerged. Maritime and mainland Southeast Asia may be drifting in different directions.[38] Conflict between Burma and Thailand worsened early in 2001, confirming the absence of a security community within the newly enlarged ASEAN membership. Acute domestic political instability in Indonesia, the association's traditional leader, raises further questions about Southeast Asia's future regional developments. Indonesian instability threatens its neighbors as conflicts and migrations spill over beyond its borders.

Many of the actors and forces that will affect the outcomes of efforts to cope with new challenges are beyond the control of the region's less powerful states. Among the more tractable variables subject to local determination, none are likely to prove more important than the natures of the economic and political regimes that emerge within Southeast Asian states and the regional and global institutions within which their interactions are embedded. On balance, the prospects for either new or significantly stronger regional institutions seem to be limited in the medium term. Enlargement, the economic crisis, and domestic political changes in key member countries have weakened ASEAN. China supports local arrangements such as ASEAN Plus Three, but may prefer global institutions such as the WTO if they afford more opportunities to play off against one another the European Union, Japan, and the United States. After all, Japan and the United States are clearly the dominant members of any Asia-Pacific economic associations and China might find it difficult to undermine a Japan-US bloc on many economic issues. In any case, Japan is unlikely to go too far in supporting regional associations that exclude the United States. Furthermore, if the region does not feature an 'Asian' variant of capitalism, the arguments in favor of exclusive regional economic arrangements assume less force.

This study argued that in several key Southeast Asian states profound political changes are underway. These shifts suggest that sustained national regulatory autonomy and closer economic integration are not likely to be achieved at the expense of participatory politics. The evidence for the other two elements of Rodrik's trilemma remains mixed, however. The playing out of the tension among these three factors will help to shape the region's medium-term future.

The context of regional economic developments today appears very different from that evident in the mid-1990s. We no longer anticipate as optimistically the onset of a borderless regional economy and the virtuous circles that drove unilateral trade liberalization across the region. In terms of the regional power balance too, the picture is murkier than it was a decade ago. Chinese and Indian power have expanded rapidly, Indonesia is in turmoil and in coming decades more middle powers such as Vietnam are apt to emerge.

The regional roles that local developing countries play will depend significantly on the trajectory of their domestic political developments. This is true also, of course, of countries such as Japan and the United States. In the former cases, however, because we have approximate historical knowledge of the nature of the transitions they will face as they urbanize, achieve economic affluence and political pluralism, we tend to believe we can better anticipate the challenges they will face. The tasks of broadening political participation, in particular, may override forces pushing in the direction of greater economic openness. The politics of economic policy making under former Presidents Estrada and Wahid in the Philippines and Thailand and Prime Minister Thaksin in Thailand as well as Malaysia's Prime Minister Mahathir all exemplify these challenges to deeper integration. Ultimately, regional stability is likely to depend in large part on the capacities of governments in Asia's developing countries to meet rising expectations and quell identity conflicts.

The region's great powers will have the greatest impact on the region's potential to facilitate national enterprises aimed at producing growth, stability, and equity. China, Japan, and the United States, however, will not operate independently in defining relations among themselves. The great powers too are context takers as well as context makers. The contexts within which they attempt to manage conflicts among them will be shaped in considerable part by political developments within Asia's developing states.

NOTES

1. Dani Rodrik, *Has Globalization Gone Far Enough?* (Washington DC: Institute for International Economics 1997).
2. Victor Mallett, *The Trouble with Tigers, the Rise and Fall of Southeast Asia* (NY: HarperCollins 1999) p.204.
3. Sheldon W. Simon, 'Asian Armed Forces: Internal and External Tasks and Capabilities', in idem (ed.) *The Many Faces of Asian Security* (Lanham, MD: Rowman & Littlefield 2001).
4. Robyn Lim, 'The ASEAN Regional Forum: Building on Sand', *Contemporary Southeast Asia* 20/2 (Aug. 1998) pp.116, 124; Amitav Acharya, 'Realism, Institutionalism, and the Asian Economic Crisis', *Contemporary Southeast Asia* 21/1 (April 1999) p.8.
5. When Li Peng visited Bangkok in Aug. 1997, a Thai editorial suggested that 'China has elevated ASEAN as a player in international relations, which Japan has refused to do'. In Simon (note 3).
6. Lim (note 4) p.114.
7. Simon (note 3).
8. Leszek Buszynski, 'Thailand's Foreign Policy: Management of a regional vision', *Asian Survey* 34 (Aug. 1994) pp.721–37.
9. Panitan explains Thai policies as an effort on the part of the Chuan government to enhance the influence of the other services at the expense of the army. Panitan Wattanayagorn, 'Thailand: the Elite's Shifting Conceptions of Security', Muthiah Alagappa (ed.) *Asian Security Practice: Material and Ideational Influences* (Stanford UP 1998).
10. Simon (note 3).
11. Felix Gilbert (ed.) *The Historical Essays of Otto Hintze* (NY: OUP 1975)
12. Clark Neher, 'Southeast Asian Security and Human Rights', in Simon, *The Many Faces of Asian Security* (note 3).
13. Acharya (note 4) p.1.
14. Simon (note 3).
15. Mely Caballero-Anthony, 'Mechanisms of Dispute Settlement: The ASEAN Experience', *Contemporary Southeast Asia* 20/1 (April 1998) p.63.
16. N. Ganesan, *Bilateral Tensions in Post-Cold War ASEAN* (Singapore: Institute of Southeast Asian Studies 1999).

17. Robyn Lim, 'The ASEAN Regional Forum: Building on Sand', *Contemporary Southeast Asia* 20/2 (Aug. 1998).
18. Philip Hirsch, 'The politics of the environment: Opposition and legitimacy', in Kevin Hewison (ed.) *Political Change in Thailand, Democracy and Participation* (London: Routledge 1997).
19. Sheldon W. Simon, 'The Economic Crisis and ASEAN States' Security', paper prepared for Strategic Studies Institute, US Army War College (Oct. 1998).
20. Richard Higgott, 'The International Relations of the Asian Economic Crisis, A Study in the Politics of Resentment', in Richard Robison, Mark Beeson, Kanishka Jayasuriya and Hyuk-Rae Kim (eds.) *Politics and Markets in the Wake of the Asian Crisis* (London: Routledge 2000) p.262.
21. *The Economist* (25 Nov. 2000) p.42.
22. Gary Hamilton, 'Asian Business Networks in Transition: or, What Alan Greenspan Does Not Know about the Asian Business Crisis', in T.J. Pempel (ed.) *The Politics of the Asian Economic Crisis* (Ithaca, NY: Cornell UP 1999) pp.52–3.
23. *The Economist* (2 Dec. 2000) pp.41–2.
24. Stephan Haggard, *The Political Economy of the Asian Financial Crisis* (Washington DC: Institute for International Economics 2000) pp.12, 219.
25. John Gerard Ruggie, 'International regimes, transactions, and change: embedded liberalism in the postwar economic order', in Stephen Krasner (ed.) *International Regimes* (Ithaca, NY: Cornell UP 1983).
26. Khoo Boo Teik, 'Economic Nationalism and Its Discontents, Malaysian Political Economy After July 1997', in Richard Robison, Mark Beeson, Kanishka Jayasuriya and Hyuk-Rae Kim (eds.) *Politics and Markets in the Wake of the Asian Crisis* (London: Routledge 2000) pp.230–1.
27. Higgott (note 20) p.262.
28. Robert Wade and Frank Veneroso, 'The Asian Crisis: the High Debt Model Versus the Wall Stree-Treasury-IMF Complex', *New Left Review* 228 (March–April 1998).
29. Bruce Cumings, 'The Asian Crisis, Democracy, and the End of "Late" Development', in Pempel, *The Politics of the Asian Economic Crisis* (note 22) p.18.
30. Kanishka Jayasuriya, 'Authoritarian Liberalism, Governance and the Emergence of the Regulatory State in Post-Crisis East Asia', in Richard Robison, Mark Beeson, Kanishka Jayasuriya and Hyuk-Rae Kim (eds.) *Politics and Markets in the Wake of the Asian Crisis* (London: Routledge 2000).
31. Teik (note 26) p.229.
32. Wade and Veneroso (note 28).
33. Acharya (note 4) p.5.
34. Acharya (note 4) pp.6–16.
35. Michael Wesley, 'The Asian Crisis and the Adequacy of Regional Institutions', *Contemporary Southeast Asia* 21/1 (April 1999) pp.56–91.
36. Etel Solingen, 'ASEAN, *Quo Vadis?* Domestic Coalitions and Regional Co-operation', *Contemporary Southeast Asia* 21/1 (April 1999) pp.48–9.
37. Ibid. pp.31–2.
38. *The Economist* (2 Dec. 2000) p.42.
39. Acharya (note 4) p.42.
40. Acharya (note 4) pp.18–23.
41. Ganesan (note 16) pp.55–6.

8

Environmental Security in East Asia:
A Critical View

M. SHAMSUL HAQUE

In the current era, the conventional discourse on international relations based on a state-centric and militaristic worldview has come under challenge due to the emergence of various local and global forces and issues that tend to diminish the role of the state and question the relevance of the military to national security. The major examples of such contemporary non-state forces and non-military issues include the globalization of transnational capital and information networks, proliferation of regional economic blocs, reinforcement of roles played by non-government organizations, and rise of concerns such as the cross-national developmental gap, universal human rights, gender equality, ethnic and religious identity, and environmental disorder.[1] The increasing influence of such newly emerging non-state actors and non-military issues may have diminished the validity of a state-centric notion of security, and reduced the explanatory capacity of the related international relations theories founded upon orthodox realist or neorealist assumptions.[2] In addition, beyond traditional military security, there are growing concerns regarding non-traditional issues such as human security, economic security, social security, information security, and environmental security.

Among these non-traditional security issues, however, environmental security stands out as one of the most critical concerns that transcends national boundaries, affects all societies, and has international conventions affecting all states. A global concern like environmental security certainly represents a serious challenge to the primacy of the state in safeguarding national sovereignty, questions the conflict of cross-national interests, and rejects the dichotomy between internal and external security suggested by conventional international relations theories.[3] The significance of this environmental security lies in various ecological disorders and natural disasters – including water and air pollution, land degradation, deforestation, global warming, ozone depletion, sea-level rise, biodiversity loss, and resource scarcity – that threaten the very sustainability of human progress and marginalize the importance of military security.[4] Thus, in recent years, there has been a massive increase in environment-related conventions, protocols, conferences, and publications, and a higher level of awareness regarding the danger of environmental insecurity caused by population pressure, poverty and inequality, industrial expansion, arms proliferation, ecological stress, use of toxic chemicals, and consumption of environmentally harmful commodities.

The conceptual articulation of this environmental security began with scholars such as Lester Brown, Richard Ullman, and Jessica Mathews, who expanded the concept of security beyond military threats, and incorporated environmental dangers into the definition.[5] However, it was only after the Cold War – which dominated the theories and practices of security in the field of international relations for many decades – that traditional security perceptions came under question, unconventional threats gained importance, and environmental security began to draw attention from top policy makers.[6]

Today the issue of environmental security is recognized worldwide by academics, politicians, and activists. The existing interpretations of environmental security can be generalized into three major categories: one set of explanations emphasizes various forms of environmental degradation affecting all humans irrespective of nationalities; another set of definitions focuses mainly on national environmental threats that spill over to other countries and cause interstate tension; and the last set of analyses pays more attention to a nation's capacity to withstand environmental threats, rectify environmental damages, and guarantee public safety from adverse consequences.[7] In fact, there is no conflict among these three sets of interpretations: they just represent different levels and dimensions of environmental security, including the human implications of global environmental disorders, cross-national conflicts arising from these problems, and state capacity to prevent and manage such disorders.

However, there are controversies with regard to how environmental threats constitute a security problem. The existing studies attempt to explain that ecological degradation and resource scarcity lead to internal social upheaval and civil strife, that internal environmental disorders affect neighboring countries and may cause external conflict and warfare, and that regional cooperation in solving environmental predicaments often enhances overall regional peace.[8] More specifically, it has been observed that environmental problems in any country (including carbon emissions, water pollution, land degradation, and natural disasters) may lead to population displacement, cross-border migration, and institutional instability, which in turn, may adversely affect other countries and create bilateral tension and armed conflict.[9] Some scholars tend to focus on the scarcity of environmental resources – often caused by overconsumption of resources (e.g. water and energy), degradation of land, and depletion of forests – as a major factor leading to conflict between states over controlling and sharing such resources.[10]

Conversely, intensive wars often involve the use of hazardous substances, contamination of air and water resources, destruction of forests and crops, thus causing environmental insecurity in the enemy territories. In short, environmental security is closely related to other forms of security in the economic and military spheres. Thus, the traditional militaristic notion of security must be reexamined and restructured to incorporate the idea of environmental security in order to reach any framework of comprehensive security.

Despite this growing evidence of the environment-security nexus from various studies, the practical security strategies continue to be guided by conventional security perception in different regions, including East Asia. The marginalization of non-traditional security issues, especially environmental security, and the dominance of military security in East Asia can be observed in the potential for armed conflict between China and Taiwan, political hostility between North Korea and South Korea, territorial disputes among various countries over the islands in South China Sea, and the expansion and modernization of national defenses in the region. Despite the irrelevance of traditional security assumptions due to contemporary changes in regional issues – including the end of the Cold War rivalries, the process of globalization affecting the state power, the rise of economic priorities over defense, and the increased influence of various civil society groups – there is still a strong tendency in the region to consider the state as the dominant actor and its military capability as the primary means to ensure national security. However, there is a growing significance of non-traditional, environmental security in the region due to the worsening forms of ecological degradation caused by population pressure, resource scarcity, industrial expansion, and hazardous production and consumption.[11] Because of these new security dynamics, there is a need to redefine security and restructure security options in East Asia based on an alternative set of assumptions.

In the above context, this study examines the following: (a) the current significance of environmental security in East Asia in terms of various forms of environmental threats and the limits of prevailing protection measures; (b) the dominant assumptions and modes of international relations pursued by East Asian countries and their critical environmental implications; and (c) the alternative set of international relations assumptions and security perceptions needed to address the emerging problems of environmental insecurity in the region. However, in order to explore these regional issues more meaningfully, the next section presents an analysis of common security perceptions in existing international relations theories, especially their limitations in addressing environmental security.

The legacy of international relations theories is characterized by certain intellectual ambiguity, fragmentation, and duplication due to the strong ideological (Cold War) underpinnings in theory-building, the use of terms borrowed from other fields and disciplines, the conversion of rhetorical tactics adopted by political leaders into theoretical models, and the close affiliation of academic experts with the state's strategic options. The fragmented and overlapping nature of these theories has been reinforced further by the development of alternative approaches in response to new challenges posed by the above-mentioned national and international events and issues that defy traditional security perception and demand non-traditional theoretical treatment. In addition, the situation is complicated by a new breed of theoretical constructs – including the critical, postmodern, and feminist perspectives – that tends to expose the inadequacies of mainstream theories or approaches in the contemporary world of international relations.[12]

There are varying taxonomies of international relations theories ranging from the simple classification of these theories into realist, liberal, and radical schools to more all-encompassing typologies that tend to consider even the specific security strategies as theories.[13] In order to avoid such tendencies of oversimplification and overgeneralization, this study presents the existing theories of international relations into four major traditions: (a) the *realist tradition* (which covers classical realism, neorealism, balance-of-power theory, and hegemonic-stability theory); (b) the *liberal tradition* (which includes classical liberalism, pluralism, and neoliberalism); (c) the *interpretive tradition* (which encompasses different versions of constructivism); and (e) the *radical tradition* (which includes critical, postmodern, and feminist theories). These theoretical traditions differ from each other in terms of their basic assumptions regarding human nature, nature of the state, state-individual relations, ethics in interstate relations, and so on. This section briefly explains these theoretical traditions and examines their intellectual positions with regard to environmental security.

Realist Tradition and the Environment

Within the realist tradition, the classical form of realism – initiated by Niccolò Machiavelli and Thomas Hobbes and reinforced by Hans J. Morgenthau, E. H. Carr, John Herz, and Raymond Aron – flourished under the Cold War characterized by superpower rivalry, arms proliferation, and distrust between the major ideological blocs. The proponents of realism, in general, hold the following assumptions: (a) human nature is predominantly guided by lust for power, and accordingly, the statesmen act on the principle of power rather than morality; (b) the atmosphere of international politics is hostile and anarchic, and thus the main goal or interest of the state is to strengthen its power to survive in such atmosphere; (c) the state, being unsure of the motives of other states, must enhance its power based on military capability in order to counter external military threats; (d) the state, guided by the instinct of survival, remains the primary actor to maintain sovereignty and shape its position in international politics; and (e) although a structure of balance of power may emerge from the desire of all states to maximize power, it is only a temporary condition under which interstate competition for power continues.[14]

The extension of classical realism to neorealism has hardly changed the above state-centric assumptions of international politics. The main departure, however, is that compared to realism, the neorealist perspective initiated by Kenneth Waltz puts greater emphasis on the balance of power. For Waltz, this balance of power results in a bipolar or multipolar structure of international system maintained by the major world powers.[15] Although the state still remains the main actor, its behavior is influenced by the structural properties (power structure) of this international system. But it is still the state's capability, based on its economic and military strengths and external alliances, which determines its position in the structure of international system.[16] Paradoxically, while the neorealists emphasize the influence of balance of power and its attendant international system on the behavior of the state, they tend to dismiss any significant role played by international institutions to regulate states and promote peace.[17]

In various ways, the above theoretical assumptions, arguments, and prescriptions offered by realist and neorealist thinkers can be found in other theoretical categories in international relations, including balance-of-power theory, deterrence theory, and hegemonic-stability theory. For instance, in extending the neorealist position, balance-of-power theory focuses on the importance counterbalancing power by forming and reforming alliances often under the auspices of a single state, especially when there are rapid changes in international power structure caused by interstate rivalries. The hegemonic-stability theory goes one step further to suggest that for ensuring the stability of the international system, there is a need for enforcing the rules of interaction among its member states. This enforcement of rules is ensured by a single dominant state or a hegemon that has strong economic, technological, and military power as well as commitment to these systemic rules. On the other hand, deterrence theory, which emerged largely during the Cold War, focuses on strategic options for major military powers, especially nuclear powers. Based on the realist assumption of states as unitary rational actors, the theory prescribes deterrence as an effective option. This deterrence is a dynamic process of continuous feedback to convince the opponents that any of their aggressive actions would invoke a response that would cause serious damage outweighing the potential benefit from the action, and thus to deter them from undertaking such action.[18] Some proponents of this theory even suggest that the proliferation of nuclear weapons would deter many states from engaging in war.

It is clear from the above description of various facets of realism, neorealism, and derivative strategic views that the realist tradition has no space for environmental and ecological questions. Its narrow state-centered and militaristic conception of security excludes non-military (especially environmental) threats to security; disregards the role of non-state actors such as non-government organizations (NGOs) in dealing with such security threats; and subordinates environmental issues to state-related categories such as national interest, sovereignty, and balance of power.[19] In fact, the assumptions, principles, and policy prescriptions of the realist tradition – which justify and encourage the expansion and use of state power through unrestrained military expenditures and defense alliances – are detrimental to environmental security due to the hazardous impacts of arms proliferation, especially nuclear weapons, and the diversion of resources to the defense sector that exacerbates resource scarcity. As discussed later, unfortunately, this environment-unfriendly realist perspective tends to dominate the security practice in East Asia.

Liberal Tradition and the Environment

The liberal tradition of international relations theories shares some of the basic principles of liberal political thinkers such as Immanuel Kant, John Stuart Mill, and David Hume. The proponents of liberalism, in general, hold a more positive assumption about human nature and collaboration, and support the protection of human liberty and equality through liberal democracy and free markets rather than state control. With regard to interstate relations, in opposition to the realist tradition, the proponents of the liberal tradition de-emphasize the unilateral role of the state, believe in interstate cooperation, encourage demilitarization, and propound collective security through international laws and institutions.[20] Extending this liberal theory further, pluralist thinkers emphasize multiple domains and actors in national and international security. They consider the state to be an embodiment of competing interest groups rather than a rational actor.

However, a more articulate attempt to extend liberal theory has been pursued by the scholars associated with neoliberalism or neoliberal institutionalism. In international relations, the neoliberals believe in most basic ideas and principles of liberalism such as interstate cooperation, non-state actors, collective security, and international law. But neoliberals have special focus on institutions – defined as sets of rules that prescribe roles, shape expectations, and outline activities – under which cooperation among states (based on their convergent interests) takes place. Among the major versions of neoliberalism, so-called 'complex interdependence' theory emphasizes the nature of interdependent relations among states and societies, the growing primacy of the economic sphere over the military dimension in such relations, and the increasing role played by non-state actors such as transnational corporations in this regard.[21]

Another version of neoliberal perspective is known as 'international regime' theory. It explains how a stable, orderly, and transparent mode of international cooperation is made possible by forming various international regimes – defined as sets of principles, norms, and rules reflecting the common expectations of actors in world politics – around specific issues like trade, security, the environment, and communication.[22] Although a regime may not be legally binding, its principles and norms, once agreed upon, shape the behavior of all participating states.

With regard to environmental security, the liberal tradition does not have a direct agenda, and its primary focus remains on international cooperation related to economic and military issues. However, the positive attitude of liberal thinkers towards interstate collaboration and their recognition of non-state actors, may create potential for considering environmental threats as security issues and accepting the beneficial roles played by various environmental groups in world affairs.[23] In addition, since neoliberal theory of international regimes emphasizes the use of various sets of agreed norms and principles to guide interstate relations in different areas, the issue of environmental security is likely to receive more favorable treatment in discourse on international security. In the case of East Asia, the potential of the liberal tradition to address environmental issues is less relevant, because there hardly exists any of the above liberal features in the region's international relations and security perceptions.

Interpretive Tradition and the Environment

The interpretive tradition of international relations theories is more recent in origin. Most theoretical arguments in this tradition stress the 'intersubjective' dimension of international relations. A major theory within the interpretive tradition is known as constructivism, which borrows from the 'social construction of reality' perspective emphasizing the intersubjective domain of human action, especially in terms of how the identities and interests of actors are socially constructed and culturally informed.[24] For Checkel, constructivism is more of an approach to social inquiry than a theory: it criticizes the existing theories for using a reductionist methodological framework, focusing unilaterally on the agents (states) and their preferences, and neglecting the influence of agents' socialization in structures (global norms) on their preferences.[25] In opposition to this agent-biased or actor-centered analysis in major international relations theories, the proponents of constructivism emphasize interaction between agents and structures.

With regard to more concrete issues in international relations such as conflict and cooperation, constructivism interprets the causes of war in terms of the conflicting identities or self-perceptions of states; and explains international cooperation as a process of interaction that often has positive outcomes, including the reexamination of preconceived interests, redefinition of identities, shared understanding of reality, and potential for collective identity and security.[26] Beyond such interstate interaction, constructivism also emphasizes the mutual constitution of the state (agent) and the international system (structure).[27] However, there are two versions of constructivist theory – 'third-image constructivism' and 'fourth-image constructivism'.[28] While 'third-image constructivism' puts more emphasis on the state's 'social' identity (its perceived identity in relation to other states) than its 'corporate identity' (its various internal features) in explaining its role in international politics, 'fourth-image constructivism' considers these two dimensions as interactive and mutually constitutive.

As far as environmental issues are concerned, constructivism does not have much to offer directly since its main focus is on the process of interaction between states and global norms, formation of states' identities and self-perceptions, shared view of reality in world politics, and potential for collective interstate identity. However, this framework may have indirect positive implications for environmental security – especially its emphasis on interstate cooperation based on shared understanding, may encourage the diversion of attention and resources from military security to environmental security. But the limitation is that constructivism remains a theoretical construct for academic discourse without much of its reflection in real-life world politics. The prevalence of a reductionist, militaristic notion of security among East Asian countries is a good example of how practical world politics is far away from the constructivist ideals of interstate collaboration and collective identity.

Radical Tradition and the Environment

The radical tradition tends to challenge and deconstruct the assumptions, principles, methods, and strategies of existing international relations theories, and suggest fundamental reforms in such theories. Within this tradition, the central intellectual tenets are borrowed from critical theory and postmodern and poststructural perspectives, and the application of these theories to international relations has been pursued by scholars such as Richard Ashley, R. B. J. Walker, and Ken Booth. For instance, in line with the original critical theory of the Frankfurt School, Booth challenges the norms of the Cold War in strategic studies, and explains security in terms of people's emancipation from war, poverty, and oppression.[29] In line with the postmodern and poststructural perspectives, Ashley suggests to question the very foundation of modern states and international politics based on geographical boundaries and geopolitical cultures, and prescribes the method of 'genealogy' in this regard.[30]

Despite certain variations among such radical scholars, in general, they postulate that there is no objective reality in world politics, and its structures and images are socially constructed. They suggest that the narratives of world politics based on modernity should be questioned, the hidden meanings of all texts and subtexts (e.g. speeches and arguments of policymakers) should be revealed, and the hegemonic theoretical traditions in international relations should be deconstructed.[31] With regard to concrete issues in world politics, they consider each state a representation of vested interests constraining the potential of a conflict-free global community, and emphasize the realization of social justice in human arenas such as culture, gender, and environment.[32] Focusing more specifically on gender, the proponents of the feminist theory of international relations tend to interpret the state as a socially constituted category that conceals its masculine identity.[33] They also encourage the critique of international studies, reexamine the existing narratives of war and peace, advocate a feminist view of politics, and demand gender equality and greater role of women in world politics.

From the above discussion, it should be clear that the radical tradition is relatively sympathetic toward the environmental question. Due to their emphasis on the multiple dimensions and interpretations of international politics, the scholars associated with this tradition are more favorable to the incorporation of non-traditional issues such as the environment into security studies. However, one of the main weaknesses of this radical tradition is that it questions the narratives of existing theories and strategies of international relations, emphasizes unconventional issues such as gender equality and environmental security in international politics, but fails to provide a set of concrete theoretical and practical guidelines. As Kegley and Wittkopf mention, critical international relations theory 'is better suited to exposing the limits of others' analyses (deconstructing their logic) than to constructing theories that might identify ways to better explaining and improving world affairs'.[34] In the case of East Asia, even this potential for deconstructing the prevailing concept of security does not exist, especially since the region's realist security perception is hardly questioned or critically examined.

Before ending this section, it should be pointed out that although some recent developments in international relations theories seem to favor issues related to environmental security, in terms of an overall intellectual scenario, the field of international relations still remains relatively indifferent or uninvolved in dealing with environmental security in a more direct and serious manner.[35] Despite the recent proliferation of various non-traditional concepts, arguments, and perspectives of world politics and international security – especially those found in critical and postmodern theories – the realist and neorealist assumptions still have the dominance over practical international relations policies and strategies.[36] As mentioned above, East Asia represents a relevant example in this regard. However, before examining the dominance of realism in East Asian security perception, the next section explores how significant the issue of environmental security is in the region.

GROWING SIGNIFICANCE OF ENVIRONMENTAL SECURITY IN EAST ASIA: THE CURRENT CONTEXT

East Asia is comprised of countries with diverse demographic, economic, political, and ideological backgrounds.[37] These various forms of cross-national diversity create both the opportunity for cooperation and the potential of conflict among these countries, and thus, have implications for regional security. The situation, of course, is complicated by other past and present issues.[38] However, one of the most common security concerns that has implications for all countries in the region, especially due to their geographic proximity, is the neglected issue of environmental security. This section examines the significance of environmental security in East Asia, especially in terms of the forms and causes of environmental degradation, the interstate dimension of environmental tension, and the inadequacies of existing policies and institutions in this regard.

Major Forms of Environmental Insecurity

The significance of environmental security in East Asia lies in its concerns regarding various forms of environmental degradation, including water and air pollution, nuclear waste, acid rain, deforestation, soil erosion, depletion of marine resources, climate change, and sea level rise. More specifically, one of the most critical issues in East Asia is water and air pollution and its subsequent adverse effects such as the greenhouse effect and ozone depletion. There is a serious problem with marine pollution in the region – covering the Sea of Japan, the Yellow Sea, the East China Sea, and the South China Sea – which is largely caused by radioactive waste disposal, industrial waste dumping, oil spills, heavy metals, and agricultural chemicals.[39]

The level of oil pollution has worsened in the Sea of Japan (its level of pollution is often 2.5 times the level found in unpolluted ocean waters); the volume of marine oil spills has nearly tripled along the coast of South Korea; and the Yellow Sea has become one of the seven 'dying seas' of the world.[40] A more alarming form of pollution, however, is the disposal of radioactive materials, and the potential for nuclear accidents in the process of producing nuclear power in China, Japan, South Korea, North Korea, and Taiwan. For example, since the introduction of nuclear power in South Korea in 1971, there have been 350 nuclear power accidents in the country.[41]

In terms of air pollution, a critical concern in East Asia is regarding the emission of sulfur dioxide. A major source of such emission is from coal-burning factories and power plants in China that emit 700,000 tons of sulfur dioxide per year, affecting other countries in the region such as South Korea and North Korea.[42] Another environmental danger emanating from sulfur emissions is acid rain to which Northeast China, Japan, North Korea, and South Korea are the most vulnerable. Chinese coal-fired power plants also emit carbon dioxide, which causes the greenhouse effect or global warming, and subsequently rise in sea level and climatic change. A significant increase in greenhouse gases has recently occurred due to the rapid pace of industrialization in China.

Other states in the region, especially Japan, Taiwan, and South Korea, are also greatly responsible for the emission of greenhouse gases since these countries are highly industrialized and urbanized. Between 1990 and 1996, the total amount of carbon dioxide emission increased from 244 million to 254 million tonnes in North Korea, 241 million to 408 million tonnes in South Korea, 1.0 billion to nearly 1.2 billion tonnes in Japan, and 2.4 billion to more than 3.3 billion tonnes in China.[43] In addition to such massive carbon emissions, the production and consumption of hazardous industrial goods in East Asia is responsible for the emission of chlorofluorocarbons (CFCs) that deplete the ozone layer.

Deforestation, which causes soil erosion and decline in biodiversity, represents another significant environmental problem in East Asia. The total area of deforestation during 1990–95 was 866 sq. km in China, 132 sq. km in Japan, and 130 sq. km in South Korea. One of the major causes of deforestation is the recent increase in demand for forest timbers in China, Japan, and South Korea.[44] With its huge timber-processing industry, Japan is considered the largest importer of raw logs in the world, and recently China has become another large consumer.[45] Today many of the forest areas – including those along the Pacific coast and the Chinese and Mongolian borders – have come under threat. Deforestation often leads to other environmental problems such as soil erosion, land degradation, and floods. For instance, in the case of China, deforestation has led to land desertification, loss of plant nutrients, and siltation of rivers – Chinese Premier Zhu Rongji has recently acknowledged the connection between deforestation and severe floods in the country.[46]

Deforestation, together with other environmental problems such as toxic pollution and acid rain, also accounts for the biodiversity loss, which has become a growing concern in East Asia. According to 1997 figures, the number of endangered mammal and bird species is 165 in China, 62 in Japan, 25 in South Korea, and 26 in North Korea; the number of such plant species is 312 in China, 707 in Japan, 66 in South Korea and 4 in North Korea.[47] In fact, the worsening situation of environmental degradation represents a threat to the human population itself due to catastrophes such as the rise of sea levels, scarcity of fresh water, destruction of crops by floods, degradation of land, and decline in agricultural production. East Asian countries are facing today some of these severe problems of environmental insecurity. One of the recent examples is the flooding of the Chang (Yangtze) River in China in June 1998, which caused 2,500 deaths, made 56 million people homeless, and affected 7 million hectares of farmland.[48]

Critical Causes of Environmental Insecurity

First, among many factors causing the above forms of environmental insecurity, population pressure is often cited as one of the most critical concerns. An increase in population causes more demand for food, water, fuel, and space; more pressure on marine and forest resources; and perhaps more likelihood of land degradation and environmental pollution. In East Asia, increasing demographic pressure has worsened resource scarcity and ecological degradation. Within a short period between 1996 and 1998, total population size increased from 1.22 billion to 1.25 billion in China, from 45.55 million to 46.43 million in South Korea, from 21.68 million to 22.08 million in North Korea, and from 125.86 million to 126.49 million in Japan.[49] Such an increase in population in these East Asian countries, especially in China, has serious implications for environmental security.

The adverse impact of population pressure on the environment is accentuated further by economic poverty, because it is often the poor who do not have any choice but to clear the forest for cultivable land, adopt intensive cultivation, and overexploit natural resources. In East Asia, the level of such 'environmentally detrimental poverty'[50] has been worsened further due to the recent economic crisis. In terms of income inequality, the shares of income for the poorest 10 per cent and the richest 10 per cent are respectively 4.8 and 21.7 per cent in Japan, 2.9 and 24.3 per cent in South Korea, 2.8 and 24.5 per cent in Mongolia, and 2.4 and 30.4 per cent in China.[51] During the period of economic crisis of 1996–98, the nominal per capita income declined in most East Asian countries except China – from $36,543 to $29,836 in Japan, $11,422 to $6,908 in South Korea, $989 to $573 in North Korea, and $460 to $436 in Mongolia.[52] The worsening condition of poverty and unemployment created by Asian economic crisis has caused a reverse migration from urban to rural areas, expanded pressure on limited land, and exacerbated resource scarcity and overexploitation of natural resources.[53] In other words, the condition of poverty accentuated by the recent economic crisis, has further worsened East Asia's environmental insecurity.

Second, a major cause of environmental degradation in East Asia is the fast and intensive process of land development and urbanization, intensifying the pressures on forest, wetland, and coastal habitats. During the past few decades, the pace of urbanization was unprecedented in East Asia, especially in Japan, South Korea, and Taiwan.[54] More recently, new mega-cities have mushroomed in China. The examples of environmental degradation caused by such a process include the modification of nearly 40 per cent of Japan's natural coastline and a significant decline in its total area of beaches and lagoons; an estimated 65 per cent loss of Korea's coastal wetlands caused by its planned reclamation; and the similar process of coastal reclamation in North Korea.[55] All of these activities have serious adverse impacts on marine resources and migratory species.

Third, most East Asian countries are well known for their most rapid and intensive rates of industrial expansion. Japan, South Korea, and Taiwan have been engaged in massive industrial development since the 1950s and 1960s. Although a latecomer, China has introduced extensive programs of industrialization since the early 1980s. This massive energy-intensive industrialization process (involving the use of coal, oil, and nuclear energy) in the region has critical consequences for its environmental security in terms of the depletion of nonrenewable resources, production of toxic waste, pollution of water and air, and emission of greenhouse gases. In this regard, it has been pointed out that China has become the second-largest electricity producer after the United States, and about 70 per cent of its total power generation capacity comes from coal and 21 per cent from oil.[56] The colossal use of such energy sources by East Asian industries poses a serious threat to environmental security, especially by producing industrial wastes and emitting deadly gases.

Lastly, one major feature that distinguishes East Asia from other regions of the world is its exceptionally high rate of economic growth (except the recent crisis period),[57] although such a distinct record of economic performance might have been achieved at the expense of environmental concerns.[58] Guided by the mission of economic growth, Japan, South Korea, Taiwan, and China have pursued policies in favor of free trade and foreign direct investment, which allegedly have adverse implications for environmental security.[59] For example, it has been pointed out that unfettered free trade in oil, timber, and minerals has often been detrimental to the environment in the region. The advocacy of trade liberalization for economic growth without raising environmental questions by the Asia-Pacific Economic Cooperation (APEC) – of which Japan, South Korea, Taiwan, Hong Kong, and China are members – has unfavorable implications for the region. In order to achieve higher growth rates, most governments in the region provide various incentives, including the withdrawal of environmental regulations, to attract foreign investors. In relation to the economic-growth fetish, the unprecedented increase in environmentally hazardous consumption (especially of cars and gasoline) also represents a major threat to the environment.[60]

Interstate Tensions Caused by Environmental Factors

Major forms of environmental degradation (e.g. pollution, global warming, acid rain, sea-level rise, and biodiversity loss), due to their regional and global scope and impacts, involve different nations and states, and it is hardly possible to keep such environmental disorders within national boundaries. In other words, environmental problems emerged or produced in one state, have spillover effects at least on the neighboring countries. In addition, environment-related problems (e.g. pollution, soil erosion, desertification, drought, and floods) in a state may accentuate resource scarcity so severely, and make human habitats so unsuitable for living, that such a state may get involved in conflict with other states over scarce resources, and part of its population may illegally migrate to other territories and provoke interstate tension.

Beyond this interstate dimension, it should be emphasized that even if one nation's environmental disorders do not spill over to other nations, environmental security still remains relevant and crucial, because, for each nation, the essence of security is to guarantee the security of its citizens against any threat (military or nonmilitary) from anywhere (internal or external). However, the main objective here is to provide some explanations – for example external spillover effects, internal resource scarcity, and motives for further resource acquisition – of how the issue of environmental security becomes an interstate concern in East Asia.

With regard to external spillover effects, one major source of environment-driven interstate tension in East Asia is the transborder pollution of air and marine resources. There are tensions among China, Japan, and South Korea over transboundary air pollution, which is largely caused by the above-mentioned pollution in China from its coal-fueled power plants and industrial facilities. The massive emission of greenhouse gases (carbon dioxide) by these power plants and industries created so much tension between China and Japan (and other industrialized nations) that during the Kyoto Protocol, China was asked to make commitment to reduce the level of its greenhouse gas emissions. China is specifically blamed for having such power plants and industries that emit acidic pollutants, and thus causes acid rain to which Japan, South Korea, and North Korea are quite vulnerable.[61] There are also controversies over the pollution of the Sea of Japan – caused by industrial waste dumping, radioactive waste disposal, and oil exploration and spills – which has coastlines with East Asian countries.

The second environment-related cause of potential interstate tension in East Asia is the situation of resource scarcity perceived and experienced by people, and which spurs their mobility within and between national borders. A major problem case of resource scarcity is China, which has a population size of nearly 1.3 billion (six times bigger than the combined population of Japan, Taiwan, and the two Koreas) with a significant percentage living in poverty. Due to the scarcity of land, water, and fuel wood caused by soil erosion, over-cultivation, and deforestation, there are millions of people (estimated 100 million to 130 million) who are on the move within the country.[62] A severe condition of resource scarcity and environmental degradation also prevails in North Korea. The subsequent cross-border migration and refugee flows from China and North Korea create apprehension among neighboring countries, especially because of the fear that such migration could spread further. It is estimated that about 100,000 to 400,000 North Koreans have fled to China owing to environmental disruption (e.g. resource scarcity) and political risk, and they intend to eventually settle down in South Korea.[63]

Another environmental reason for interstate tension among East Asian countries is their motive of increasing control over environmental resources beyond national borders. Such a scenario is exemplified in the continuing disputes over fishing in the regional seas, which are often caused by the tendency of these countries to take unilateral action to maximize their share of fishery stocks. Often these disputes are not resolvable by existing bilateral agreements.[64] Similar motivations can be seen in the continuing territorial disputes (mostly over islands) of Japan with China, South Korea, and Taiwan; the maritime boundary dispute between China and Vietnam; and the dispute over the Spratly Islands, especially, between China and Taiwan (each claiming itself as the sole legitimate authority to exercise control over these islands).[65] The motives of these countries to acquire these environmental resources represent one of the most primary factors behind such disputes.

Current Environmental Measures and Their Limits

The significance of environmental security in East Asia lies not only in its forms, causes, and interstate implications, but also in the inadequacies of existing protection measures practiced by these countries. First, at the global level, there are various international conventions and protocols related to transboundary pollution, ozone depletion, waste disposal, and biological diversity.[66] There are also international institutions such as the United Nations Environment Programme, the United Nations Commission on Sustainable Development, the Intergovernmental Panel on Climate Change, the Secretariat of the Convention on Biological Diversity, and so on. As with other countries, these international legal and institutional measures have certain influence on East Asian countries in favor of environmental security.

At the regional level, there is the so-called Northeast Asia Environment Programme, which organizes conferences and invites high-level officials (mostly from foreign ministries), so that they can get involved in dialogue on common environmental problems and pursue regional cooperation in sharing information, conducting research and training, and monitoring the conditions of marine pollution, biodiversity, and acid rain. Another initiative is the Northwest Pacific Action Plan in which East Asian countries are participants. Its agenda is to produce a regional convention to protect the coastal and marine resources in the Sea of Japan and the Yellow Sea.

There is also the Tumen River Area Development Program (TRADP) comprised of participants such as China, Russia, North Korea, South Korea, and Mongolia. One of its main objectives is to promote environmental protection, initiate joint projects for environmental management, and raise sensitivity among these member countries regarding the environmental implications of domestic economic and industrial activities for their neighbors.

In addition, the Intergovernmental Oceanographic Commission's Sub-Commission for the West Pacific has member states from various regions, including China, Hong Kong, South Korea, North Korea, and Japan from East Asia. Its purpose is to develop local skills in research on geological conditions and resources. There are also regional initiatives such as the South Pacific Regional Environment Programme and the Lower Mekong Basin Development Environment Program, which involve environmental cooperation between Southeast Asia and Northeast Asia. In addition, regional economic institutions such as APEC have incorporated environmental issues in their agendas of cooperation. Beyond these regional-level plans, programs, and initiatives, there are bilateral treaties or agreements involving China, Japan, South Korea, and North Korea; environmental think tanks and movements in Japan, South Korea, and Taiwan; and government agencies, ministries, and/or commissions in all these countries to address various forms and causes of environmental threats and ensure environmental security.[67]

Despite the availability of the above initiatives for environmental security in East Asia, there are contradictions and limitations inherent in most of these measures. For example, in the case of TRADP, competing national interests have prevailed over the broader regional concerns, and the legacy of conflicting relations between North Korea and Japan has prevented the latter from participating in the program.[68] The intention of economic institutions like APEC to support environmental concerns, contradicts their broader policies of free trade and foreign investment as they often degrade the environment. On the other hand, a major limitation of existing environmental measures in East Asia is that they are mostly unilateral regulatory means and voluntary bilateral or multilateral programs rather than legally binding multilateral conventions and treaties. As a result, regional cooperation in environmental security remains relatively uncertain and ineffective, especially due to the absence of specific legal measures and enforcing agencies at the regional level and the continuing emphasis on national-level strategies and institutions. In fact, the potential for environmental protection through such individualistic national initiatives has recently come under challenge due to the lack of finances accentuated by the recent Asian economic crisis. Although East Asian countries were adopting laws and regulations in compliance with international demands and pressures in the past, the post-crisis period witnessed a decline in such environmental legal standards in the region.[69]

In addition, the prevailing measures hardly take into account various environmentally relevant issues such as poverty, arms proliferation, industrial expansion, economic growth, consumerism, free trade, and foreign investment. As stated above, in various ways, these issues represent indirect threats to the environment. For instance, poverty and inequality (especially in China, North Korea, and Mongolia) force the poor to deplete environmental resources while allowing the rich to consume expensive but environmentally harmful industrial goods. Arms proliferation (especially in China, North Korea, and Taiwan) multiplies radioactive waste and diverts resources from human and environmental needs to military purposes. Economic growth based on industrial expansion, free trade, and consumerism often depletes resources, pollutes air and water, produces toxic waste, and endangers the overall environment. One may list other non-environmental issues with serious environmental consequences, but the problem remains that these issues are not taken seriously by most East Asian countries obsessed with industrial growth, consumerism, foreign investment, and military expansion.

In East Asia, one of the major reasons why factors related to regional environmental security receives less attention than national economic safety and military security, could very well be the legacy of traditional security perception based on the realist assumptions of interstate relations. In the region, individual states are overwhelmingly concerned with their performance in economic growth and national defense, which may create adverse environmental impacts (discussed above) and encourage interstate competition rather than cooperation. In other words, there is a dilemma between the drive for economic growth and consumerism that adversely affects the environment and intensifies interstate competition on the one hand, and the need for environmental security requiring a reduction in growth and consumerism and an expansion of interstate cooperation on the other.

The dilemma also exists between long-established perceptions or habits of traditional (military) security and the worsening ecological situation that needs adequate attention to non-traditional (environmental) security. For example, it is unrealistic to expect smooth cooperation between China and Taiwan, between South Korea and North Korea, and between Japan and China in the sphere of environment when these countries already have a legacy of conflictual interstate relations in the sphere of military security. The continuity in such strained interstate relations in East Asia, which largely reflects the realist perception of international relations, is likely to constrain regional cooperation needed for environmental protection. Thus, the next section explains the dominant international relations outlook and its implications for environmental security in the region.

DOMINANT INTERNATIONAL RELATIONS OUTLOOK IN EAST ASIA: IMPACT ON ENVIRONMENTAL SECURITY

Despite the end of the Cold War and emergence of a globalized multipolar world, the dominant outlook of interstate relations in East Asia still appears to be founded upon realist or neorealist assumptions. The legacy of the realist tradition in the region's international relations can be found in the continued dominance of states as the main actors in regional politics, preoccupation with traditional security and marginalization of non-traditional security issues, expansion of military apparatus and defense expenditure, use of bilateralism rather than multilateral institutions, mutual negative perceptions among states, and apprehension about interstate military threats.[70] This section examines some of the major symptoms of realist underpinnings in East Asian international relations, the reasons or rationales for this realist outlook, and the critical implications of realist perspectives for environmental security in the region.

Indicators of the Realist Perspective in East Asia

First, with regard to the dominant realist outlook in international relations, one major indicator in East Asia is the dominance of states as the main actors in regional and international affairs. Despite the diminishing role of the state in domestic economic management due to recent market-oriented government reforms, the state remains the central actor in international relations, especially in regional economic relations and security strategies. The state still plays the leading role in pursuing nation-building, articulating national identity, and promoting nationalism – all of which considerably affect security perceptions in East Asia. State-centric nationalism and sovereignty, although they may constrain regional cooperation, often shape the nature of foreign policy in China, North Korea, South Korea, and Japan. Although certain segments of society, including business managers, economic experts, and academic professionals, may have liberal, pluralist, or constructivist viewpoints; the main forces in actual foreign policy making (such as top political and military leaders) still hold the state-centric realist assumptions of sovereignty in international affairs.[71] This dynamics is most prominent in China and North Korea.

Second, in terms of regional security perceptions, countries in East Asia are mostly guided by the conventional realist notion of state power based on military expansion for encountering external threats. This militaristic view of security is evident in the continuous increases in defense expenditures in countries like China and Japan. China has modernized its military and increased defense spending by 10 per cent each year since 1989, while the continual expansion of military expenditures in Japan during the recent decades has made its defense budget the second largest in the world.[72] However, the tension between the two Koreas, exacerbated by their potential nuclear threats and missile programs, has led to massive concentration of troops along their shared border.[73] The overall size of military forces and the amount of weapons in East Asia is quite alarming, and such an expansive defense system implies the dominance of a realist, militaristic security perception in the region, which is reinforced further by the formation of strong bilateral military alliances with the United States by Japan, South Korea, and Taiwan. Such alliances are observed suspiciously and cautiously by China and North Korea.

Third, realist security assumptions in East Asian countries become obvious when their mutually negative perceptions are considered. One prime example of such negative perceptions is the apprehension about the 'China threat' in other countries of the region, which is largely their perceived threat of China caused by its nuclear power, military capability, significant territorial and demographic size, permanent seat on the UN Security Council, strong nationalistic attitude, and desire to get control over the disputed South China Sea.[74] There is also a negative perception about Japan due to its colonial past, its formidable economic strength, and its potential revival of military power. Such negative interstate perceptions are often reinforced by the above-mentioned territorial and border disputes among various East Asian countries. For all these disputes, the unilateral use of military force remains one of the most preferred options in these countries.

Last, another indicator of realist or neorealist assumptions under-girding the international relations outlook of East Asian countries (except Mongolia) is their preference for a national security realized through bilateral security arrangements rather than multilateral institutions.[75] For instance, China is unwilling to pursue multilateral regional cooperation,[76] especially because of its state-centric nationalism that tends to rule out multilateralism due to its potential constraint on its sovereignty. Similarly, Japan has a tradition of engaging itself in bilateral ties, although its security cooperation with the United States may constrain its multilateral cooperation within the region.[77] It is true that East Asian countries have created certain multilateral institutions such as the TRADP and the APEC. But, as mentioned above, multilateral cooperation through such institutions has been constrained by the particularistic national interest of each member country. On the other hand, although an institution like the ASEAN Regional Forum involves some East Asian countries (China, Japan, South Korea, and North Korea), it does not address security issues that are unique to East Asia.[78] This relative absence of genuine and direct multilateral cooperation in East Asia reflects the realist assumption that the balance of power is less stable when it involves more than two states.

Reasons Behind the Realist Perspective

What are the major reasons for the dominance of realist assumptions in the practice of East Asian international relations? The most frequently mentioned reasons are the history of Japan's military aggression against other East Asian countries during World War II and the legacy of Cold War rivalries, which still continue to perpetuate mutual distrust, perceived external threats, and negative attitudes toward the neighboring countries.[79] For instance, there has been tension between Japan and other countries in the region (especially China) due to their demand for an apology from Japan for its war crimes and Japan's reluctance to comply. Similarly, the Cold War – which created tension between the communist bloc (China and North Korea) and the capitalist bloc (Japan, South Korea, and Taiwan) – continues to influence contemporary security perceptions and practices in the region. Concrete examples of this Cold War legacy include the current tension between China and Taiwan, and between South Korea and North Korea.

The second major reason for the realist framework's dominance in East Asia is the unequal regional power structure in both economic and military domains. More particularly, Japan is the regional economic power, although in recent years, China has become a potential giant mainly due to its huge markets, enormous enterprises, and high growth rates. Although South Korea and Taiwan have higher rates of per capita income than China, their economies are much smaller in size. Meanwhile, the poorest economies are Mongolia and North Korea. This uneven economic power – reinforced by the membership of Japan and South Korea in the WTO and the OECD (inaccessible to North Korea and China) – exacerbates economic tension, and makes multilateral cooperation less likely.[80] In the military sphere, China has become a formidable global power, and it possesses a military capability in terms of personnel, organization, and conventional and nuclear weapons that surpasses the total defense capabilities of all other East Asian countries. The military power of North Korea, especially its missile development program and potential nuclear capability, also represents a regional threat, especially to South Korea and Japan.[81]

Another major reason for a realist view of international relations in East Asia may be found in internal problems such as economic decline, poverty, unemployment, and class conflict. These factors often lead states to use the rhetoric of nationalism, external threat, and militarism in order to deflect public attention away from the politically damaging domestic problems. For example, China is facing an increase in unemployment (from 10 million to 16 million during 1998–99), a growing income gap and urban-rural divide, and political challenges from its Muslim population and religious sects such as Falun Gong.[82] One should not discount the pressure caused by these domestic problems, and the temptation for the government to divert public attention elsewhere by overemphasizing external security threats. Similarly, North Korea is suffering from severe poverty and hunger and South Korea has the worsening problem of unemployment and labor strikes. It is easier for both states to maintain public confidence in governance by portraying each other as a security threat than to resolve internal socioeconomic problems.

Finally, the realist perception of regional security in East Asia is also perpetuated by the presence of external actors, especially the extensive military presence of the United States, in the region. Since US foreign policy and security perception continue to be guided by a predominantly realist worldview, its trusted military allies such as Japan, Taiwan, and South Korea also are psychologically influenced. The United States assists these allies not only by providing advanced weapons and military training but also by maintaining its thousands of troops within their territories. The presence of the US army creates certain distrust between China and Taiwan, North Korea and South Korea, and Japan and China. Such distrust, in turn, encourages a realist security perception among these East Asian countries, and encourages them to expand and modernize their military capabilities. Thus, the US presence or influence remains one of the major factors reinforcing the realist view of security in the region. Although there is a strong belief that this US presence is essential for security and stability in East Asia, the fact remains that such a notion of regional security and stability is in line with the aforementioned balance-of-power and hegemonic-stability theories within the realist tradition.

Impacts of the Realist Perspective on Environmental Security

During and after the Cold War, most East Asian states, especially China, South Korea, North Korea, and Taiwan, pursued the expansion and modernization of defense based on a realist assumption of security emphasizing the need for state power to encounter external threats. Such a one-dimensional security outlook precludes the non-traditional dimensions of security such as the environment.

In addition, due to the primacy of military security based on a realist perspective in East Asia, there has been a proliferation of conventional, chemical, biological, and nuclear weapons that are detrimental to the environment. While there is already a problem of disposing nuclear waste and radioactive materials from the production of missiles and nuclear weapons in China, the missile development program and potential nuclear warheads in North Korea are likely to increase the volume of such hazardous materials. In addition, the current strategy of maintaining a US-led military superiority in South Korea and Taiwan also involves the transfer of hazardous weapons and equipment to the region. Beyond these examples, there are indirect environmental implications of such a military expansion. More specifically, as the increase in defense expenditures in East Asian countries diminishes their available resources needed for reducing poverty and satisfying people's basic needs, the impoverished population may have no other choice but to over-cultivate land and overexploit forest and marine resources. This risk is more serious in relatively poorer countries such as North Korea and China.

Another adverse implication of a realist view of security in East Asia is the perpetuation of a state-centric bilateralism at the expense of building collective security through multilateral cooperation. The absence of multilateral cooperation is not conducive to environmental security because the cross-boundary nature of various environmental problems requires multilateral initiatives. However, the traditional habits of East Asian states to manage security problems by themselves or by establishing bilateral defense ties with external actors such as the United States, are not easy to change even in this post-Cold War world. The hegemonic influence of the United States itself is a critical factor discouraging its allies (Japan, South Korea, and Taiwan) to engage in any multilateral cooperation with its adversaries such as China and North Korea. Such a barrier to multilateral cooperation in military security has negative spillover effect on the potential for such cooperation in environmental security. In other words, if East Asian countries remain adversaries, and cannot achieve regional cooperation with regard to military security, one should not expect them to achieve a collective regional security for the environment. Thus, in order to realize environmental security, East Asian countries must question their traditional, realist view of security founded upon the assumptions of state power, external threat, and military expansion, and make a paradigm shift toward an alternative security perspective that values interstate cooperation, emphasizes multiple actors, and recognizes non-traditional security issues like the environment. The next section attempts to explore the major constituents of such an alternative.

CHANGING THE INTERNATIONAL RELATIONS PERSPECTIVE FOR ENVIRONMENTAL SECURITY

As discussed earlier, a new direction in thinking of international relations has emerged in terms of redefining security to encompass non-military security issues and multiple actors under new terms such as comprehensive security and non-traditional security.[83] In line with this intellectual shift, various international conventions, protocols, and institutions have been introduced in relation to different forms of environmental insecurity. Unfortunately, this current trend of re-conceptualizing security and creating international institutions for environmental security is not yet reflected in the perception and practice of regional security in East Asia. There is hardly any effective legal and institutional means at the regional level to deal adequately with environmental problems. In this context, what steps should be taken by East Asian countries to ensure environmental security in the region?

First, it is essential to rethink and take initiative to resolve the legacies of traditional conflicts – arising from events and issues such as Japan's role of aggression in World War II, the Korean War affecting the current inter-Korean relations, intraregional divisions created during the Cold War, and age-old territorial disputes – which tend to overshadow more crucial contemporary concerns such as environmental security. More specifically, it is necessary for China and Korea to question the practical significance of Japan's apologizing for its past role, and for Japan to question why it is so difficult to do so. All East Asian countries also need to reexamine their Cold War identities in this post-Cold War world, use pragmatic and rational rather than obsolete ideological criteria in their interstate relations, reassess the need for external actors (especially the United States) in shaping their security perceptions, and sort out their interstate rivalries by themselves. In this process, a critical factor is the demystification of negative perceptions that East Asian countries hold about each other, which requires diverse mechanisms – such as formal confidence-building measures, informal meetings and dialogues, and information and knowledge exchanges – to build mutual trust based on sincerity and commitment. They should increasingly replace the negative perceptions arising from historical conflicts with positive attitudes towards issues of common interests, and adopt a 'win-win' rather than 'win-lose' approach.[84] By overcoming negative perceptions, rebuilding trust, and complementing mutual needs, East Asian countries can divert attention away from military security and move to non-military security problems such as the environment.

Second, after changing mutual perceptions and attitudes among East Asian countries, the next step is to reexamine and restructure the traditional institutional frameworks predominantly based on unilateral defense strategies (except bilateral ties with the United States in a few cases). Once the above measures of replacing mutual misperception with trust are effective and the significance of military security is diminished, these countries have to find ways to restructure the existing security arrangements, especially in terms of reducing the defense sector (budget, personnel, weapons). In this regard, being the largest power in the region, China has to set examples for other states. Although China encourages the two Koreas to reduce potential nuclear proliferation in the Korean Peninsula,[85] it has to demonstrate its sincerity by reducing its own nuclear arsenal. On the other hand, countries like Japan, South Korea, and Taiwan have to rethink their military alliance with the United States (one of the central factors causing interstate distrust), and take initiatives to establish a collective regional security. In other words, based on mutual trust, these countries need to replace unilateral or bilateral security, and build institutions for multilateral security involving all states in the region

With regard to environmental security, this reduction in the defense sector and expansion of multilateral regional collaboration will not only mitigate the problem of hazardous arms production, it will also release considerable financial and human resources from the military to satisfy basic needs of the poor, and thus, minimize their dependence on environmental resources. In addition, such a regional collaboration in military security will set an example or precedence of multilateralism needed for environmental security in East Asia. In fact, there is an urgent need for regional cooperation to address various forms of environmental problems in the region, including transboundary air pollution, acid rain, marine pollution, deforestation, and potential nuclear catastrophe.[86] However, it is necessary to add that multilateral cooperation for environmental security should involve various levels of stakeholders – including governments, NGOs, research institutions, and environmental experts – so that it becomes mutually reinforcing. More importantly, multilateralism in environmental security must result in legally binding regional environmental conventions requiring strict compliance of all states in the region.

Third, beyond the direct measures of regional cooperation and institution-building for environmental security, East Asian countries need to address critical issues such as population pressure, poverty, and inequality that have adverse implications for environmental security. Although there are extensive programs for controlling population growth in these countries, these programs must be supplemented by nationwide publicity, access to information, basic education, and adequate health care, so that people are motivated rather than coerced to follow such programs. With regard to poverty, states in East Asia must undertake comprehensive anti-poverty programs – especially to ensure the satisfaction of people's basic needs such as food, health care, education, transport – which, as stated above, can easily be financed by money saved from cuts in defense expenditure. In addition, a reduction in income inequality by adopting various redistributive measures can contribute to poverty alleviation. If effective, these policies and programs to reduce population pressure and poverty are likely to minimize the overuse and depletion of natural resources by the poor.

Fourth, for greater environmental security, East Asian countries should reexamine and readjust their policy priorities. More specifically, recent state policies in these countries (except North Korea) have mostly been guided by the objective of economic growth. During the period since World War II,

Japan, South Korea, and Taiwan experienced extremely high rates of economic growth, and more recently, China has become another high-performing economy in the region. As discussed in this study, such a high growth rate – mostly based on expansive industrial production, massive consumption, and trade liberalization – is often achieved by worsening environmental degradation. Thus, it is necessary to revise the objectives of economic growth, reexamine the current market-centered policies undertaken in the name of economic growth, and adopt more environment-friendly economic policies. More specifically, East Asian governments should revise the policies guided by economic growth, and adopt policies based on the principle of 'sustainable development' that favors environmental security.[87] If certain market-led policies and reforms are really unavoidable, each government in the region must adopt strict regulations for environmental protection, introduce measures to incorporate the environmental costs into the costs of concerned commodities,[88] and empower various environment protection agencies to enforce such regulations and measures.

Finally, all the above initiatives and policy measures are less likely to be adopted if there is no basic change in the realist security assumptions held by East Asian states. In this regard, it is imperative for the top policy-makers of these countries to reexamine the validity of realist assumptions underlying their security perceptions, assess the environmental (and other) costs of holding such a realist outlook in security strategies, and explore alternative theories or paradigms of international relations that are conducive to all forms (traditional and non-traditional) of security. As discussed earlier, there are other approaches to international relations with varying environmental implications.

With regard to environmental security, while the liberal tradition has certain potential (but otherwise indifferent), the interpretive tradition is accommodative (but without specific policy agenda), and the radical tradition is sympathetic (but without a concrete theory of its own). In considering these diverse international relations perspectives to articulate and promote an environment-friendly approach to security, the academic scholars and experts in the region can play a crucial role through publications, conferences, and media networks. In this regard, however, the academics themselves may have to critically examine their own preconceived assumptions regarding international security in general, and environmental security in particular.

NOTES

1. Shin-Wha Lee, 'Safeguarding the Environment: An Agenda for Regional Cooperation in South Korea, Northeast Asia, and Beyond', in Carolina G. Hernandez and Gill Wilkins (eds.) *Population, Food, Energy, and the Environment: Challenges to Asia-Europe Cooperation* (Tokyo: Council for Asia-Europe Cooperation 2000) p.182; Tsuneo Akaha, 'Non-Conventional Security Cooperation in Northeast Asia', paper presented at the workshop of Inter and Intra-Regional Cooperation and Institutions Research Group, University of Hong Kong (11–12 Dec. 2000).

2. Rowland T. Maddock, 'Environmental Security', in M. Jane Davis (ed.) *Security Issues in the Post-Cold War World* (Cheltenham: Edward Elgar 1996) pp.160–80.

3. Geoffrey D. Dabelko and David D. Dabelko, *Environmental Security: Issues of Concept and Redefinition,* Occasional Paper No.1 (College Park, MD: Department of Government and Politics, Univ. of Maryland 1993).

4. M. Shamsul Haque, 'The Fate of Sustainable Development Under the Neoliberal Regimes in Developing Countries', *International Political Science Review* 20/2 (1999) pp.199–222; and Patricia M. Mische, 'Security Through Defending the Environment: Citizens Say Yes', in Elise Boulding (ed.) *New Agendas for Peace Research: Conflict and Security Reexamined* (Boulder, CO: Lynne Rienner 1992) pp.103–19.

5. Lester Brown, *Redefining Security*, Worldwatch Paper No.14 (Washington DC: Worldwatch Institute n.d.); Richard H. Ullman, 'Redefining Security', *International Security* 8 (Summer 1983) pp.129–53; and Jessica T. Mathews, 'Redefining Security', *Foreign Affairs* 68 (Spring 1989) pp.162–77.

6. NISSD (Nautilus Institute for Security and Sustainable Development), *Energy, Environment and Security in Northeast Asia: Defining a U.S.-Japan Partnership for Regional Comprehensive Security* (Berkeley, CA: NISSD, Dec. 1999); see also >www.nautilus.org/papers/energy/ESENAfinalreport.html<

7. R. Perelet, 'The Environment as a Security Issue', in Dutch Committee for Long-term Environmental Policy (ed.) *The Environment: Towards a Sustainable Future* (The Hague: Kluwer Academic Publishers 1994) pp.147–73; Daniel Esty, 'Pivotal States and the Environment', in Robert Chase, Emily Hill, and Paul Kennedy (eds.) *The Pivotal States: A New Framework for U.S. Policy in the Developing World* (NY: Norton 1999) pp.290–314; NISSD (note 6).

8. Patricia M. Mische, 'Ecological Security in a New World Order: Some Linkages between Ecology, Peace and Global Security', in UNESCO (ed.) *Non-military Aspects of International Security* (Paris: UNESCO 1995) pp.155–95; NISSD (note 6).

9. Jack Goldstone, 'Demography, Environment and Security: An Overview', Guest Lecture by Prof. Jack Goldstone, The MIT Project on Demography and Security (Oct. 1999); Thomas F. Homer-Dixon, 'On the Threshold: Environmental Changes as Causes of Acute Conflict', *International Security* 16 (Fall 1991) pp.76–116; Ullman (note 5).

10. Thomas F. Homer-Dixon, 'Environmental Scarcities and Violent Conflict: Evidence from Cases', *International Security* 19/1 (1994) pp.5–40.

11. Carolina G. Hernandez, Jorge V. Tigno, and Crisline G. Torres, 'The Asian Overview: Population, Food, Energy, and the Environment', in Carolina G. Hernandez and Gill Wilkins (eds.) *Population, Food, Energy, and the Environment: Challenges to Asia-Europe Cooperation* (Tokyo: Council for Asia-Europe Cooperation 2000) pp.122, 130–31.

12. Jim George, *Discourses of Global Politics: A Critical (Re)Introduction to International Relations* (Boulder, CO: Lynne Rienner 1994); Christine Sylvester, *Feminist Theory and International Relations in a Postmodern Era* (Cambridge: CUP 1994); R.B.J. Walker, *Inside/Outside: International Relations as Political Theory* (Cambridge: CUP 1993).

13. Dennis Pirages, 'Ecological Theory and International Relations', *Indiana Journal of Global Studies* 5/1 (1997) pp.53–64; Charles Kegley Jr and Eugene R. Wittkopf, *World Politics: Trends and Transformation*, 5th ed. (NY: St Martin's Press 1997).

14. Raymond Aron, *Peace and War: A Theory of International Relations* (NY: Doubleday 1966); Robert Jervis, 'Cooperation under the Security Dilemma', *World Politics* 30/2 (1978) pp.167–214; Scott Burchill, 'Realism and Neo-Realism', in Scott Burchill and Andrew

Environmental Security 231

Linklater (eds.) *Theories of International Relations* (NY: St Martin's Press 1996) pp.67–79; Dabelko and Dabelko (note 3).

15. Kenneth N. Waltz, Theory of International Politics (Reading, MA: Addison-Wesley 1979); idem 'Realist Thought and Neorealist Theory', in Charles W. Kegley Jr (ed.) *Controversies in International Relations Theory: Realism and the Neoliberal Challenge* (NY: St Martin's Press 1995) pp.67–83.
16. Kegley and Wittkopf (note 12).
17. John Mearsheimer, 'The False Promise of International Institutions', *International Security* 19/3 (1994–95) pp.5–49.
18. National Research Council, *Post-Cold War Conflict Deterrence* (Naval Studies Board, National Research Council, National Academy of Sciences 1997).
19. Dabelko and Dabelko (note 3).
20. Kegley and Wittkopf (note 12).
21. Kegley and Wittkopf (note 12) pp.31–5; Robert Keohane, 'International Institutions: Two Approaches', *International Studies Quarterly* 32 (1988); Robert Keohane and J. Nye, *Power and Interdependence: World Politics in Transition* (Boston: Little, Brown 1977).
22. Robert Wolfe, 'Rendering Unto Caesar: How Legal Pluralism and Regime Theory Help in Understanding Multiple Centres of Power', in Gordon S. Smith and Daniel Wolfish (eds), *Who Is Afraid of the State?* (Univ. of Toronto Press 2001); S. Krasner, *International Regimes* (Ithaca, NY: Cornell UP 1983).
23. However, for Pirages, although liberalism may hold a positive attitude toward ecological issues and prescribes interstate alliances in this regard, it does not offer concrete theoretical and practical guidelines to deal with growing biological and ecological challenges. See Pirages (note 13) pp.53–64.
24. J. Ruggie, 'What Makes the World Hang Together? Neo-utilitarianism and the Social Constructivist Challenge', *International Organization* 52/4 (Autumn 1998).
25. Jeffrey T. Checkel, 'The Constructivist Turn in International Relations Theory', *World Politics* 50 (Jan. 1998) pp.324–48.
26. Alexander Wendt, 'Constructing International Politics', *International Security* 20 (Summer 1995) pp.384–96; Checkel (note 25).
27. In this regard, Reus-Smit mentions that within the context of globalization, constructivism highlights the 'mutually constitutive relationship between states and emerging global structures and processes'. Christian Reus-Smit, 'Beyond Foreign Policy: State Theory and the Changing Global Order', in Paul James (ed.) *The State in Question: Transformations of the Australian State* (NSW, Australia: Allen & Unwin 1996) p.163.
28. Ibid.
29. Ken Booth, 'Security in Anarchy: Utopian Realism in Theory and Practice', *International Affairs* 67 (1991) pp.527–45.
30. Richard Ashley, 'The Geopolitics of Geopolitical space: toward a critical social theory of International Politics', *Alternatives* 12 (1987) pp.403–34. Genealogy is a method of philosophical analysis – introduced by Friedrich Nietzsche and extensively used by Michel Foucault – which questions the existing moral and truth claims, explores their historical origins and process of normalization, reveals their fragmented and localized nature, and thus demystifies their altruistic appearances. See Friedrich Nietzsche, *Beyond Good and Evil* (Harmondsworth: Penguin 1990); Michel Foucault, *Discipline and Punish: The Birth of the Prison* (NY: Vintage Books 1979); Michel Foucault, *Power/Knowledge: Selected Interviews and Other Writings* (NY: Pantheon 1980).
31. Richard Devetak, 'Critical Theory', in Scott Burchill and Andrew Linklater (eds.) *Theories of International Relations* (NY: St Martin's Press 1996) pp.145–77; and Richard Devetak, 'Postmodernism', in Scott Burchill and Andrew Linklater (eds.) *Theories of International Relations* (NY: St Martin's Press 1996) pp.179–209.
32. Eric Laferriere and Peter J. Stoett, *International Relations Theory and Ecological Thought* (London: Routledge 1999) pp.12, 148.
33. Christine Sylvester, 'Feminist Theory and Gender Studies in International Relations', *International Studies Notes* 16–17/3-1 (1991–92) pp.32–8; Jacqui True, 'Feminism', in Burchill and Linklater, *Theories of International Relations* (note 14) pp.229–32.

34. Kegley and Wittkopf (note 12) p.28.
35. Pirages (note 13) pp.53–64.
36. Dabelko and Dabelko (note 3); Iftekharuzzaman, 'South Asia', in Paul B. Stares (ed.) *The New Security Agenda: A Global Survey* (Tokyo: Japan Center for International Exchange 1998) pp.273–4.
37. For instance, demographically, China has a total population of 1.25 billion, Japan 126.5 million, South Korea 46.4 million, North Korea 22.1 million, and Mongolia 2.4 million; and in economic terms, the nominal per capita GDP is $29,836 in Japan, $6,908 in South Korea, $910 in China, $573 in North Korea, and $436 in Mongolia. In politico-ideological term, there is a democratic tradition with advanced capitalist market in Japan, a process of democratization and a developed market system in both South Korea and Taiwan, a move towards market-led reforms and expanding democratic forces in China and Mongolia, and a rigid system of communist rule and an underdeveloped market system in North Korea. See M. Shamsul Haque, 'How Critical is "Environmental Security" as a Non-Traditional Security Issue in Northeast Asia?', paper presented at the workshop of Inter and Intra-Regional Cooperation and Institutions Research Group, University of Hong Kong, 11–12 Dec. 2000; Akaha (note 1).
38. Some of these issues include the memory of Japan's colonial intervention in other East Asian countries; the remembrance of the Korean War; the legacy of the Cold War mind-set; the strong alliance of the US with Japan, South Korea, and Taiwan, but rivalry with China and North Korea; and the nuclear power of China and North Korea. Peter Hayes and Lyuba Zarsky, 'Environmental Issues and Regimes in Northeast Asia', *International Environmental Affairs* 6/4 (Fall 1994).
39. Hernandez, Tigno, and Torres (note 11) pp.130–2; NISSD (note 6); SCFA (The Standing Committee on Foreign Affairs), *Crisis in Asia: Implications for the Region, Canada, and the World*. Report of the Standing Committee on Foreign Affairs, Dec. 1998, Canada.
40. Hayes and Zarsky (note 38); Lee (note 1) p.188.
41. Hernandez, Tigno and Torres (note 11) p.133.
42. Hayes and Zarsky (note 38); Lee (note 1) p.188.
43. World Resources Institute, *World Resources 2000–2001* (Washington DC: World Resources Institute 2000).
44. World Bank, *World Development Report 2000–2001* (NY: OUP 2001) p.291.
45. Hayes and Zarsky (note 38).
46. Mao Yu-Shi, *The Economic Cost of Environmental Degradation in China: A Summary.* Occasional Paper of the Project on Environmental Scarcities, State Capacity, and Civil Violence (Univ. of Toronto 1997) >www.library.utoronto.ca/pcs/state/chinaeco/summary.htm<; Matsushita Kazuo, 'Environment and Development in Asia', *Japan Echo* 27/3 (June 2000).
47. World Bank (note 44) p.222.
48. Kazuo, 2000.
49. Akaha (note 1).
50. Among the poorer countries in East Asia, the percentage of people earning less than one US dollar a day was 18.5 per cent in China in 1996, and 13.9 per cent in Mongolia. World Bank (note 44) pp.280–81.
51. World Bank (note 44) pp.282–3.
52. Akaha (note 1).
53. Lyuba Zarsky and Simon Tay, 'Civil Society and the Future of Environmental', in D. Angel and M. Rock (eds.) *Asia's Clean Revolution: Industry, Growth and the Environment* (Sheffield: Greenleaf 2001).
54. Lee (note 1) p.187.
55. Lyuba Zarsky, 'The Domain of Environmental Cooperation in Northeast Asia', paper prepared for the Sixth Annual International Conference Korea and the Future of Northeast Asia: Conflict or Cooperation?, Portland State University, Portland, OR, 4–5 May 1995.
56. NISSD (note 6).
57. The average rate of economic growth was 9.8 per cent in Japan during 1956–73, 8.95 per cent in South Korea during 1963–91; and 9.7 per cent in China during 1979–99. Li Kai, 'The

Impact of Expanding Population and Economic Growth ... in the People's Republic of China', in Carolina G. Hernandez and Gill Wilkins (eds.) *Population, Food, Energy, and the Environment: Challenges to Asia-Europe Cooperation* (Tokyo: Council for Asia-Europe Cooperation 2000) p.141.

58. As pointed out by World Bank, 'East Asian countries have been pursuing rapid economic growth, industrialization, and modernization with little consideration of environmental issues.' World Bank, *Environmental Implications of the Economic Crisis and Adjustment in East Asia* (Washington DC: World Bank 1999) p.2.

59. Hernandez, Tigno, and Torres (note 11) p.130; Zarsky and Tay (note 53); Gill Wilkins, 'The European Overview', in Hernandez and Wilkins, *Population, Food, Energy, and the Environment* (note 57) pp.9–10.

60. Between 1990 and 1996, the number of cars per 1000 people increased from 1 to 3 in China, 283 to 373 in Japan, 48 to 151 in South Korea, and 5 to 12 in Mongolia; and between 1987 and 1997, the consumption of motor gasoline per person increased from 20 to 35 liters in China, 308 to 422 liters in Japan, and 39 to 245 liters in South Korea. World Resources Institute (note 43).

61. Zarsky (note 55); NISSD (note 6).

62. SCFA (note 39).

63. Lee (note 1) p.202.

64. Zarsky (note 55).

65. SCFA (note 39); Deng Yong, 'The Asianization of East Asian Security and the United States' Role', *East Asia: An International Quarterly* (Autumn 1998). Christopher C. Joyner, 'The Spratly Islands Dispute: What Role for Normalizing Relations between China and Taiwan?' *New England Law Review* 32/3 (Spring 1998).

66. The examples include the Convention on the Prevention of Marine Pollution by Dumping of Wastes and other Matter (1972), Convention on Long-Range Transboundary Air Pollution (1979), Vienna Convention for the Protection of the Ozone Layer (1985), Montreal Protocol on Substances that Deplete the Ozone Layer (1987), Convention on Biological Diversity (1992), Framework Convention on Climate Change (1992), Convention to Combat Desertification (1994), Comprehensive Test Ban Treaty (1996), the Kyoto Protocol (1997).

67. For the examples of national-level initiatives in China and South Korea, see Yi-Chi Wang, 'Republic of China', in Asian Productivity Organization (ed.) *Asian Approach to Resource Conservation and Environment Protection* (Tokyo: Asian Productivity Organization 2000) pp.43–56; Kyung-Ho Maeng, "Republic of Korea', in Asian Productivity Organization (ed.) *Asian Approach to Resource Conservation and Environment Protection* (Tokyo: Asian Productivity Organization 2000) pp.142–6. For such initiatives in Japan, see Organization for Economic Co-operation and Development, *OECD Environmental Performance Reviews: Japan* (Paris: OECD 1994).

68. Akaha (note 1).

69. Due to the growing concern for recovery from economic crisis and increase in international competitiveness on the one hand, and the diminishing financial capacity of the state to enforce comprehensive environmental regulations on the other, the regulatory measures are being eroded or deemphasized in the region. Zarsky and Tay (note 53).

70. NISSD (note 6); and Haque (note 37).

71. Akaha (note 1).

72. Ibid.

73. Deng (note 65); Masashi Nishihara, 'Japan's New Search for Security', Department of Foreign Affairs and International Trade, Canada, 1999.

74. SCFA (note 39); Lee Lai To, *China and the South China Sea Dialogue* (Westport, CT: Praeger 1999) p.10.

75. In the environmental domain, the examples of bilateral arrangements include the Agreement on Cooperation in the Field of Environmental Protection (1993) between South Korea and Japan, the Agreement on Environmental Cooperation (1995) between China and South Korea, and the Environmental Cooperation Treaty (1994) between Japan and China. Hernandez, Tigno, and Torres (note 11) pp.135–6.

76. Lee (note 74), pp.72, 80.

77. Japan's bilateral cooperation with China in terms of providing foreign assistance has largely been based on the domestic interests and pressures within both countries. Quansheng Zhao, 'Japan's Official Development Assistance to China: A Bilateral Megapolicy', in John D. Montgomery and Dennis A. Rondinelli (eds.) *Great Policies: Strategic Innovations in Asia and the Pacific Basin* (Westport, CT: Praeger 1995) p.194.
78. Akaha (note 1).
79. Hernandez, Tigno and Torres (note 11) p.136
80. It is mainly because, since Japan and South Korea already have access to global economic forums and are participants in international financial agencies, they have lesser interests to form any multilateral financial arrangement primarily for East Asian economies. Akaha (note 1).
81. For example, in 1998, the launch of a missile over Japan by North Korea considerably intensified Japan's security concern. Ibid.
82. Nishihara (note 73).
83. Eric K. Stern, 'The Case for Comprehensive Security', in Daniel H. Deudney and Richard A. Mathew (eds.) *Contested Grounds: Security and Conflict in the New Environmental Politics* (Albany: State Univ. of NY Press 1999) pp.127–54; Maddock (note 2) pp.160–80.
84. East Asian countries can complement each other based on their individual strengths. For example, Japan and South Korea have the technological and financial advantages, North Korea and Mongolia have primary resources, and China has a large labor force. Hayes and Zarsky (note 38).
85. Quansheng Zhao, 'How China Views Korea: A Balanced Act Tilting Toward the South', in Wang Gungwu and John Wong (eds.) *China's Political Economy* (Singapore UP 1998) p.318.
86. Zarsky (note 55); NISSD (note 6).
87. Haque (note 4) pp.199–222.
88. According to the World Bank, in East Asia, one of the major reasons of excessive resource exploitation and pollution is the underpricing of natural resources and the exclusion of negative environmental externalities. World Bank (note 58) p.3.

PART V

CONCLUSION: FUTURE TRENDS IN EAST ASIAN
INTERNATIONAL RELATIONS

Asian-Pacific International Relations in the 21st Century

QUANSHENG ZHAO

The world has undergone significant change since the end of the Cold War. One such development is that the Asia-Pacific has become increasingly prominent in international affairs. In order to comprehend the dynamics of the region at the beginning of the twenty-first century, it is imperative for scholars, practitioners, and policy-makers to identify central issues in the region and examine the future directions of strategic, political, and economic trends.

To meet this demand and challenge,[1] this collection has brought scholars from North America, Europe, and Asia to undertake this task in regard to East Asian international relations. Taken together, these authors represent a variety of theoretical as well as policy stances. This diversity of opinion serves to promote further conceptualization of empirical developments in the region and to provoke discussion. Despite the cessation of the Cold War, traditional analytical frameworks in the field of international relations still remain valuable. A realist perspective, for example, continues to be instrumental when analyzing Asian-Pacific international relations. Of course, newer approaches also may reveal issues previously unconsidered.

POST-COLD WAR TRENDS IN THE ASIA-PACIFIC

There have been two fundamental transformations in world affairs since the end of the Cold War.

First, with the collapse of the Soviet empire, the international system has been altered from a bipolar to a unipolar power structure. That is to say, the United States has become what Samuel Huntington has termed 'the lonely superpower',[2] dominating all dimensions of world affairs – strategic, political, economic, and technological. In his examination of the unipolar world structure, Michael Green focuses on the dynamics of unilateralist US foreign policy as carried out by the George W. Bush administration in its initial stages. Green also captures the essence of the changes since the end of the Cold War era in his critical assessment of former President Bill Clinton's foreign policy. Furthermore, he analyzes debates within the foreign policy establishment in Washington between mainstream and anti-mainstream schools. One of the central concerns of Green's argument is how to sustain the 'American unipolar moment'. He argues that despite the potential for conflict in the region with respect to the strategic competition between Beijing and Washington in particular, 'US engagement in Asia will long remain an indispensable source of stability in the region'. Green also goes into detailed analysis of American foreign policy toward other key players in the region such as China, Japan, Korea, Russia, Southeast Asia, and Australia, and advocates that the United States engages in 'minilateralism' with some of these powers.

The second global trend is that multilateralism and regional community-building efforts have intensified, as demonstrated by the successful formation of the European Union (EU) and the North American Free Trade Association (NAFTA). Similar developments also have been seen in the Asia-Pacific, as represented by ASEAN (Association of Southeast Asian Nations) and APEC (Asia-Pacific Economic Cooperation). Robert Scalapino presents a current overview of the region, focusing upon the movement toward multilateralism, as represented by such regional organizations and mechanisms as APEC, ASEAN, as well as the US-Japan-Republic of Korea (ROK) alliance. Scalapino also pays close attention to the linkage between domestic developments and foreign policy concerns of major powers in the region, such as the United States, China, Japan, and Russia, followed by a detailed discussion of their key bilateral relations.

The two trends discussed above – the United States' unilateralism and regional multilateralism – present a seemingly contradictory dynamic. Nevertheless, one can predict that, for the foreseeable future, the world's unipolar structure will remain. At the same time, multilateralism will increasingly be emphasized, which is especially true in the wake of the terrorist attack on the US on 11 September 2001. Questions worth contemplating for the future are how the unilateralism and multilateralism will interact, and under which circumstances one trend will prevail over the other. To clarify this picture, we must conduct detailed analyses of each of the main dimensions of international relations, as discussed below.

STRATEGIC AND SECURITY DYNAMICS

Ever since the end of World War II, East Asia – along with Europe and the Middle East – has remained a major flashpoint of regional conflict. Several regional wars, such as the Korean War, Vietnam War, and Taiwan Strait crisis, also have had global implications as they drew great powers into military confrontation.[3] At the beginning of the new millennium, East Asia has emerged as the most likely theater of all these conflicted regions for the next military confrontation among major powers. The Taiwan Strait and Korean Peninsula, for example, are sites that may trigger larger confrontation in the future.

There are many perspectives from which one may investigate security issues in international relations. One way is to examine the relative dynamics of power among major players in a region. This type of analysis provides a comprehensive strategic picture of the region. Along this analytical line, Quansheng Zhao argues that tremendous changes in power status have taken place in the post-Cold War era. He defines this power reconfiguration as comprising 'two ups' and 'two downs', referring to the rise of the United States and China, and the downturn of Russia and Japan. Zhao emphasizes that a shift in relative power distribution significantly changes perceptions among major powers, thereby effectively impacting upon international relations in the region and beyond. The author argues that the ability to adapt to this new power configuration will not only be crucial to major powers but also will have significant influence on medium and small actors in the region.

A second approach is to consider the impact of critical components on regional security. For example, nuclear weapons management and missile defense implementation, such as theater missile defense (TMD; also known as national missile defense, or NMD) affect the relative balance of power. More specifically, the issue of TMD has triggered significant controversy among the US, Russia, China, Japan, and European powers. By focusing on what he describes as 'the second nuclear age' of Asia, Victor Cha analyzes the complicated situation regarding nuclear proliferation in South and East Asia. He looks into the relative nuclear capacity not only of major powers such as China and India, but also medium or smaller players such as the two Koreas, Pakistan, and Taiwan. In his investigation of nuclear proliferation issues, Cha presents an assessment of the nuclear security environment in Asia and argues that 'sober optimism' rather than 'proliferation pessimism' is merited in terms of future prospects. In all, Zhao and Cha's contributions are complementary in the sense that Zhao provides a macro analysis of the strategic shift in power distribution in East Asia while Cha examines the region's concrete nuclear security issues.

In terms of regional and even global security, a key issue confronting all powers in the Asia-Pacific is how to manage the relationship between the two ascendant powers – the United States and China. Virtually all regional controversies, such as cross-strait relations between Taiwan and the PRC, the resolution of the tensions on the Korean Peninsula, the evolving nature of the US-Japan security alliance (and the future direction of Japanese foreign policy), and the potential conflict over the South China Sea dispute, are all closely linked to major-power relations, particularly the ongoing dynamics of the Washington-Beijing relationship. The Asian-Pacific security environment will continue to be affected by this shift in power distribution for the time to come, despite the events of 11 September 2001. At the same time, the necessity for an anti-terrorist coalition will also provide a fresh opportunity to inspect the overall dynamics of the major power relationships. The spirit of this new framework may be reflected in the joint anti-terrorism statement signed by Asian-Pacific leaders in the Shanghai APEC meeting in October 2001. Along this line, the issues of management of strategic weaponry, such as nuclear proliferation and missile defense systems, appear even more crucial to regional security and stability.

POLITICAL AND DIPLOMATIC DYNAMICS

If power distribution and arms management are key concerns in the strategic and security dimension, institutions, influence, and prestige, are some of the central considerations to be investigated in analysis of political and diplomatic issues.

One diplomatic issue is how to deal with relationships between countries with asymmetric power. Are there circumstances in which political influence in world affairs does not function according to the relative 'size' of a country's power? Brantly Womack's contribution is geared toward answering this question. By focusing on two major powers, the United States and China, Womack examines the asymmetric relationship between the two countries as well as their strength in comparison to their respective neighbors. For example, China's Asian regional context leads to comparisons between China and its neighbors such as Japan, South Korea, Russia, India, Pakistan, Vietnam, Kazakhstan, and Mongolia. Meanwhile, the United States is placed in both regional and global contexts, thereby promoting comparisons with not only other countries in the Americas

(Canada, Mexico, Brazil, and Argentina) but also other global powers, such as the United Kingdom, France, Germany, Russia, Japan, and China. In examining these cases, Womack discusses the respective asymmetric situations in terms of relative political and diplomatic influence. He also addresses such crucial issues as how to deal with misperceptions and how to manage an asymmetric relationship more effectively.

The decision-making process is another central focus of study in diplomacy and foreign policy analysis. Various conceptual approaches have proved instrumental in this regard, such as 'two-level games'[4] and 'macro-micro linkage'analyses.[5] When it comes to East Asian politics more specifically, one has to pay special attention to the distinction between formal and informal channels in diplomatic relations.[6] Therefore, it is important not only to look at a country's policy-making process in the context of domestic politics (such as political parties, institutions, and interest groups) – but also examine a country's political culture and historical legacies, which may provide deeper understanding of foreign policy issues and enhance cross-cultural communication. In his study of Japanese foreign policy toward Taiwan, Philip Deans examines informal politics and virtual diplomacy by discussing the important and often overlooked relationship between Japan and Taiwan (also known as the Republic of China, or ROC). Given Taiwan's historical status as a former Japanese colony and the fact that they both followed a similar developmental strategy in the post-war era, a strong connection has remained between the two entities despite Japan's formal recognition of the PRC. Deans investigates the institutional mechanism – the Japan-ROC Diet Members' Consultative Council, *Nikkakon* – through which this informal relationship has been maintained, even though mainland China exerts significant diplomatic pressure on Japan. Of course, given the fact that the decision-making process in Japan is becoming more institutionalized and transparent – especially with recent political reform under the leadership of Prime Minister Junichiro Koizumi and Foreign Minister Makiko Tanaka – one may wonder how much weight informal politics and channels will continue to carry in Japan's future diplomatic relations.

Other political issues that have drawn increasing attention include human rights concerns and the function of non-governmental organizations (NGOs). The issue of human rights is no longer regarded as an exclusively internal matter to be discussed only within a country's sovereign borders. Rather, it has become a foreign policy issue, frequently appearing in diplomatic negotiations.[7] The heated debate over 'universal human rights' versus 'Asian values' has highlighted the complicated nature of this issue, as there probably is more than sheer ideology at stake. Instead, such perspectives may be more related to historical and cultural context.[8]

ECONOMIC AND ENVIRONMENTAL DYNAMICS

When it comes to East Asian economics, one may be struck by the dramatic shift that occurred over the last quarter of the twentieth century, from Asia's spectacular 'economic miracle' to the financial crisis of 1997–98 and the subsequent recovery – to varying degrees. Many key issues are involved in the East Asian political economy, such as, for example, the extent of deregulation in the Japanese economy and whether it amounts to what T.J. Pempel describes as 'regime change'.[9] Other central concerns include the transformation from a state-controlled to market-oriented economy in China – with special attention to the reform of state-owned enterprises (SOEs)[10] – as well as the impact of the economic crisis on Southeast Asia and Korea.[11]

Given an environment of globalization and economic interdependence, regional integration and multilateralism comprise one of the most significant trends of development in international affairs. In providing a political economic overview of Asia's potential for regional order, Danny Unger emphasizes that a regional economic organization could contribute significantly to stability and prosperity in the Asia-Pacific. As a lens into Asian prospects for economic integration, Unger refers to Dani Rodrik's argument that at best, state economies can hope to achieve two of three possible aims: increased economic integration, enhanced democratization, and maintenance of the nation-state as the central player in economic integration. Thus, Unger is less than optimistic that a robust regional order could be created and sustained in Asia. Lastly, Unger emphasizes that, in the management of their relations, great powers also must take the roles played by 'Asia's developing states' – namely, small- and medium-sized powers – into consideration.

In general, economic issues are diverse, including many crucial debates regarding developmental strategies, trade disputes, technology transfer, and environmental protection. M. Shamsul Haque examines environmental security by linking the issue not only to various schools of thought in international relations but also to more general security issues known as 'comprehensive security'.[12] Haque calls for redefining 'security' so that it encompasses non-military security issues and the involvement of non-state actors. In his view, worsening environmental degradation and catastrophes make environmental security a crucial human concern. According to Haque, the United States plays a negative role as a 'barrier' to multilateral cooperation in East Asia not only in military security but also environmental security, challenging the conventional positive assessment of the US presence in East Asia.

In conclusion, the ultimate question for the future direction of Asia-Pacific international relations is whether the world is heading into a new Cold War between the US and China; alternatively, there could be a new post-Cold War or post-11 September 2001 framework under which major powers may share a constructive atmosphere. In the first scenario, many international observers believe that the most likely trigger point is the conflict across the Taiwan Strait.[13] Given the location, losses and damage would be inflicted primarily on East Asian players – namely, Taiwan, mainland China, and Japan. Meanwhile, the second scenario may present a 'win–win' situation for all parties concerned. Thus, while remaining fully prepared for a negative turn of events, less confrontational gestures and policies from the United States may actually facilitate internal transformation in China toward a more pluralistic society,[14] thereby providing more common ground for the two powers on which to cooperate. This crucial debate, along with other key issues such as the future direction of Japanese foreign policy, the evolving situation on the Korean Peninsula, and the political economic direction of Southeast Asia, will call for attention from academics and practitioners for decades to come.

Questions also can be asked from more conceptualized perspectives when envisioning the future directions of East Asian international relations, such as:

- What is the relationship between a country's perceived national interests and ideological considerations? Will democratization reduce the chance of conflict among powers in the Asia-Pacific?[15]
- Is the 'developmental state'[16] a form of a crony capitalism, or is it merely a different style of capitalism from the predominant Anglo-Saxon type?
- Are there 'Asian values' and what is their relationship with universal human rights?[17]
- How distinctive is an Asian style of politics when comparing *guanxi* (in Chinese), *tsukiai* (in Japanese), and other social-networking mechanisms to the concept of 'social capital' often mentioned in Western societies?[18]
- Is it true that the notion of national sovereignty has become obsolete and that countries should not deem it necessary for territorial disputes to represent part of their key national interests?[19]
- To what degree will world confrontation be shaped by 'the clash of

civilizations'[20] rather than considerations of national interest or ideology?[21]

- How should we re-conceptualize the meaning, scope, and impact of so-called 'irregular warfare' in the forms of terrorism, drug smuggling, human trafficking, and the joint efforts of the international community to fight these negative transnational trends?

All of the above questions are crucial to our understanding of the future directions of the Asia-Pacific, and they will reemerge over time in a variety of forms and settings. Indeed, each question may deserve a full-length work for further study and examination. This collection has touched upon virtually all of the issues mentioned, but is not intended to provide comprehensive analysis nor answers to those questions. Rather, it provides some useful analytical frameworks for future examination and debate.

With this comprehensive study of *Future Trends in East Asian International Relations*, one will get a detailed understanding of key issues, crucial actors, and future trends in the region. This broad awareness of East Asian international relations is particularly significant given the continued rising status of the region in world affairs and the ongoing redefinition of major-power relations in the post-Cold War era.

NOTES

1. Examples of previous studies on East Asian international relations, albeit from different analytical perspectives, include Robert S. Ross (ed.) *East Asia in Transition: Toward a New Regional Order* (Armonk, NY: M.E. Sharpe 1997); Suisheng Zhao, *Power Competition in East Asia: From the Old Chinese World Order to the Post-Cold War Regional Multipolarity* (NY: St Martin's Press 1998); Samuel S. Kim (ed.), *East Asia and Globalization* (Lanham, MD: Rowman & Littlefield, 2000); and Michael Yahuda, *The International Politics of Asia-Pacific, 1945–1995* (London: Routledge 1996).
2. Samuel P. Huntington, 'The Lonely Superpower', *Foreign Affairs* 78/2 (March–April 1999) pp.35–49.
3. For a comprehensive overview of the security environment in Asia, see Muthiah Alagappa (ed.) *Asian Security Practice: Material and Ideational Influences* (Stanford UP 1998).
4. See Robert D. Putnam, 'Diplomacy and Domestic Politics: The Logic of Two-Level Games', *International Organization* 42/3 (Summer 1988) pp.427–60.
5. See Quansheng Zhao, *Interpreting Chinese Foreign Policy: The Micro-Macro Linkage Approach* (Hong Kong and NY: OUP 1996).
6. An excellent source in this regard is Lowell Dittmer, Haruhiro Fukui and Peter N.S. Lee (eds.) *Informal Politics in East Asia* (Cambridge: CUP 2000).
7. For further reading on Chinese foreign policy and human rights, see Ann Kent, *Between Freedom and Subsistence: China and Human Rights* (Oxford: OUP 1995); and Ming Wan, *Human Rights in Chinese Foreign Relations: Defining and Defending National Interests* (Philadelphia: Univ. of Pennsylvania Press 2001).
8. For a recent elaboration on this issue, see Joanne R. Bauer and Daniel A. Bell (eds.), *The East Asian Challenge for Human Rights* (Cambridge: CUP 1999).

9. See T.J. Pempel, *Regime Shift: Comparative Dynamics of the Japanese Political Economy* (Ithaca, NY: Cornell UP 1998); and Steven K. Vogel, *Freer Markets, More Rules: Regulatory Reform in Advanced Industrial Countries* (Ithaca, NY: Cornell UP 1996).

10. See Andrew G. Walder (ed.) *China's Transitional Economy* (Oxford: OUP 1996).

11. For further information, see Gregory W. Noble and John Ravenhill (eds), *The Asian Financial Crisis and the Architecture of Global Finance* (Cambridge: CUP 2000) and T.J. Pempel (ed.) *The Politics of the Asian Economic Crisis* (Ithaca, NY: Cornell UP 1999).

12. The concept of comprehensive security in Asia was discussed extensively at a conference held by the Tsukuba Advanced Research Alliance at the University of Tsukuba, Japan, on 15–16 March 2001. The author attended and made a presentation at this conference.

13. For a detailed and powerful analysis, see Kurt M. Campbell and Derek J. Mitchell, 'Crisis in the Taiwan Strait?' *Foreign Affairs* 80/4 (July–Aug. 2001) pp.14–25.

14. This argument was forcefully made by George Gilboy and Eric Heginbotham in 'China's Coming Transformation', *Foreign Affairs* 80/4 (July–Aug. 2001) pp.26–39.

15. There recently has been a significant amount of discussion and debate regarding the relationship between democracy and peace. Representative arguments may be found in Bruce Russett, *Grasping the Democratic Peace* (Princeton UP 1993); Tony Smith, *America's Mission: The United States and Worldwide Struggle for Democracy in the Twentieth Century* (Princeton UP 1994); Michael E. Brown, Sean M. Lynn-Jones and Steven E. Miller (eds.) *Debating the Democratic Peace* (Cambridge, MA: MIT Press 1996); Michael Doyle, *Ways of War and Peace* (NY: Norton 1997); Michael Cox, G. John Ikenberry, and Takashi Inoguchi (eds.) *American Democracy Promotion: Impulses, Strategies, and Impacts* (Oxford: OUP 2000).

16. The best argument along these lines is Chalmers A. Johnson, *MITI and the Japanese Miracle: The Growth of Industrial Policy, 1925–1975* (Stanford UP 1982).

17. As early as the 1980s, scholars already were paying close attention to this question of 'Asian values' and their relationship to human rights issues. See James C. Hsiung (ed.), *Human Rights in East Asia: A Cultural Perspective* (NY: Paragon House 1985).

18. For a study of informal mechanisms in the Japanese context, see Quansheng Zhao, *Japanese Policymaking the Politics Behind Politics: Informal Mechanisms & the Making of China Policy* (Hong Kong and NY: OUP 1995). For application of the concept of 'social capital' to Western societies, see Robert D. Putnam with Robert Leonardi and Raffaella Y. Nanetti, *Making Democracy Work: Civic Traditions in Modern Italy* (Princeton UP 1993).

19. For one of the most vocal challenges to the notion of sovereignty, see Stephen D. Krasner, *Sovereignty: Organized Hypocrisy* (Princeton UP 1999).

20. A controversial and provocative notion raised by Samuel P. Huntington, *The Clash of Civilizations and the Remaking of World Order* (NY: Simon & Schuster 1996).

21. There are many critiques of Huntington's 'clash of civilizations' thesis. For example, by providing systemic empirical data over three periods – the pre-Cold War period (1816–1945), the Cold War era (1946–88), and the post-Cold War era (1989–92) – Errol A. Henderson and Richard Tucker argue that these data contradict Huntington's thesis. See Henderson and Tucker, 'Clear and Present Strangers: The Clash of Civilizations and International Conflict', *International Studies Quarterly* 45 (2001) pp.317–38.

Abstracts

Trends in East Asian International Relations
ROBERT SCALAPINO

Despite certain serious problems, relations among and between Asia-Pacific nations at present are more positive than in earlier times. Three factors are centrally involved: the primacy of domestic issues, especially the economy; an absence of immediate threats; and the existence of multilateral structures allowing dialogue. Each nation now must deal with internationalism, nationalism and communalism. Multilateral institutions are still incomplete, but serve useful purposes. Nationalism is rising in virtually all nations. And domestic problems are numerous. The major powers each illustrate these basic facts in terms of both their domestic situation and their bilateral relations. Finally, given the problems of faltering or failing states, 'humanitarian intervention' will continue to be a contentious issue for the foreseeable future, yet war between major powers seems unlikely.

The United States and East Asia in the Unipolar Era
MICHAEL J. GREEN

United States' foreign policy in East Asia has been driven by a mix of idealism and realism. Asian observers may have seen a confusing jumble of priorities in US foreign policy in the region. But there has been, and still remains, a clear and consistent hierarchy to US interests in East Asia that has its roots in the forming of the Republic over two hundred years ago. While idealism and global regime-building are central elements in American foreign policy in East Asia today, realism and power still trump idealism. This essay examines the enduring US interests in East Asia with a particular focus on (a) its historical roots; (b) what has changed since the end of the Cold War; and (c) competing definitions of security in the US debate. The essay also examines how these interests affect US relations in East Asia, both in terms of broad regional themes and specific bilateral relations. The essay will conclude by stating that the United States will achieve its strategic, economic and ideational objectives in Asia only by leading or joining in coalitions of the willing. This effort must begin with strengthening bilateral relations with key allies in the region, but increasingly the coalitions will have to expand beyond traditional allies. For this reason the United States will have to put more energy into 'minilateralism' and not give up entirely on broader regional multilateralism, even if the short-term pay-offs seem negligible.

The Shift in Power Distribution and the Change of Major Power Relations
QUANSHENG ZHAO

In analyzing international relations in East Asia from the perspective of the changing dynamics of power distribution, this essay argues that the shift in power status is one of the most significant factors that changes perceptions among major powers, thereby impacting upon international relations in the region. This dynamic is demonstrated by the important effects of the 'two ups and two downs', in which the United States and China are rising in power whereas Russia and Japan are experiencing a downward trend. Clearly, stability and prosperity in the Asia-Pacific are in the best interests of all concerned parties in the region. Nevertheless, without properly handling shifts in power distribution, a peaceful international environment in East Asia will not be able to be maintained. The ability to adapt to new power configurations is crucial not only to major powers, but also to medium and small actors in the region.

The Second Nuclear Age: Proliferation Pessimism versus Sober Optimism in South Asia and East Asia
VICTOR D. CHA

This study makes two arguments with regard to the second nuclear age in Asia. First, I argue that the causes of proliferation are *overdetermined*. As was the case in the first nuclear age, profileration derives largely from the intersection of security-scarcity, resource constraints, and domestic forces. The combination of these drivers not only ensures that profileration is overdetermined in Asia, but also means that rollback of these capabilities is not likely. Second, I make a case for 'sober optimism' regarding the prospects for stability. Swaggering, competitive testing, and outright conflicts may certainly occur, but there is no reason to expect that the likelihood of this behavior escalating to a nuclear exchange is any more probable than was the case for the first nuclear age.

How Size Matters: The United States, China and Asymmetry
BRANTLY WOMACK

China as a regional power and the United States as a global power are in similar situations of relating to countries that are in general smaller in terms of population, economic capacity and military expenditures. Leadership in asymmetric relations is difficult because compliance can rarely be forced, and yet disparity creates a sense of vulnerability in the less powerful that can be exacerbated by the insensitivity of the powerful. This essay presents a general theory of asymmetric leadership and applies it to China's regional role and the American global role. It concludes with an analysis of the US-China relationship.

Taiwan in Japan's Foreign Relations: Informal Politics and Virtual Diplomacy
PHIL DEANS

The absence of diplomatic relations since 1972 has made the use of informal channels of contact vital to the maintenance of effective links between Japan and the Republic of China on Taiwan. Japan and Taiwan have evolved a 'virtual diplomatic relationship' that exploits aspects of informal politics common in much of East Asia. This contribution addresses the activities and motivations of pro-Taiwan figures in Japan over the last 25 years and argues that while this link has been extremely effective, the lack of institutionalised ties makes it a vulnerable mechanism for contact.

A Regional Economic order in East and Southeast Asia?
DANNY UNGER

The region's great powers will have the greatest influence on the region's potential to facilitate national goals of growth, stability, and equity. The contexts within which they attempt to manage conflicts among them, however, will be shaped in considerable part by political developments within Asia's developing states. The economic and political regimes that emerge within Southeast Asian states and the regional and global institutions within which their interactions are embedded will shape the wider East Asian region's geopolitics. The prospects for either new or significantly stronger regional institutions seem to be limited in the medium term. Enlargement, the economic crisis, and domestic political changes in key member countries have weakened ASEAN. The tasks of broadening political particip·.tion may override forces pushing in the direction of greater economic openness. The politics of economic policy making in the Philippines, Indonesia, Thailand, and Malaysia all exemplify these challenges to deeper integration. Ultimately, regional stability is likely to depend in large part on the capacities of governments in Asia's developing countries to meet rising expectations and quell identity conflicts.

Environmental Security in East Asia: A Critical View

M. SHAMSUL HAQUE

The existing international relations theories have increasingly come under challenge due to unprecedented global events or issues, among which environmental security is one of the most widely known and discussed. The conventional theories and approaches are inadequate to deal with environmental security, because it involves multiple actors, transcends national borders, requires interstate collaboration, and needs alternative theoretical explanations. The increasing significance of environmental security is evident in the proliferation of related international conventions and organizations, research and academic institutions, and theoretical approaches and models. In more practical terms, the worsening forms of environmental degradation and catastrophe make environmental security a crucial human concern. However, this non-traditional security issue has not gained much attention in East Asian countries that are still influenced by traditional security perception. In this context, the main purpose of this contribution is to explore the significance of environmental security in East Asia, the dominant realist perception of security in East Asia and its environmental implications, and the articulation of an environment-conscious approach for greater environmental security in the region.

About the Contributors

Quansheng Zhao is Professor and Division Director of Comparative and Regional Studies, and Chair of the Interdisciplinary Council on Asia at American University. He is also Associate-in-Research at the Fairbank Center for East Asian Research of Harvard University. He received his BA from Beijing University and his MA and PhD from the University of California, Berkeley. A specialist in comparative politics and international relations in East Asia, Dr Zhao is author of *Interpreting Chinese Foreign Policy*, and *Japanese Policymaking* (selected as 'Outstanding Academic Book' by *Choice*). He also co-edited *Politics of Divided Nations: China, Korea, Germany and Vietnam*. He has published three books in Chinese, two books in Japanese, and one book in Korean. He is chair of the American Political Science Association's Conference Group on China Studies, editor of the 'Comparative Perspective in Modern Asia' book series for Palgrave (St Martin's Press) and a member of the editorial advisory board of *The Journal of Strategic Studies*, *The Journal of Contemporary China*, and *The China Review*.

Robert A. Scalapino is currently Robson Research Professor of Government Emeritus of the University of California at Berkeley. He received his BA degree from Santa Barbara College and his MA and PhD degrees from Harvard University. From 1949 to 1990 he taught in the Political Science Department of the University of California at Berkeley, and was department chair from 1962 to 1965 and Robson Research Professor of Government from 1977 to 1990. In 1978 he founded the Institure of East Asian Studies and remained its director until his retirement in 1990. He has published some 518 articles and 38 books or monographs on Asian politics and US Asian policy. These include *Major Power Relations in Northeast Asia* (1987) and *The Last Leninists: The Uncertain Future of Asia's Communist States* (1992). He was editor of *Asian Survey* from 1962 to 1996.

Michael J. Green has been a senior fellow at the Council on Foreign Relations and has taught at the Johns Hopkins School of Advanced International Studies. He received his BA from Kenyon College, and his MA and PhD from the Johns Hopkins University Paul H. Nitze School of Advanced International Studies. His recent publications include *Reluctant Realism: Japanese Foreign Policy in an Era of Uncertain Power*, 'Japan: The Forgotten Player' (2000), *Arming Japan: Defense Production, Alliance Politics and the Postwar Search for Autonomy* (1995). Since writing this article he has joined the US National Security Council under the George W. Bush administration. The views expressed here are his own and not those of the US Government.

Victor D. Cha is Associate Professor in the Department of Government and School of Foreign Service, Georgetown University, Washington, DC. He holds a PhD from Columbia University (1994); an MA/BA (Hons) in PPE from the University of Oxford and an AB in economics from Columbia College (1983). He is the author of *Alignment Despite Antagonism: The United States-Korea-Japan Security Triangle* (1999), which was the 2000 winner of the Masayoshi Ohira Memorial Foundation Main Book Prize for best books on the Pacific Basin/East Asia, and a nominee for the 2000 Hoover Institution Uncommon Book Award. Dr Cha serves as an independent consultant and lectures to various branches of the US Department of Defense (Office of the Secretary of Defense), Department of State, and SAIC. In 1999, he was the Edward Teller National Fellow for Security at the Hoover Institution on War, Revolution and Peace at Stanford University and a recipient of the Fulbright Senior Scholar Award. His current research projects look at the future of American alliances; and globalization and military modernization in Asia.

Brantly Womack is Professor of Government and Foreign Affairs at the University of Virginia. He received his PhD from the University of Chicago. His publications include *Contemporary Chinese Politics in Historical Perspective* (1992), *Politics in China* (with James Townsend, 1986), and *Foundations of Mao Zedong's Political Thought*

(1982). His current research concentrates on asymmetry in international relations.

Phil Deans is Lecturer in Chinese Politics at the University of London, School of Oriental and African Studies. He was previously Lecturer in the International Relations of East Asia at the University of Kent. He has just completed a book on Japan-Taiwan relations and is currently working on a study of nationalism and the origins of the Cold War in Asia.

Danny Unger teaches comparative politics and international relations in the Department of Political Science at Northern Illinois University. He received his BA from Stanford University and his PhD from the University of California, Berkeley. He writes on issues of comparative political economy and international relations with a regional focus on Japan and on Southeast Asia. Among his publications are *Building Social Capital in Thailand* (1998), *The Politics of Open Economies* (1997), *Friends in Need, Burden Sharing in the Gulf War* (1997) and *Japan's Emerging Global Role* (1993).

M. Shamsul Haque is Associate Professor, Department of Political Science, National University of Singapore. His articles have appeared in numerous journals. He is the author of *Restructuring Development Theories and Policies: A Critical Study* (1999). He serves on editorial boards of several journals, including *Public Organization Review: A Global Journal, International Review of Administrative Sciences, Innovation Journal, Korean Journal of Policy Studies, Politics, Administration and Change*, and *Asian Journal of Political Science*.

Index

For Product Safety Concerns and Information please contact our EU
representative GPSR@taylorandfrancis.com
Taylor & Francis Verlag GmbH, Kaufingerstraße 24, 80331 München, Germany

www.ingramcontent.com/pod-product-compliance
Lightning Source LLC
Chambersburg PA
CBHW050704280326
41926CB00088B/2526